☐ America's Search
for Economic Stability
Monetary and Fiscal
Policy Since 1913

TWAYNE'S EVOLUTION OF AMERICAN BUSINESS SERIES

Industries,

Institutions,

and

Entrepreneurs

Edwin J. Perkins

SERIES EDITOR

UNIVERSITY OF

SOUTHERN CALIFORNIA

☐ AMERICA'S SEARCH FOR ECONOMIC STABILITY,

Monetary and Fiscal Policy Since 1913

Kenneth Weiher

America's Search for Economic Stability: Monetary and Fiscal Policy Since 1913
Kenneth Weiher

Twayne's Evolution of American Business Series:
Industries, Institutions and Entrpreneurs No. 9

Twayne Publishers   Maxwell Macmillan Canada, Inc.
Macmillan Publishing Company   1200 Eglinton Avenue East
866 Third Avenue   Suite 200
New York, New York 10022   Don Mills, Ontario M3C 3N1

Macmillan Publishing Company is part of the Maxwell Communications Group of
Companies.

10 9 8 7 6 5 4 3 2 1 (hc)
10 9 8 7 6 5 4 3 2 1 (pb)

The paper in this publication meets the minimum requirements of American National
Standard for Information Sciences—Permanence of Paper for Printed Library
Materials, ANSI Z39.48-1984. ∞™

Printed and bound in the United States of America.

Library of Congress Cataloging-in-Publication Data

Weiher, Kenneth E. (Kenneth Edward), 1949–
    America's search for economic stability : monetary and fiscal
policy since 1913 / Kenneth Weiher.
        p.   cm. — (Twayne's evolution of American business series :
9)
    Includes bibliographical references (p.   ) and index.
    ISBN 0-8057-9813-7 (hc). — ISBN 0-8057-9819-6 (pb)
    1. Monetary policy—United States—History—20th century.
    2. Fiscal policy—United States—History—20th century.   I. Title.
    II. Series: Twayne's evolution of American business series ; no. 9.
HG538.W36   1992
336.3'9073'0904—dc20   91-40061
                                                                  CIP

For Diane and my parents, Anna Mae and Charles Weiher

CONTENTS

PREFACE

IN OCTOBER 1987, FOLLOWING THE BIG-GEST stock market crash since 1929, the whole country held its breath and waited to see how the economy would react to this shock. The question in almost everyone's mind was, Would this Wall Street calamity be followed by a replay of the Great Depression? After all, was the 1929 crash not the major cause of the depression? I knew the 1987 crash would not be followed by even a recession let alone a replay of the depression, and it was not. My confidence about the postcrash economy in 1987 was the product of my knowledge about the Great Depression. Contrary to popular opinion, the 1929 crash was only a minor contributor to the severity of the depression; the overwhelming majority of the blame for the cause and depth of the Great Depression must go to ill-advised government stabilization policy. The government caused the Great Depression, and the depression caused the crash. Yet so many people have learned or concluded otherwise over the years that when the 1987 crash occurred, fears of a depression sequel were rampant though totally unwarranted.

The events of 1987 are an excellent example of how important it is to understand the past in order to interpret the present and anticipate the future. Another, more recent example came in 1990, when predictions abounded that the Mideast crisis, and the accompanying rise in oil prices, would set off a recession just as similar events had supposedly triggered recessions in 1974–75 and 1980–82. Those two recessions in the preceding decades, like the one in 1990, most likely would have occurred regardless of what had happened in the Mideast. Those recessions were caused at least as much by government stabilization policy changes as they were by the oil prices shocks. Although the effects of the hikes in oil prices made matters worse in all cases by raising production costs and lowering output, the preponderance of the blame resided in Washington, D.C., not the Mideast. Americans have historically tended to blame everything but their own government's policy for episodes of economic instability. The irony is that the source of most of these episodes can be traced to government policy moves designed to promote stability. The reason Americans have developed such a confused picture of the source of instability in their economy is that they know too little about the history of government stabilization policy and its effects on the economy. The goal of this book is to help correct that fault. After getting an accurate picture of the history of American stabilization policy, a reader will be much better able to understand and cope with the crises the economy may encounter in the future.

At the beginning of the twentieth century, the American economy had established itself as a highly productive machine. Its capacity to produce was the envy of the world. Nevertheless, in terms of two other standards of evaluation—equity and stability—many believed the economy could stand serious improvement. The industrializing economy was growing robustly and generating rapidly rising average living standards, but it was highly susceptible to damaging business contractions born primarily out of financial panics. Furthermore, a widening schism was developing between the rich and the poor. This century has been marked by efforts, often quite unsuccessful, to correct these two flaws through government intervention. The search for economic stability in America began with the creation of the Federal Reserve in 1913 and has been carried on with the development and implementation of discretionary monetary and fiscal policies. This book tells the story of that search.

We will find that in the process of seeking stability, lawmakers and economists have developed many theories and several tools of stabilization policy. In the application of the theories and tools, policymakers have sought to conquer unemployment and inflation, and at times they have been somewhat successful. Unfortunately, more often the government has produced the opposite results and added to the instability. For example, most if not all of the recessions the U.S. economy has endured since 1920, including the Great Depression, must be blamed on bad government policy. It is difficult to find any significant economic contraction that was not preceded by a notable shift to contractionary policy—primarily at the Fed. Furthermore, the inflation policymakers battled throughout the 1960s, 1970s, and 1980s was a product of their own mistakes as money growth was allowed to double output growth from 1961 well into the 1980s. The double-digit inflation and unemployment rates of the early 1980s and the uninterrupted deficits of the past 20 years stand as testimony to the failures of stabilization policy. Yet by the latter part of the 1980s, there were promising signs that government policy might be bringing the economy closer to stability than it had been during the entire search.

By the 1990s, America's long journey in search of economic stability—a journey that had taken many detours into increased instability and had visited a variety of policy approaches—had come full circle back to the Federal Reserve. But the Fed of the 1980s was far more knowledgeable than the one that had been relied on in the 1920s and 1930s and had failed so badly. Nevertheless, as the 1990s began, there was still plenty of doubt about whether the search for stability had been successful. Stabilization policy had certainly earned the cynicism with which the public viewed it. It could only be hoped that the many lessons that had been revealed over the previous eight decades, including the ones just listed, would be incorporated into a policy approach that could maintain stability well into the future.

The evolution of stabilization policy in the United States is a story that has attracted a great deal of research and debate. It is difficult to become casually acquainted with the process because of an abundance of material and no shortage of disputes. This book provides a relatively brief synthesis of the large amount of work that has been done on the subject and makes the story as understandable and interesting as possible, given the limitations of the dismal science. Economists have a knack for making many issues more difficult and mysterious than necessary, possibly because it makes our profession more imposing. I have made every effort to simplify and clarify what might at first glance appear complicated and obscure. One of the most valuable assets in accomplishing that task is historical perspective. Those who have analyzed the economy throughout the century in the present tense, or by looking into the very recent past, have often suffered from myopia—a lack of historical perspective. I have discovered that understanding all periods, even the present, is made easier when that period is viewed as part of a continuum of experiences. You will find that I have used my economic history perspective to interpret the past, not just to report on it.

My account of the history of American stabilization policy starts just before the Federal Reserve was created in 1913 and extends into the 1990s. After an initial summary chapter, the eight decades are covered in detail over eight chapters with subperiods: 1913–21, 1921–30, 1930–

33, 1933–40, 1940–50, 1950–60, 1960–80, and 1980–90. The final chapter looks at the lessons of the past and assesses the current state of policy-making. The Bibliographic Essay describes for each chapter the sources I relied on the most and believe are the most highly recommended for further reading. The Selected Bibliography provides the master list of references that could be investigated to learn more about the topic. This list, while lengthy, is not exhaustive but is, by design, a selection of the best sources I discovered in researching the book.

I have addressed this book to students and teachers of both history and economics at all levels, as well as to a general audience of interested readers. Although I have tried to keep things as simple as possible, I have assumed the reader has a rudimentary understanding of macroeconomics. Specifically, the aggregate demand/aggregate supply model is the basis of analysis, and a reader should have some idea of how aggregate demand and aggregate supply determine the level of output and prices in the economy. Furthermore, I have assumed an awareness of the concepts of inflation, unemployment, and full employment. But since jargon is defined and theories are explained when they are first introduced, even a weak background in macroeconomics should not be a major handicap.

Writing this book would probably have been impossible without the support and guidance of Professor Edwin Perkins of the History Department at the University of Southern California. He has been far more than just the series editor. Whatever good this book accomplishes owes a great deal to his input, and I am immensely grateful. I also owe a debt to Carol Chin and Barbara Sutton, Twayne's in-house editors, and their staffs, for their many helpful suggestions. Their efforts lifted the finished product to a higher level of quality. I am sure, however, that errors and questionable interpretations remain hidden from my view, and I take full responsibility for them. Finally, my gratitude goes also to the three persons to whom the book is dedicated: my wife, Diane, without whom none of the efforts would be worthwhile, and my parents, Anna Mae and Charles Weiher, who have lived to watch almost the entire history covered by this book and who are responsible for the development of its author.

1

The Big Picture

BEFORE PLUNGING DIRECTLY INTO A more detailed study of the evolution of stabilization policy, it is helpful to gain a bit of perspective by looking at the whole process from afar. After the Federal Reserve was created, the mechanisms for both monetary and fiscal policies existed, but the actual development of the policy procedures took some time. Gradually policymakers got used to the idea of employing government powers to influence the level of activity in the private sector. The application of newly legislated or discovered powers became increasingly more active until, by the 1960s, both monetary and fiscal policies were being used aggressively—sometimes in concert, sometimes in opposition. Developing coincidentally with the increased use of the policy tools was a rising public expectation that not only had it become the government's responsibility to try to use monetary and fiscal policies to aid the macroeconomy, but also presidents and other policymakers could be held accountable for unsatisfactory economic conditions. That marks a significant conversion in the public's view of the government's role in the economy, as well as its faith in the government's ability to perform that expanded role. But the misconceptions about the past persist.

□ Lessons from History

The 80-year evolution of stabilization policy covered in this book is marked by a trial-and-error process by which policymakers have learned many lessons, some the hard way. Improvements in policy have benefited from and incorporated these advances, and our historical survey will uncover many of those insights. Moreover, we will also discover other lessons, ones that were not apparent to policymakers or analysts in the past and have continued to escape their detection today. These finds become evident only under the light of historical perspective and serve to further justify our study. Listed as follows are the most important lessons that have been or should have been learned in the past 80 years.

□ Contrary to the opinion of people within the Treasury and the Federal Reserve at the time, World War I inflation was caused by rapid money growth designed to hold down interest rates. The much-delayed overreaction, which caused the money supply to plunge in 1920, sent the economy into the century's second worst contraction.

□ The Fed's apparent success at warding off recessions in 1924 and 1927 was the inadvertent result of policy designed to help Great Britain return to the gold standard, not of purposeful countercyclical policy.

□ Ill-advised efforts by the Fed to rein in the stock market in 1928 and 1929 halted money supply growth and produced an economic contraction in 1929 that precipitated the crash of 1929 and turned into the Great Depression.

□ The Great Depression was caused by a catastrophic drop in aggregate demand that must be blamed on the Fed's failure to stop the enormous decline in the money supply produced by the series of panics that befell the banking system. Contrary to contemporary opinions and some that still linger today, money was extremely scarce and expensive, as real interest rates exceeded 10% throughout the contraction. The depression was not the product of some chance drop in consumption. Capital investment disappeared in the face of tight money, and consumption was dragged downward as an aftereffect.

□ Federal Reserve policy mistakes in the 1930s and continued incorrect evaluations by economic historians were the product of policymakers' misinterpreting signals on interest rates (real versus market) and excess reserves.

□ Many New Deal policies based on a reflation strategy hampered economic recovery by artificially raising prices and thereby reducing aggregate demand.

☐ The Roosevelt administration never adopted the Keynesian policy prescription of major increases in government expenditures. What spending increases occurred were reluctantly accepted and minor compared with the full employment gap.

☐ A combination of budget-balancing efforts on the part of Roosevelt and reserve requirement increases on the part of the Fed set off the 1937 relapse contraction.

☐ The economy's miraculous wartime recovery and subsequent prosperity throughout the 1940s emphasized how much bad policy in the 1930s had crippled the economy; these events also propelled Keynesian economics and fiscal policy to the forefront of stabilization policy strategy. Furthermore, it created the false impression that wars are typically good for the economy.

☐ After gaining independence from the Treasury's deficit-financing constraints in 1951, the Fed established a policy of slow money growth that produced slow inflation in the 1950s. Triggered by obsessive inflation fears alternating with excessively low unemployment goals, variations in money growth contributed to four recessions during the Truman and Eisenhower years and to a general dissatisfaction with the economy's performance.

☐ Apparently motivated by the quest for lower unemployment and interest rates, the Fed locked in on significantly higher money supply growth rates during the first half of the 1960s. Annual money growth averaged nearly 8%—more than twice the economy's long-term average for output growth—from 1960 to 1965. The inflation acceleration that began in 1964 was born out of this seldom-recognized monetary policy change—not the Vietnam War deficit spending, which postdated the acceleration by at least two years.

☐ Most of the credit usually given to the 1964 tax cut for boosting the economy to full employment should probably be given instead to the money-fueled expansion that was at least four years old at the time of the earliest possible effect of the tax reduction.

☐ Convincing evidence suggests that because none of the tax changes of 1964, 1968, 1975, and 1981–83 had a significant effect on aggregate demand, fiscal policy was not nearly so potent a stabilization tool as was believed. Furthermore, as government spending became progressively more a captive of political forces in the 1960s and 1970s, less and less faith was placed in the practicality of fiscal policy.

☐ The upward trend in the inflation rate during the 1960s and 1970s was the product of a similar upward trend in the money supply growth rate, which reached well over 10% in the 1970s. Changes in the inflation rate consistently lagged changes in the money supply growth rate by close to three years. An inability to recognize this lag and to discern the difference between real and market interest rates led the Fed to pursue a monetary policy characterized by rapid and inconsistent money growth.

☐ A slowdown in the money supply growth rate to 1960s levels, beginning in late 1977 and continuing into Paul Volcker's chairmanship of the Fed (commencing in August 1979), eventually brought the inflation rate down to 1960s levels starting in 1981. The credit for the disinflation should go to the change in monetary policy, but Volcker's predecessors deserve as much credit as he, since the policy change was started two years before he took office.

☐ The much-delayed recession of 1981 and 1982 was also caused by the monetary slowdown and the double-digit real interest rates spawned by the combination of slower money growth and Fed-fueled inflationary expectations.

☐ The best way to understand the influence of monetary policy on the economy over the past 40 years is to track movements of M2 (the money supply definition that includes currency plus checking and savings accounts) and the velocity of money and to remember that, while velocity has experienced wide swings, the net change of velocity over any extended period during those years has been zero.

☐ Of the four main planks of the Reaganomics plan for revamping the relationship between government and the economy—that is, lower taxes, lower government spending, less government regulation, and slower monetary growth—only tax reductions and slower money growth were accomplished. The result was large federal budget deficits in the early 1980s.

☐ Relatively high U.S. interest rates attracted foreign financial investors to American markets, and the value of the dollar skyrocketed from 1980 to 1985. The expensive dollar—not unproductive American industry—drove imports up and exports down and resulted in a burgeoning balance of trade deficit.

☐ In spite of a variety of destabilizing forces—such as enormous budget deficits, Third World debt crises, the large balance of trade deficit, a major stock market crash of 1929 proportions, and the ever-worsening savings and loan debacle, the economy accomplished a degree of stability in the latter 1980s that defied pundits' predictions of imminent recessions and inflation surges. Such stability was primarily the result of monetary policy's having achieved a degree of consistency that had evaded the Fed for years.

☐ Trends and Patterns

As we delve into the evolution of government stabilization policy in the upcoming chapters, it will become apparent that certain trends and patterns have developed over the past 80 years. To help make those concepts stand out, we should identify some of the more important ones at this time.

☐ **The Evolving Role of the Government**   One of the most apparent trends has been the secular increase in government involvement in policymaking to stabilize the economy. At the beginning of the century, the government had essentially no stabilization role. Since there was no central bank and the country was on the gold standard, changes in the money supply were accidents of international gold flows or the result of unusual wartime policy, such as occurred during and after the Civil War. Fiscal policy was confined to annually matching tax revenues to expenditures, much in the manner that most state and local governments follow today, with no consideration of macroeconomic ramifications. Economists, businesspeople, and government officials all tended to believe in laissez-faire.

The Great Depression changed all that when the Roosevelt administration portrayed the economy as a complex, troubled machine that needed government guidance in many forms. By 1946, when the Full Employment Act was passed, Congress had decided it was the government's responsibility to use fiscal and monetary policies to promote stable prices, full employment, and economic growth. During the Eisenhower years, both fiscal and monetary policymakers accepted this new role, but they tried to reduce the degree of government intrusion into the economy relative to the 1930s and 1940s. The 1960s brought an increase in policy activity with the 1964 tax cut, the 1968 surtax on income, heavy doses of government spending, and the efforts by the Fed to hold down unemployment and interest rates with a rapidly growing money supply.

The peak of government involvement came in the 1970s. The Nixon administration started the decade with wage and price controls, and the Federal Reserve ended it with its efforts to slow inflation. In between, the economy experienced major swings in monetary policy and 10 straight years of federal budget deficits. Fiscal policy, the darling of the 1960s, was essentially abandoned as a stabilization tool by 1980.

Reaganomics promised reduced government intervention in the economy for the 1980s, but the burgeoning budget deficits caused by tax cuts and spending increases affected the state of the economy as much as any policy moves in the 1970s. The only difference was that policy remained essentially on one fixed course in the 1980s (even with the advent of the Bush administration), in stark contrast to the 1970s, when it was changed repeatedly. By the end of the 1980s, the consensus held that government policy greatly influenced the economy and that this influence carried with it major responsibilities for controlling both fiscal and monetary policies, as well as relationships in the international trade sphere.

☐ **Keynesians versus Monetarists**   Intertwined with the changing role of government policy in the economy was the battle between the Keynesians, who called for highly involved countercyclical fiscal and monetary policies, and the monetarists (or, in their earlier form, neoclassicals), who contended that little government policy is ever needed. These two groups have battled for policymaking supremacy for at least the past 60 years, with the neoclassicals/monetarists dominating in the early years, the Keynesians controlling the top of the mountain in the middle years, and the monetarists gaining the advantage in more recent years, The fundamental difference between the two camps is their opposite views of the inherent stability of the economy. Whereas the neoclassical/monetarists believe the economy is inherently stable and self-correcting, the Keynesians contend it is inherently unstable and prone to cyclical swings between prosperity and depression. Whereas the monetarist view requires little governmental meddling and looks on such meddling as a probable source of instability, the Keynesian position calls for the government to counteract the swings that occur naturally in order to keep the economy on a steady course.

The neoclassical view was orthodoxy in the period up to the New Deal. Most economists and policymakers believed the economy had self-healing mechanisms that should be permitted to operate without government policy to hamper the process. They simply embraced the idea that intermittent periods of contraction were occasionally necessary to purge the economy of inefficiencies. Any efforts by policymakers to intervene might slow the cleansing process and delay the return to prosperity.

When the Fed carried benign neglect to its absurd limit in the early 1930s and destroyed any hope the economy had of healing itself, people rallied around the New Deal. Unfortunately, most of the policies hurriedly enacted prolonged the depression by exacerbating the lack of aggregate demand. The inability of New Deal policies to promote recovery and prosperity confirmed some of the neoclassical contentions, even though very few saw it at the time. Furthermore, the government's ineptitude in dealing with the depression stimulated the development and eventual acceptance of John Maynard Keynes's policy solution, countercyclical fiscal policy, which he offered in his book *The General Theory of Employment Interest and Money*, published in 1936. The form of government policy Keynes called for was far different in concept from anything attempted in the 1930s. He called for major temporary increases in government spending, not major government intrusion in the marketplace. Keynes believed the economy needed only some aggregate demand pump priming, not restructuring.

The disappearance of the depression in the face of increased government spending in the 1940s vindicated Keynes and his policy prescriptions, and these prescriptions gradually began to be accepted. Eisenhower agreed to deficit spending during mild recessions in the 1950s, in an effort to buoy aggregate demand. Policymakers who came to Washington, D.C., with the Kennedy administration during the 1960s were hard-core Keynesians. Even president Nixon, an avowed conservative on most matters, announced around 1970 that he was now a Keynesian. That may have disturbed even Keynes in his grave, but there is no doubt that Keynesian policymaking dominated the 1960s.

While Keynesians had gained access to policy controls, a revival of neoclassical ideals in the form of monetarism was developing. Milton Friedman, the leading monetarist, began this renaissance in the early 1960s with his reinterpretations of American economic history in *A Monetary History of the United States* (coauthored with Anna Schwartz) and his warnings against Keynesian policy. He contended that catastrophically tight monetary policy caused the Great Depression and that the rapid money growth of the 1960s was destined to produce inflation. The monetarists drew supporters slowly at first, but the deterioration of the economy in the late 1970s vindicated Friedman and sent many fleeing from the Keynesians' camp to the monetarists'. By 1980, the monetarist interpretation of the past and present was very convincing.

But just when the monetarists were riding high, some of their equations and predictions, which had been so reliable for the preceding 25 years, apparently began to miss the target. In the middle of the 1980s, monetarist views were coming under severe attack. Hints of a Keynesian reinterpretation of recent years circulated. But Keynesian economics revolved around compensatory fiscal policy. That tool had been shelved by the Reagan administration because policymakers had no faith in it and because the budget had got so far out of control. Keynesian policy would remain a hostage to the uncontrollable deficits. By the end of the decade, monetarism had regained some stature when it was realized that monetarists, but not monetarism, were mistaken. The economy's record for the decade continued to support the notion that slower and steadier money growth would breed less inflation and more stability. As the 1990s began, stabilization policy was once again the sole province of the Federal Reserve, even if it was by default.

☐ Political and Individual Influences

One of the most influential factors over what form policy took was who the policymakers were as well as what political or philosophical preferences they held. Many times policy changed drastically simply because a new person had assumed the office of president or chairmanship of the Federal Reserve. The evolution of macroeconomic policy was carried on by a cast of characters who significantly shaped the course that evolution took.

From the conception of the Federal Reserve into the 1930s, no one packed more monetary clout than Senator Nelson Aldrich and Congressman Carter Glass, the principal designers of the Fed system and critical watchdogs over its operation. Until reforms in the 1930s established a true chair of the Board of Governors of the Fed, no specific person could be singled out as *the* person who directed monetary policy. That is why the legislators continued to exert influence and why whoever was secretary of the treasury and the head of the New York Federal Reserve Bank tended to dominate decision making. Benjamin Strong's views at the New York Federal Reserve Bank pushed Fed policy toward more countercyclical involvement in the 1920s. His death and the inability of his successor to pack as much clout left the Fed without a leader during its most trying times of 1929 to 1933. That void in leadership contributed to a lack of direction in Fed policy during the Great Depression.

As fiscal policy gradually took on more importance during the Great Depression, the identity of the president began to have a greater impact. Herbert Hoover is unfairly given too much blame for the depression by many historians, but his relatively conservative fiscal goals were not particularly helpful. The juxtaposition of Hoover's administration with that of his activist successor established an apparent, if not always actual, dichotomy between the policies associated with the two political parties. Roosevelt brought with him a long list of government interventions into the economy. From the 1930s to the 1980s, the Democrats have been associated, sometimes incorrectly, with far greater government involvement than the Republicans have.

Presidents Truman, Kennedy, Johnson, and Carter to varying degrees continued the traditions established by the New Deal, while Presidents Eisenhower, Ford, Reagan, and Bush have tried to reduce and limit government involvement. It is still not "perfectly clear" where to classify President Nixon, who at the beginning of his term appeared to be heir to the Eisenhower tradition but who also introduced policies one might associate with the relatively liberal side of the Democratic party. His already-mentioned conversion to Keynesian economics may explain his duality. Exceptions can be raised with the records of each of these presidents. For example, Truman was a fiscal tightwad; Reagan's tax cuts and tax reforms took on a decidedly populist form; and all presidents after Nixon abandoned the balanced budget. Nevertheless, the preferences toward more or less government intrusion still separates the two parties' candidates.

Who sat as the chair of the Federal Reserve Board of Governors became vitally important starting in the 1950s, when the Fed reestablished its bureaucratic independence and its influence over the money supply. William M. Martin, whose policy in the 1950s would have been given fairly high marks by monetarists, became progressively more accommodating to fiscal and political pressures in the 1960s and helped set off the acceleration of inflation. His policy was molded by efforts to hold down unemployment and by Keynesian notions of interest rate targeting. Arthur Burns, who took over in 1970, led the economy through some extremely wide swings in monetary policy. It went from tight in 1970, to very easy in 1971–73, to very tight in 1973–74, and back to very easy in 1975–77. Efforts to fight inflation in one year and unemployment in the next led to the wide swings in the growth rate of the money supply.

Paul Volcker took over the reins of the Fed from G. William Miller in 1979 and promised to concentrate on stabilizing and slowing the growth rate of the money supply by de-emphasizing interest rate targets. He then proceeded to steer the money supply on a two-year course that topped Burns for volatility. In doing so, he contributed to higher inflationary expectations, higher interest rates, and the severity of the 1981–82 recession. By the mid-1980s, however, Volcker had gained far better control over the money supply and the inflation rate settled in at 3% to 4% for more than six years. By the end of his term, in 1987, Volcker's early mistakes were mostly forgotten, and his success in fighting inflation was the legacy he passed on to his successor, Alan Greenspan, another avowed inflation fighter.

Since monetary and fiscal policy have become such an integral part of the macroeconomy, whoever is sitting in the White House or Federal Reserve chair automatically becomes a leading character in shaping the state of the economy. Since the Federal Reserve actually possesses more autonomy over economic policy, the Fed chair is likely to be more powerful than the president in effecting policy changes. And since the president shares taxing and expenditure power with Congress, congressional leaders as well as presidential advisers play an important though lesser role in shaping policy. The names of some of these influential people will also come up in our discussions. Finally, influential economists are often associated with policy formats that become popular and push their names into prominence. Although the two prime examples, Keynes and Friedman, have already been mentioned, others, ranging from Parker Willis in the 1910s to Arthur Laffer in the 1980s, will receive a measure of attention.

Table 1 provides a summary of the movements of three important variables—output, prices, and the money supply—over the eight decades covered in the chapters to follow. The differences in the figures from decade to decade are telling in themselves. In the periods when money growth was less than output expansion, prices fell. Whenever

Table 1. Economic Indicators, 1914–1990

	Real GNP	M2	Price Level
1914–20	11	112	107
1920s	30	27	−17
1929–33	−29	−35	−23
1933–40	55	87	16
1940s	56	162	84
1950s	38	39	29
1960s	45	101	36
1970s	32	160	104
1980s	33	100	56
1914–90	3.1/yr	6.65/yr	3.57/yr

Real GNP = Percent change in real GNP
   M2 = Percent change in M2 (currency plus checking and savings accounts)
Price Level = Percent change in GNP Implicit Price Deflator

Sources: See Bibliographic Essay.

money growth greatly outpaced output, prices rose substantially. Monetary growth in the 1970s closely resembled that of the wartime 1940s, but because output grew more slowly in the 1970s, inflation was worse during that decade. The 1980s resembled the 1960s in money growth, but slower output expansion in the 1980s produced more inflation. It should be noted that throughout the entire period the average annual rate of increase in nominal GNP was 6.75%, only slightly higher than the 6.65% rate for the money supply. At the same time, the growth rate for output was 3.1% per year, and the average annual inflation rate was 3.57%. The sum of those two rates is 6.67%. In other words, the amount by which money growth exceeded output growth over time was matched by the inflation rate. That relationship will show up numerous times for shorter subperiods. Now that we have the big picture, it is time to go back to the beginning and study the whole process more carefully.

2

Struggle for Control:
1913–1921

IN 1912 THE NEWLY ELECTED PRESIDENT
Woodrow Wilson instructed Congress that it was about time the United
States had something that virtually every other industrialized country
already had, namely a central bank. Congress had been seriously considering the concept ever since the panic of 1907, a crisis that had finally
convinced most observers that the economy desperately needed some
central financial leadership. But it was not until 1913 that Congress
drew up the Federal Reserve Act, and the country had a genuine central
bank in operation for the first time. Until this innovation, the economy
had been periodically buffeted about by a highly unstable financial
system. The designers of the Fed hoped to reduce this instability without giving the central bank too much power. This was a tricky path to
walk—enough power to maintain stability but not so much as to be
excessively threatening—but Congress completed a compromise that
became the Federal Reserve System in 1913.

No sooner had the Fed started operating than war broke out in
Europe, and emergency policy was needed. All the conditions under
which the Fed was designed to operate were thrown into disarray. The
international gold standard fell apart, and the Fed was faced with inflation problems it had no weapons to combat. Then the United States
entered the war, and the Fed was thrust into the unenviable position of
being servant to the Treasury in financing wartime deficits. Efforts to
hold interest rates down led to rapid money growth and inflation. The

Table 2. Economic Indicators, 1914–1920

	Q	M1	M2	P	GE	GR	Surplus Deficit	Prime Rate
1914	−4.3	na	3.2	2	725	725	0	5.5
1915	−0.8	15.5	16.6	4.6	746	683	−63	4
1916	7.9	16.4	18.4	12.1	713	761	48	3.8
1917	−0.7	17.3	14.2	24.1	1,954	1,100	−854	5.1
1918	12.3	13.7	12.4	12.5	12,662	3,645	−9,017	6
1919	−3.5	13	15.9	14.1	18,448	5,130	−13,318	5.4
1920	−4.3	−2.3	2.9	14	6,357	6,648	291	7.5

Q = Percent change in real GNP (output)
M1 = Percent change in M1 (currency plus checking account deposits)
M2 = Percent change in M2 (currency plus checking and savings accounts)
P = Percent change in GNP Implicit Price Deflator
GE = Federal government expenditures (millions of dollars)
GR = Federal government revenues (millions of dollars)
Surplus/Deficit = GR minus GE
Prime Rate = Average prime rate of interest (percent)

Sources: See Bibliographic Essay.

deficits and Federal Reserve-fed monetary inflation continued for a year after the war ended (see Table 2). In 1920 money supply growth was abruptly halted then reversed, and the country was thrown into a severe contraction.

□ Life before the Fed

Until 1914, the size of the American money supply and the regulation of a major portion of the banking system were both outside the control of the federal government. Since 1879, the United States had operated on the gold standard, which basically meant the money supply rose or fell in direct proportion to the amount of gold that entered or exited the country. The money supply was essentially determined by external forces of international trade and finance rather than any government policy. Contributing to this lack of governmental control over the money supply were the loose reins by which the government directed the banking system. A minority of the banks had national charters and were subject to minimal federal influence. Bank lending expanded and contracted at the collective whims of the thousands of banks and their many customers. Thus, a primary determinant of the level of aggregate demand, the money supply, tended to rise and fall with the level of economic activity and thereby pushed aggregate demand up and down in such a way as to exacerbate an already-damaging business cycle. In addition, given the rules of maintaining reserves under the national banking system, the financial markets were highly susceptible to panics, which could drain the banks of funds and send the level of aggregate demand plummeting.

☐ **Operating on the Gold Standard**   During the 1988 presidential campaign, one candidate called for the return of the United States to the gold standard. He was quite serious, but many people responded in puzzlement, "What is a gold standard?" At the beginning of this century, America's currency was tied directly to gold. The Currency Act of 1900 (often called the Gold Standard Act) set the value of the dollar at 23.22 grains of gold and therefore the price of an ounce of gold at $20.67 (480 grains equals an ounce), the market price at the time. Gold (or gold coins) was the basic unit of the money supply, and all other forms of money—that is, government gold certificates, bank notes, and bank deposits and checks—were simply substitutes for gold that could be converted into gold at will. The responsibility of the government was to keep the value of the dollar fixed so that the price of gold stayed at almost exactly $20.67 an ounce. To accomplish this feat, increases and decreases in the money supply had to be in direct proportion to changes in the quantity of gold available in the country.

One might ask, "What did Americans carry in their pockets, wallets, and purses at the turn of the century?" First, they carried gold coins minted by the government. Anyone who found gold in the Yukon or Colorado could take it to the Treasury and get gold dollar coins in return. Gold also entered the country from other countries in payment for products and assets. Foreign gold coins could also be traded in for gold dollars. Because gold is heavy, most people preferred to receive and carry paper gold certificates from the Treasury instead. These certificates were like warehouse receipts and were totally convertible into gold coins. Gold coins and certificates could also be deposited at national banks in exchange for national bank notes, which looked a lot like today's Federal Reserve notes. These notes were usually "as good as gold," but during panics (as we will discuss later) they circulated at a discount. Finally, Americans also carried at state and national banks deposit accounts that were subject to withdrawal by check. These checks were not as readily acceptable in 1900 as they are today, but in many cases they took the place of gold, coin, and currency for convenience.

Suppose, under such a system, the gold supply increases owing to the sale of goods to foreign buyers who pay with gold, and that the exporter deposits that gold in a national bank in exchange for bank notes. The bank would set aside a percentage (15–25%) as a required fractional reserve, which it could not lend, but it would use the rest (excess reserves) as the basis for a loan to one of its customers. The loan would be given in the form of bank notes or bank deposits. The proceeds of that loan would probably be spent and deposited in another bank, and the gold reserves would be transferred to the second bank. Eventually a series of loans would be made in the form of notes and deposits based on the original deposit of gold. Thus, the money supply rises by some multiple of the gold inflow.

The total money supply is always equal to some multiple of the gold supply, and the size of that multiple depends on two things: (a) the ratio of bank deposits to reserves held by the bank and (b) the ratio of bank deposits to currency carried by the public. The first ratio is set by national and state laws regarding banks' required reserves or the habits of bankers themselves in maintaining even higher reserves. The second is determined by preferences of individuals to hold their money in the form of currency versus deposits (remember the "less cash received" line on checking deposit slips). As long as those two ratios remain steady, the money supply will stay in a fixed proportion with the gold stock, and the value of the dollar will stay fixed at its original setting.

If a given economy pumped up its money supply without proper gold backing, the increase in the money supply spurred aggregate demand to race ahead of output and thereby cause inflation. The rise in domestic prices encouraged that country's consumers to buy more imports and foreigners to buy fewer of that country's exports. That shift in trade flows caused gold to flow out of the country to pay for the trade deficit until the money supply and prices returned to their original levels. The result of any attempt to artificially increase the money supply was no change in the money supply at all but a decline in the gold stock within the country and in the value of the country's currency. With exchange rates and currency-to-gold ratios both kept fixed, automatic gold flows owing to balance of payment deficits and surpluses kept the money supply out of the control of the government and punished any efforts by a government to circumvent the mechanism.

The rate of change of a country's money supply, up or down, was primarily determined over the long run by changes in the world gold stock. For example, from 1879 to 1913—the longest unbroken period of American participation in the gold standard system—65% of the money supply increase was due to increases in gold in the United States. The rest was due to increases in the two deposit ratios mentioned earlier. Virtually none of the U.S. money supply growth was due to any government policy designed to change the overall stock of money. The country's money supply was in the impersonal hands of the gold flows. Because gold supplies throughout the world were rising faster than output during the period 1896–1913 (as a result of gold discoveries in South Africa, Alaska, Colorado, and elsewhere), participants in the gold system experienced moderate inflation from 1896 to 1913. Not surprisingly, relatively stagnant world gold supplies had caused deflation in the 20 years before 1896, because output tended to rise faster than the world stock of gold.

When the designers of the Federal Reserve drew up their blueprints, they expected the Fed to be functioning within the parameters of the rules of the gold standard. Under such circumstances, it would be the central bank's job to make sure money supply changes moved in proportion to changes in the gold supply. There would be room for short-term variations in either direction, and these variations could be engineered by the government. Extra money might be created, for example, to avoid panics. Other deviations, such as changes in bank deposit ratios, would have to be monitored and counteracted if they persisted.

As a case in point, suppose the money supply begins to shrink relative to the domestic gold stock, as occurs during a panic. Banks start calling in their loans, thereby reducing deposits, while individuals rush to teller windows to convert their deposits into currency. At such a time, a central bank could step in and supply additional reserves to the banking system. That action would encourage lending and mitigate the panic atmosphere. Failure to take such action would cause aggregate demand, output, and prices to fall. These are the ingredients for starting a recession. Of course, the price decline would soon boost export demand and discourage imports, which in turn would cause gold to flow into the country to settle accounts. Eventually the money supply would return to its original level. Even without a central bank, gold flows would automatically act to end the recession. That is not a bad system of adjustment. But with a central bank acting to maintain a steady, reliable money-supply-to-gold ratio, the recession might be avoided altogether.

That is how the Fed's designers pictured the central bank's role in the economy. It would support the gold system by maintaining a steady money-supply-to-gold ratio. The rest would be left up to gold flows.

Financial panics could conceivably become obsolete. There would be little need or desire for the Fed to make discretionary changes in the money supply over the long run. Given the general philosophy of the time, the less discretionary action the Fed took, the better. This hands-off view fit in perfectly with the gold standard. Unfortunately, as we will see later in the chapter, the international gold standard system fell apart with the beginning of World War I just as the Fed was opening its doors.

☐ **A Panic-prone Banking System**   The primary reason Congress was finally pushed to institute a central bank, despite continued hesitancy on the part of many members of Congress, was the unstable performance of the banking system. Part of that instability was a direct result of the lack of a central bank. Individual bankers had a tendency to expand loans during economic good times and to be rather stingy during bad times. As a result, the money supply tended to vary in a manner that was procyclical—that is, it added to the volatility of swings in aggregate demand and economic activity. Contributing to the swings in bank loans and the money supply was the design of the national banking system. The peculiar inverse-pyramid, reserve requirement system that Congress devised during the Civil War had a nasty habit of turning minor liquidity drains in rural areas into full-blown panics in major urban centers. When the drain from depositors' accounts became too great for the banks to meet, they suspended payment—that is, the banks stayed open for business but would not convert deposits into bank notes or notes into gold. This was the system Congress felt obliged to repair. Let us briefly examine its flaws.

Banking is a tricky and risky business. The most fundamental rule that guided turn-of-the-century bankers in deciding whether to lend money, for how long, and for what purpose was called the real bills doctrine, or commercial loan theory. By either name, the rule bankers followed was to lend mostly in the form of short-term, commercial notes. The borrowers were supposed to use the loan proceeds to buy real goods, such as raw materials or finished products, for their inventories. What made these loans attractive was that they were supposedly self-liquidating: sale of the goods by the borrower would generate the cash to cover repayment of the loan in a matter of weeks or months. Such loans were perceived to be low risk even though in reality a business contraction could lead to a default on these loans as much as on other kinds of loans.

As long as bank portfolios were made up almost exclusively of these real bills (the promissory notes given by the business to the lending bank), banks were likely to remain a source of trouble for the economy. First, the real-bills-only approach precluded banks from supporting capital formation with long-term loans, but that is not what is relevant here. More important to our discussion was the pattern of change in the money supply that this practice produced. The demand for commercial loans rose and fell with the level of economic activity. The bankers were happy to oblige because loans made during expansions are more likely to be repaid than those made during contractions. As a result of these loan practices, the money supply rose rapidly during expansions and declined during contractions as the deposits-to-reserves ratio rose and fell. The aggregate monetary policy of individual bankers inflated aggregate demand when it was already rising and deflated it when it was falling. Bank lending practices added to the instability of the economy.

The system of reserve requirements established with the National Banking Act of 1864 made matters worse. A liquidity crisis could easily spread from one bank to another as depositors withdrew funds from their accounts. None of the banks had any outside source to turn to in order to acquire more cash reserves. The only choice was to cut back loans and deposits, which caused the money supply to shrink. A panic in a small town could send shock waves all the way to New York City and back again.

The problem with required reserves is that they cannot be used to satisfy surges in currency withdrawals. Reserve requirements limit and standardize bank lending activities, but the required reserves themselves cannot be a source of liquidity and are thus useless in an emergency. They must stay where they are, backing remaining deposits. Banks needed a source of reserves to draw on during liquidity crises (panics). Without a central bank, no institution was available to replenish reserves when widespread currency withdrawals left banks short of cash and in violation of the reserve requirements. As a result, the money supply plummeted whenever a liquidity crisis rippled through the banking system. Financial panics turned into economic contractions in short order, because bank managers cut back their loans.

The banking system had no separate source of funds available to replenish or supplement the banks' supply of currency. It was said that the banking system lacked *elasticity* with respect to currency. That is, when currency demand rose during a liquidity panic, the supply of currency could not be expanded to meet the exaggerated demand of depositors. What currency existed was hoarded or held as required reserves. There was no room for temporary currency expansion—that is, no elasticity—and no easy convertibility between currency and deposits such as we are accustomed to today.

What, then, did all the banks do when their depositors asked for more currency than the banks had on hand? Did they close down the bank? No, they just said no. They refused to pay out currency, but they did not close the banks' doors. The banks continued to conduct all business in checks but refused to pay out specie or currency. This course of action was called a suspension of payment; it was a suspension of depositors' right to convert deposits to currency. Bank checks continued to circulate, but no currency did. The checks and currency that were in circulation were often accepted by merchants at a discount—that is, a $100 bill would buy only a $90 product—but business continued. Some banks eventually failed when, owing to the economic contraction, too many of their loans were not repaid. But most banks continued to operate on the basis of checks and deposits without having to close their doors.

When the surge in depositors' demand for currency subsided in a matter of days or months, the liquidity crisis ended. The banks resumed convertibility, and the system returned to normal. In the meantime, the economy suffered because of the decline in the money supply as loans contracted and the value of bank notes shrank. The drop in the money supply had set off a drop in aggregate demand, and output and prices soon declined as well. A depression with all its harmful effects usually followed a liquidity panic, all of which could have been avoided had the banking system been provided with an independent source of currency and reserves during the emergency. Without such a source, the banking system and the entire U.S. economy were prone to panics that in turn led the nation into unnecessary depressions.

☐ Designing a Central Bank

Since the days of Thomas Jefferson and Andrew Jackson, many Americans had been suspicious of anyone who called for a central bank in the United States, because of the concentration of financial power in the hands of a small number of people that was implied. It was assumed that this power, regardless of where it was geographically housed or in whom it was entrusted, would emanate from the wealthy money barons and money trusts of New York City. During the panic of 1907, when the actions of J. P. Morgan to loan funds to troubled brokerage houses and banks saved the economy from a far worse collapse, the concept of some form of centralized bank or common source of reserves became much more appealing to even the most stubborn foes of central banking. In 1908 Congress passed the Aldrich-Vreeland Act, which established a system for emergency increases in currency during a panic (the National Currency Association), as well as the National Monetary Commission. The latter provision was the official beginning of the search for a central bank, a search that after five years of conflict and compromise culminated in passage of the Federal Reserve Act.

☐ **Conflicts and Compromises**   Although a large number and a wide variety of people put their two cents worth into the act, a relatively small group actually created the Fed. This group included congressmen, bankers, academics, and a president. The primary goal of the creators was to establish currency elasticity, and that required some centralized authority. Whether it would be a government or private sector body was debatable, but the need was no longer a matter of dispute after the 1907 experience.

One plan was offered by Paul Warburg, a banker who brought with him from Germany his own experience with a central bank. In 1907 he proposed "A Plan for a Modified Central Bank," which among other things called for a centralized reserve system reminiscent of the privately owned German Reichsbank. Warburg (who would eventually learn not to use the C-word in his plans, to avoid inciting the anti-central-bank forces) also proposed a system whereby liquidity could be injected into the system by allowing regular banks to discount their normal business loan notes (their real bills) at offices of the central bank. The centralized reserve plan would allow reserves to flow easily throughout the banking system. Thus, local problems were less likely to result in national problems. The discounting provision would allow banks that were hard-up for currency to borrow it from the central bank, using their real bills (commercial paper) for collateral. The provision for shifting reserve deficiencies from one regional district to another meant this truly was going to be a central bank regardless of what its framers called it.

Ultimately, the Warburg plan became the skeleton of the Federal Reserve Act, and Warburg himself served on the Fed's first board, but the political process sent the plan through many hoops and molds. Sen. Nelson Aldrich, via the learning process generated by the National Monetary Commission, became convinced that the Warburg plan was essentially sound. He used it as the basis for the Aldrich Bill, which he offered in 1911. This plan drew fire from all directions but primarily from that of the Democrats in Congress and the Populists because it favored a central bank run by bankers. Even though bankers like Morgan and Warburg seemed to be the only people with a clear view of the big financial picture, it was politically impossible to create such a banker's bank. It looked too much like putting the fox in charge of the henhouse, even if the idea did work in other countries.

Whereas the Democrats took control of the House of Representatives in 1910 and the White House in 1912, their opposition to the Aldrich Bill doomed this particular version of a central bank. They set out to draw up their own under the leadership of Rep. Carter Glass, the chair of a House subcommittee on the banking system, and President Woodrow Wilson. Glass enlisted the aid of Professor Parker Willis, a banking expert at Columbia University, and by early 1913 they had drafted a plan for a noncentralized central bank—that is, a central bank made up of multiple regional branches. This draft looked very much like the Aldrich Bill with a different signature. The new plan called for a fractional required reserve system run by the comptroller of the currency (the office that regulates the national banking system). Wilson substituted a Federal Reserve Board to run the system—an idea suggested by Professor J. Laurence Laughlin, Willis's onetime teacher, and Victor Morawetz, an influential figure in the business sector. Ultimately, the Federal Reserve Act was primarily the creation of Warburg, Aldrich, Glass, Willis, Wilson, Laughlin, and Morawetz, plus the result of a lot of political maneuvering.

The Glass Bill drew a great deal of suspicion and debate. Glass purposely kept it under wraps until the House was ready to debate it as a whole rather than piece by piece. Bankers were suspicious because of the secrecy, when in actuality they would have supported the bill had they known how similar to the Aldrich Bill it was. Their lack of enthusiasm was probably a blessing (anticipated by Glass) because that kept the anti-central-bank forces calmer—the main reason for keeping its similarities to the Aldrich Bill quiet. Congressional debate centered on the number of regional reserve banks and the composition and power of the Federal Reserve Board. The key strategy was to create a central bank that did not look like one, but to avoid going too far in dissipating its powers so that it no longer functioned as a central bank.

The House passed a "decentralized" bill, and the Senate chose to be more honest and pass a "central bank" bill. Because the Democrats and Republicans could not agree on whether to give control to bankers, Wilson chose the compromise course that pleased only the Populists. He granted ultimate power to the federal government while eliminating any mention of a central bank. The two congressional houses agreed on 8 to 12 reserve bank districts and a seven-member Federal Reserve Board that included the comptroller and the secretary of the treasury, with all members to be appointed by the president. On 23 December 1913 President Wilson found a long-awaited present for the economy under his tree, and he signed the Federal Reserve Act into law.

☐ **Tools at the Fed's Disposal**   The creators of the Federal Reserve believed they were giving birth to an institution that would act as a source of stability in troubled times for a banking system that was self-regulating the rest of the time. During these troubled times, it was the Fed's responsibility to inject currency into the system so that a shortage of currency would not set off a panic and thereby send the money supply and level of aggregate demand tumbling downward. By making the supply of currency more elastic—that is, more able to expand when demand for currency rose unpredictably—it was hoped that the entire money supply would be less likely to contract and trigger a recession. The Fed could make the banking system panic-proof by being the source of extra currency during a liquidity crisis.

During the periods of normal, nonpanic operations, the Fed was expected to function within the guidelines set by the real bills doctrine and the gold standard. According to the former, the "needs of trade" would bring businesspeople to banks in search of money to finance short-term business activities. The banks, in turn, would turn to the Fed to acquire more currency or reserve deposits to accommodate the commercial borrowers. The promissory note given by the borrowing business to the bank would be carried by the bank to the Fed, where it could be discounted for reserves or currency. Since a business supposedly would not seek the loan if it did not have real customers to serve, the Fed could be satisfied that increases in the money supply tied to such loans would be in proportion to genuine economic activity, rather than, say, speculation. In a sense, the Fed need only "go with the flow," and the money supply would grow at an appropriate rate. The other guideline was set by the gold standard. A country on the gold standard, as we discussed earlier, agreed to have its aggregate money supply determined by gold flows resulting from foreign trade and capital movements. Ultimately, the rule for the Fed was that it had to maintain a 40% reserve of gold backing for the Federal Reserve notes it issued.

It was not apparent to the framers of the Federal Reserve that these two rules of operation would not always be consistent with each other. If gold flowed rapidly into the country, the gold standard rule required that the money supply rise proportionately at a rate that could easily outstrip the needs of trade of the U.S. economy. Inflation would result. Or the needs of trade could rise without a commensurate increase in the gold stock. An increase in the money supply at such a time would violate the gold standard. Regardless of the inherent contradictions, these were the rules of the game the Fed vowed to follow. The tools and powers provided to the Fed did not seem all that expansive in this context. As it turned out, however, the framers were wrong about the rules; the tools turned out to be much more influential and the powers more extensive than they had anticipated.

The main avenue for increasing the money supply, as the designers saw it, was discounting, and therein lay the Fed's original tool for exercising its influence over the money supply. The Federal Reserve was allowed to lend reserves or the newly created Federal Reserve notes to banks that were members of the Federal Reserve system. To secure the loan, the borrowing bank presented the Fed with one of the promissory notes it had acquired in the process of routine lending activities. Those notes which were eligible for discounting were primarily those which resulted from commercial loans (those real bills again), but government securities could also be used. The bank might exchange $100,000 worth of commercial IOUs for $99,500 worth of currency or reserves. This way, the Fed could increase the money supply by discounting commercial paper. The numerical difference between the face value of the note and the amount of the loan—that is, the discount—was the interest charged by the Fed for the loan. The percentage by which the loan was discounted was the *discount rate*, the rate of interest charged by the Fed for a loan to the bank.

The Fed could exert its influence over the money supply by changing the level of the discount rate. An increase in the discount rate would discourage banks from borrowing from the Fed and, in turn, from lending to their regular business customers. That would slow the flow of reserves or currency into the banking system and thereby slow the growth of the money supply. On the other hand, a decrease in the discount rate would encourage banks to borrow from the Fed, thereby stimulating the growth of the money supply. In the Fed's early years, the discount rate received the most attention from policymakers at the Fed, but open market operations gradually climbed in importance.

An *open market operation* is a purchase or sale by the Fed of a government security in the open money market—the market for short-term securities. When the Fed buys securities, it adds reserve deposits to the banking system. The banks, in turn, transform those reserves into money through loans to their customers. Therefore, a purchase of government securities by the Fed will result in an increase in the money supply. Should the Fed sell government securities, on the other hand, it would cause reserves, loans, and the money supply to fall. The Federal Reserve Act gave the new central bank the power to conduct open market operations because government securities were its main assets. In the early years of the Fed, open market operations took a backseat to discount rate changes as the main tool in controlling the money supply. It was several years before the people at the Fed realized the power and applicability of this tool. Today, open market operations are the dominant policy option by far.

When the Fed opened its doors in 1914, it had these two instruments at its disposal to conduct monetary policy—that is, the power to control the money supply and influence interest rates. Today economists are so accustomed to talking about rates of growth of the money supply that it is easy to forget that such a perspective is a fairly recent development. Indeed, the Fed itself rarely spoke of such numbers until the late 1960s. It must be remembered that from the outset, Fed policy was oriented toward observing the levels of interest rates, assessing the state of the credit markets, and using the Fed's power to influence interest rates. It must also be emphasized that most contemporaries thought that involvement of the Fed in expanding the money supply would actually occur only during those precarious times of potential panic for which the Fed was originally designed. Little did any of the framers of the Federal Reserve Act realize how much the Fed would eventually influence daily economic activity and the financial news.

☐ Christening under Fire

The people who took on the roles of the inaugural crew of the newly christened Federal Reserve must have felt as if they had boarded the wrong ship. The creators of the Fed had envisioned a monetary system based on the gold standard and had designed the Fed accordingly. No sooner did the Fed get out of port, though, than most of Europe became embroiled in war. As a consequence, European governments abandoned the gold standard. Gold came pouring into this country as never before. Standard operating procedures required reassessment. About two and a half years later, the United States joined the war, and the Fed was faced with the problem of helping the government pay its bills. The Fed had to help the Treasury find owners for billions of dollars of government securities at reasonable interest rates. Then, once the dust had settled after the war, the Fed was called on to halt the inflation that had persisted well past the end of the war, but to do so without damaging the postwar economy. The Fed's first seven years of existence were stormy for reasons primarily beyond its control. Its crew performed about as well as could be expected for a group of green sailors on a cruise that was quite unlike what they had signed up for. They made some mistakes but brought the ship back to port in one piece.

☐ **Golden Neutrality**   When Europe went to war, the United States became a supplier to Britain and its allies. Those countries began importing far more from the United States than they exported to it. To pay for that imbalance, gold flowed from Europe into the United States. That should have driven down the money supplies of those nations, but they abandoned the gold standard instead. That way, they could push up their money supplies in an effort to pay for the war. The United States remained on the gold standard, with enormous amounts of gold flowing into its economy, and the Fed was left trying to figure out what to do with it all.

As the gold entered the U.S. economy, it was deposited in banks and/or turned into the Fed in exchange for Federal Reserve notes or bank reserve deposits. Currency and reserve deposits and, back then, gold, when lumped together, formed what is called the monetary base, or high-powered money. Increases in the monetary base usually translate into increases in the money supply because (a) currency is part of the money supply; (b) gold is convertible into currency or bank deposits; and (c) reserve deposits are the stuff from which loans are made by banks—and every bank loan adds to the money supply by increasing checking account deposits at the bank or placing currency in circulation. In fact, a one-dollar increase in the monetary base will result in a money supply increase of much greater magnitude because of the bank deposit multiplier, whereby a dollar's worth of specie, currency, or reserves supports more than one dollar's worth of loans throughout the banking system. For example, in 1991 an addition of $100 in reserves to the banking system would have resulted in an increase in the money supply of about $260.

The World War I inflow of gold caused the American money supply to rise rapidly, and the Fed was powerless to stop it. Raising the discount rate would have been fruitless because banks were simply not borrowing reserves from the Fed at any price. They had a plentiful supply that was constantly being supplemented by deposits of currency and gold. Why borrow from the Fed? Indeed, the Fed actually lowered the discount rate in 1915 and 1916, and the banks paid no attention.

One might ask why the Fed was lowering the discount rate when the appropriate policy would have been to raise it. The Fed had a problem. When it opened for business in 1914, it had no interest-earning securities in its portfolio of assets. The Fed had no ability to earn income until it acquired some assets. Fed boardmembers had assumed that normal banking business would bring banks to the Fed, offering commercial paper in return for reserves, and that the Fed would thereby naturally accumulate interest-earning securities. The Fed expected to earn enough interest to pay its costs of operation plus pay dividends to its stockholders (the banks that were members of the Federal Reserve system). The flood of gold into the United States changed the rules of operation before the Fed even had a chance to work under the original rules. In an effort to draw some banks into borrowing at its discount windows, the Fed was forced to try the lower discount rate—even though this move ran contrary to correct monetary policy principles. The good news for the economy was that the banks ignored the reduced discount rate and did not borrow more reserves from the Fed. As it happened, the Fed did not further accelerate the money supply growth rate with its discount rate policy.

The news was not so good in the area of open market operations. Because the Fed's efforts to acquire earning assets through the discount window were so unsuccessful, it was forced to turn to its other tool of policymaking, open market operations, as a means of obtaining government securities. In this case, the Fed would not have to rely on the preferences of banks; it could simply go into the money market and buy securities. Having the power to create reserves at will is the ultimate in clout. That is precisely what the Fed did in 1916 and 1917. Of course, these actions added reserves to a banking system already swollen with reserves created by the gold inflow. To slow bank lending, the Fed should have been selling securities in the open market and thereby absorbing the excess supply of high-powered money that was fueling the money expansion and inflation. But the Fed started out owning no securities. It needed to acquire securities before it could sell them. Thus, during a period of rapid inflation caused by excessive growth of the money supply, the Fed was forced into a posture that fueled the growth. One can hardly blame the leadership at the Fed. They were powerless to slow the money supply growth; they had been given a ship that at first could be turned in only one direction. Soon, however, they possessed a collection of securities that exceeded their worst nightmares.

In the spring of 1917 the United States joined the war against Germany. That brought an end to the inflow of gold, and the president banned the export of gold for the duration of the war. The Fed no longer had to worry about gold inflows causing inflation. Instead, it had to contend with the needs of paying for a very expensive war.

☐ **Financing the War**   The fiscal orthodoxy of the times was that a balanced budget was appropriate during peacetime years, but that strategy did not carry over to wartime. World War I required levels of government spending that had not been seen since the Civil War, and the Treasury found it impossible to pay for all the spending out of current tax receipts. Federal expenditures were more than $30 billion ($300 billion in 1991 dollars) during the 20-month period of U.S. engagement in the war, from April 1917 to November 1918, compared with less than $1 billion annually before 1917. Tax revenues managed to cover about 30% of that total. That left the Treasury needing to borrow in excess of $23 billion in slightly more than two years. The method chosen to finance war expenditures brought the Treasury and the Federal Reserve to the brink of a war of their own.

The conflict between the two departments derived from the original design of the Fed's governing board. The law established the Federal Reserve Board to oversee the operations of the Fed. The board comprised two ex officio members—the secretary of the treasury and the comptroller of the currency (the head of the national banking system)—and five board members to be appointed by the president to staggered terms of 10 years each. The chair of the Federal Reserve Board was the secretary of the treasury, and the headquarter offices for the new "central bank" were tucked away inside the Treasury building. While many of the framers of the Federal Reserve Act envisioned an independent bank, it was obvious that in practice the Fed was very much under the influence of the Treasury and its boss. Although the independent board members were inclined to steer the Fed on a course of increased control over the credit markets, the policymakers inside the Wilson administration, including the president himself, foresaw a much more subordinate role for the Fed and its crew. This disagreement on the role of the Fed was critical to the paths taken by fiscal and monetary policies during and immediately following the war.

When the United States entered the war in 1917, William McAdoo, the secretary of the treasury, had a big task before him: finding the funds to pay for the expenditures of billions of dollars beyond regular tax revenues. He clearly planned to sell Treasury securities to finance a major share of the anticipated shortfall. GNP at this time measured just over $50 billion annually. To balance the budget, taxes would have had to rise to a level equal to approximately 25% of GNP. By today's standards of taxes eating up close to 20% of GNP, that would appear to be a reachable figure—at least under an emergency. But prior to World War I, federal tax revenues and expenditures were equal to only a tiny 1% of GNP. While expenditures climbed to 25% of GNP during the war, tax revenues never exceeded 10% of GNP.

Hindsight and current standards tell us that taxpaying households could probably have afforded to pay a larger share of the war bill, but the Treasury chose not to force such a method of current finance on the country. The Treasury tried instead to offer an alternative to involuntary taxes by selling Treasury securities. Funds to finance the government expenditures could then come out of consumer savings, as households put their savings into government securities rather than corporate ones.

The Treasury issued $23 billion in securities called Liberty Bonds during the two years of active military involvement. McAdoo did not want the interest rates paid on these securities to be any higher than the rates paid by banks on savings accounts. To do so, it was feared, would set off a mass withdrawal of funds from banks—in modern jargon, financial disintermediation—and create a financial crisis. It became clear, however, that the 3.5% rate set on the first set of bonds issued would not be high enough to attract enough funds to finance the war. Indeed, current savings, even in their entirety, were probably not great enough to fund such a large undertaking. Since the Treasury chose not to raise taxes any further, there arose a dilemma. How could the Treasury sell all the Liberty Bonds when current savings appeared inadequate?

The McAdoo solution was to convince the American people to lend the government their future savings in addition to their current savings. If households were able to borrow money from their local banks in order to buy Liberty Bonds, they could use their interest earnings plus the cash value of the bonds to pay back the loans in the future. The banks simply had to lend consumers money at the same interest rate that the government was paying on the bonds. But where would the banks get all this money to lend to Liberty Bond buyers? If the banks had to rely only on the funds already in the pool of loanable funds, a great shortage would exist. The enormous demands of wartime spending had already pushed the demand for funds billions of dollars beyond the supply. Under normal circumstances, that would send interest rates sky-rocketing. McAdoo would not stand for that solution, however. He had nightmares about rising interest rates sending the value of already-issued bonds plummeting. Nobody who observed that happening to the price of existing bonds would ever buy new bonds from the Treasury.

The only way to prevent interest rates from rising under these circumstances was to greatly increase the pool of loanable funds. That is where the Federal Reserve came into the picture. The Fed may have been a conscientious objector to the plan, but it was drafted into supplying reserves to the banks. Bankers borrowed reserves from the Fed and made Liberty Loans to their customers, who in turn used the proceeds to buy Liberty Bonds. McAdoo used his power over the Federal Reserve Board and his unparalleled influence in the White House and Congress to convince board members to go along with his plan. The discount window became a limitless source of bank reserves. The Fed created large quantities of high-powered money that the banks turned into loans to prospective bond buyers. In modern terminology, the Fed *monetized* the deficit. That is, it added enough reserves to the money market that the supply of loanable funds kept up with the demand for funds, and interest rates were held down.

As a result, the money supply ballooned by 19% in less than two years. The secretary of the treasury took great pride in the fact that the overwhelming majority of the Liberty Bonds were purchased by individuals rather than banks or the Fed, but he failed to see that this was just a facade. Most of the bond purchases were done with money created by the Federal Reserve. The Fed lent banks reserves, and the banks turned those reserves into money. The Fed acquired stacks of commercial paper from the banks (through discount loans) instead of the Liberty Bonds themselves, but the result was the same as if the Fed had directly purchased the Treasury's bonds in the open market: government expenditures were to a great extent financed by the creation of money. The government did not print greenbacks as it had during the Civil War; things were more subtle in 1917 than in 1863. But the result was nearly the same.

With the economy already operating at full employment in 1917 and the money supply growing at annual rates of more than 10%, the economy was a sure bet to experience more inflation. The wholesale price index rose 17% during the 20-month period. From 1914 to 1917, the inflow of gold had caused the money supply to rise faster than output, and inflation was the result. After the United States entered the war, it was the method of financing the unusually high level of government expenditures that sent the money supply racing further upward and led to continued rapid inflation.

Quite remarkably, neither McAdoo nor his influential assistant secretary, Russell C. Leffingwell, connected the policy they imposed on the Fed with the inflation. This was in sharp contrast with the opinion of the members of the Fed board, particularly Adolph Miller, the board's only economist. He saw that as long as taxes and current savings were not sufficient to cover expenditures, increases in the money supply would have to make up the remainder of the necessary funds. Furthermore, he argued that if the purchases of bonds or the payment of taxes was financed by the creation of credit by the banks, this increase in purchasing power would be in monetary terms rather than in terms of actual output. The result would be inflation. His arguments were based on the Quantity Theory of Money, which states that money supply growth in excess of output expansion will in the long run result in inflation.

But the people at the Treasury disagreed. First, they did not equate inflation with rising prices, as we do today. In modern terminology and economic analysis, inflation and rising prices are the same thing. To some people in 1918—and, as we will see later, throughout the 1920s and the 1930s—inflation meant an excessive growth in the supply of available credit or money. What made a particular growth rate of credit excessive varied from situation to situation. Interestingly enough, Leffingwell did not include checking account deposits in his definition of the money supply, and so the money supply by his definition did not grow nearly so fast as that by the Fed's measurement. Moreover, Leffingwell did not believe the excess aggregate demand and rising prices were the results of the rapid rise of the money supply. He held that the rising prices were caused by the excess of aggregate demand (the results of the enormous government expenditures) over output, and he stubbornly maintained that the rapid rise in the money supply (the "inflation," in his terms) came about as a logical *result* of all this spending. Thus, according to his analysis, the fact that prices were rising was not a consequence of his method of financing the wartime spending.

The price rise was caused by aggregate demand growing faster than output. But the ability of aggregate demand to rise at such a rate was tied to the rate of growth in the money supply. Spending cannot be growing unless the amount of money or its rate of circulation is rising. Government spending cannot rise the way it did during World War I unless funds are borrowed from the private sector or new funds are created. If funds are borrowed from the private sector, inflation is unlikely to occur, because total spending will not be rising faster than output; the government simply spends more and the private sector spends less of national income. But if the government spends more without causing the private sector to spend less in an economy at full employment, aggregate demand will race ahead of output. The only way that can be accomplished in a full-employment economy such as existed in 1917 is for government spending to be financed by increases in the money supply.

Because the funds collected by the Treasury out of consumer taxes and savings were insufficient to cover all the war expenditures, the rest was financed through money supply increases. That means all excesses in aggregate demand over output must be attributable to money supply increases. Therefore, the inflation during the United States' engagement in the war was the direct result of the Fed monetizing the budget deficits by creating bank reserves that were used to create loans that in turn were used by individuals to buy the Liberty Bonds. The people at the Fed were right in their analysis, but the secretary of the treasury and other administration officials were running their agency, and the conflict of interpretations was to carry over to the postwar era.

☐ **The Postwar Inflationary Bubble**   The war ended in November 1918, but it took a while to dismantle the enormous government that had grown up during the war. As a result, government spending continued at a high level relative both to prewar levels and to tax revenues. Monthly expenditures figures of $1–2 billion continued well into 1919. By the summer of 1919, monthly expenditures were still twice as high as tax revenues, and it was not until the end of 1919 that expenditures fell to a level sustainable by tax revenues. Thus, for a full year deficit spending continued just as it had during the hostilities. Consequently, the Treasury found it necessary to issue a final $6 billion batch of securities to finance these deficits. Though the postwar bonds were called Victory Bonds, they were exactly the same as the Liberty Bonds they succeeded, and they caused the same difficulties for the Treasury and Federal Reserve as their wartime cousins.

The new secretary of the treasury, none other than Carter Glass, a principal architect of the Federal Reserve Act, was faced with the same problems McAdoo had encountered during the war. Any hopes that this cocreator of the Fed would treat the Fed differently from McAdoo were dashed quickly. Glass made it clear that his number-one priority was to issue the last package of bonds without damaging the market price of previously issued bonds. This meant once again that the secretary of the treasury wanted to hold down interest rates while new bonds were being marketed. Rising interest rates would mean falling prices for previously issued bonds. Glass feared that a significant erosion of bond prices would so undercut the creditworthiness of the government that it would have to issue new bonds to replace all the old ones.

Falling bond prices actually harm only those people who do not hold the bonds to maturity but instead sell at the current market price, which can be below the face value of the bonds. Those who do hold their bonds to maturity, however, get the face value regardless of where interest rates have gone. And because most of the bonds in question were held by individuals, most bonds would probably have been held to maturity—especially those purchased with bank loans. Anyone selling a bond at a price below its face value—that is, at a discount—would be unable to pay back the bank loan from the sale proceeds alone. That sounds like a good reason to hang onto the bond until maturity. Nevertheless, McAdoo and Glass shared the fear that falling bond prices might set off a frenzy of selling. As we look back now, having lived through the 1970s and 1980s, when the financial markets experienced wide interest rate swings in both directions without an erosion in public confidence in Treasury securities, we can see that their fears were probably unjustified.

Right or wrong, the Treasury refused to allow a rise in interest rates for a year after the war ended. The Treasury even used some of its own funds to buy securities in the open market to prop up bond prices and help hold down interest rates. The Fed would not yet be allowed to function independently when the Treasury was invading its turf. Just as during the wartime months, the Fed, in order to keep interest rates steady in the face of major government borrowing, had to push the money supply upward through loans to member banks and open market purchases of securities. During the one-year period following the armistice, M1 (the sum of currency and checking deposits) rose by about 20%, while output rose very little if at all. No wonder wholesale prices climbed by more than 20% between November 1918 and May 1920.

What is striking about this surge in the money supply is that it occurred despite the fact that gold was flowing out of the country. The president had lifted the embargo on gold exports. Gold began to flow out of the country immediately. This is no surprise. The wartime inflationary increases in the money supply were accomplished without an increase in the gold stock—as opposed to the preceding period of neutrality, when the inflationary money supply increases were fueled by gold imports. When a country on the gold standard expands its money supply without a proportional increase in the stock of gold, the resulting domestic inflation will send gold flowing out of the country because imports rise and exports fall. The winding down of the war worked to magnify this tendency. Had the United States followed the gold standard rules, it would have allowed the money supply to shrink in proportion to the decline in the gold stock. This would have left the ratio of money to gold steady. Instead, the money supply was pushed upward, sending the ratio of money to gold upward. The Fed was forced by the needs of the Treasury to take a stance that was contradictory to the rules of the gold standard.

Recognizing the inflationary nature of their interest rate policies, some of the people at the Fed argued in favor of an increase in the discount rate throughout 1919. Those favoring such a move included William Harding, Adolph Miller, and Benjamin Strong (at the New York City Fed). But Secretary Glass was opposed. The position of the Treasury continued to be that the increase in the money supply was the result of the inflation, not the cause. Much has been studied and written about the failure of the Fed to slow the growth of the money supply during this period. Indeed, a congressional commission looked into the matter in 1922 after the recession of 1920–21. The consensus is that while the people at the Fed were aware that going along with the wishes of the Treasury was dangerously inflationary, the Treasury was in a superior position of power. Had push come to shove during the first six months after the war, the president could have employed the Overman Act wartime powers to put the control of the Fed under any government agency he wanted. That left the Fed with little or no leverage on this policy debate. Besides, the people at the Fed were not entirely unsympathetic to the problem facing the Treasury, even if they did not agree completely with the perception of those needs.

There is little doubt that the Fed, had it been free to do so, would have raised the discount rate sometime earlier in 1919 and would have pursued a far less expansionary policy in the year after armistice. It was not until December 1919 that the Treasury agreed to a discount rate increase from 4% to 4.75%. Meanwhile, people at the Fed (particularly Strong) were beginning to feel uneasy about the near future of the economy. They anticipated that the inflationary bubble might soon burst, and a depression would soon follow. They did not want to raise interest rates too much now that the expansion was showing signs of stalling. Strong believed the time to act in a seriously restrictive manner had passed. Moderate restriction was now what he called for from the Fed.

Just as the Fed's zeal for raising the discount rate began to soften, the Treasury did a sharp about-face and began to call for a big interest rate hike. The exports of gold had shrunk the ratio of gold reserves to Federal Reserve notes and deposits at the Fed from the 48% level, where it had stood at the end of the war, to below 43% in January 1920. Had the Treasury not violated the rules of the gold standard and forced the Fed to increase the money supply when gold left the country throughout 1919, this problem would not have arisen. Of course, at that time the Treasury was more worried about financing deficit spending. But now that federal budget deficits had disappeared, the Treasury decided it was time to begin following the rules of the gold standard again. The only way to stop the outflow of gold was to raise interest rates. The discount rate was hiked from 4.75% to 6% in January 1920—an exceptionally large onetime increase. As some at the Fed had feared, the interest rate increase came just when economic activity was peaking. The inflationary expansion ended; a deflationary contraction began; and the latter soon turned into a wicked recession.

☐ **The 1920–1921 Contraction**   The downturn that began in January 1920 started out looking rather mild. Industrial production fell but not drastically during the first half of the year, while
wholesale prices did not begin to fall until May. From the middle of the
year onward, however, the economy slid into a serious contraction and
severe deflation. During the one-year period from mid-1920, industrial
production slumped 21%, unemployment climbed from 4% to 11.9%,
and wholesale prices plummeted an incredible 56%. The economy dramatically demonstrated its reaction to a swing in fiscal and monetary
policies from exceptionally expansionary to unusually contractionary.
What is striking is how perverse monetary policy continued to be
throughout the contraction.

The discount rate increase that was effected in January 1920 was
not enough to bring a halt to the growth of the money supply. Loan
demand at banks continued at such a strong pace that bankers could
afford to borrow reserves from the Fed at 6% and still make a profit on
loans. As a result, the gold problem that so worried the Treasury and the
Fed did not go away. The only thing that would ease the gold reserve
crunch was an improvement in the gold reserve ratio, and that required
either an inflow of gold or a decline in the money supply. The January
interest rate increase was not enough to cause either change to occur –
at least not fast enough to satisfy the Treasury, which was nervous about
the danger of not meeting gold convertibility requirements, even
though the 40% requirement could have been temporarily lifted.

In June 1920, just as gold had begun to flow back into the United
States, the Fed raised the discount rate again to 7%, its highest level to
that date. Six months into an economic contraction, the Fed was moving
further in the direction of contractionary policy. It is no surprise that
the relatively mild contraction evident during the first six months of the
year turned into such a severe one at midyear. The money supply did
not begin to actually fall until September, but from that time until mid-
1921 M2 (the sum of currency and both checking and savings accounts)
fell 9%. Figure 1 shows the dramatic change in monetary policy that
occurred in 1920. As the money supply fell, aggregate demand dropped
even faster. Sales dropped off, and producers responded by cutting production and lowering prices—substantially.

During the year starting in the summer of 1920, the Fed earned all
the criticism it has since received for inaction. In the face of such a
severe contraction, accompanied as it was by unprecedented deflation,
the Fed did nothing. It left the discount rate at 7% until May 1921. By
that time, as a result of gold inflows and a shrinking money supply, the
gold reserve ratio had reached 56%, apparently a comfortable enough

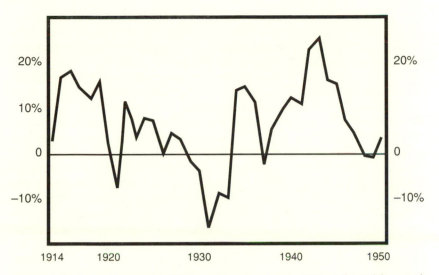

Figure 1. U.S. money supply (M2) growth rates, 1914–1950. Adapted from Milton Friedman and Anna J. Schwartz, *A Monetary History of the United States, 1867–1960* (Princeton, N.J.: Princeton University Press, 1963).

level to satisfy the Treasury and the Fed that the U.S. financial system was safe. Thus, despite the severity of the contraction, the Fed did not move to use its powers to turn the money supply around and fight the contraction.

Interestingly enough, as late as March 1921 most everyone concerned at the Treasury and the Fed did not think the time had come to lower the discount rate. Benjamin Strong, certainly one of the wiser participants at the Fed, thought it was still too soon to take action. He did not believe the deflation had properly run its course; he was concerned wages had not fallen as far as prices. Until they did, Strong contended, a healthy recovery could not begin, for real wages (wages adjusted for current price levels) would be substantially higher than they had been before the contraction began.

Strong's position was part of a larger theory or point of view that was held by many contemporaries. It was believed that every once in a while, particularly after a hefty expansion and/or inflation, the economy was due for—and indeed needed—a deflation that would bring the structure of all prices back to a more appropriate level. During this deflation certain firms and banks might be driven out of business, but that was a necessary by-product of the cleansing process. As a result, there was no sense of urgency at the Fed to turn monetary policy around in 1920 and early 1921. The cleansing process was not completed. Besides, the real bills doctrine dictated that the economy would signal the Fed through the banking system when more money was desired. To act before that would have been artificial and—perish the thought—"inflationary," because doing so would add to the supply of bank reserves before there was an equal demand. That is the whole idea of expansionary monetary policy as we see it today: to create an excess supply of money that spurs increased spending. But this was 1921, long before the concept of countercyclical policy was accepted or even understood.

In spite of the severity of the economic contraction, the banking system survived the 1920–21 period fairly unscathed. Bank failures, which in general were more common in this time period than they would be in the years after Federal Deposit Insurance Corporation was instituted, did rise from more than 100 a year to more than 500 in 1921. But there seems to be little evidence of overly excited depositors trying to cash in their deposits. The Fed was not really called on to act as the lender of last resort to the banking system, because the system never faced a major liquidity crisis. Why such relative calm existed compared with the situation in earlier contraction periods is unclear. The mere existence of the Fed may have created some new sense of public security, although the average depositor was probably too unfamiliar with the Fed to derive either comfort or anguish from its presence. Though the Fed was soon to develop a good reputation as a stabilizing force during the remainder of the 1920s, as of 1921 it had no reputation at all.

That the banking system traveled so smoothly through the contraction does not change the fact that the Fed's policies were greatly to blame for the timing, depth, and length of the economic downturn. The postwar inflationary bubble was the product of the same kind of policy that produced the wartime inflation, and the big problem was that the accommodative stance the Fed took toward the Treasury's financing troubles extended the inflationary policy through most of 1919. There is no doubt that the Fed waited too long to slow the growth rate of the money supply with the only tool it really knew how to use, the discount rate. Had the Fed raised that rate sooner and more gradually, a significant portion of the postwar inflation could have been avoided. Instead, the Fed waited until the expansion had already begun to stall to raise the discount rate in January 1920. That policy would have been enough to gradually accomplish its twin goals of slowing inflation and rebuilding the gold reserve ratio. But the people at the Fed and the Treasury were not satisfied with the results by midyear, and they hiked the rate even further. The result was a sizable drop in the money supply. Whenever the Fed causes the money supply to fall, it has gone too far with contractionary policy; only a painful contraction can result. And then, as if to make sure that economic historians would have plenty to criticize, the Fed stuck with its contractionary policy for almost a year—long enough to leave a lasting impression.

It had taken a long time for the United States to get itself a central bank. That was because the country was divided over what it wanted or what form it should take if accepted. This ambivalence led to a Federal Reserve Act that was vague and noncommittal in important respects and that created a central bank that easily came under the influence of the Treasury. As a result, during its first seven years of existence the people running the Fed were constantly feeling their way along, trying to find the proper path for this uniquely American central bank to take. The timing of the war made it that much harder for the Fed to get its feet on the ground. But after the war, when the Fed should have been showing the way to a new kind of policy-making—one that would indicate how much better the economy could function with the Fed than without—it was able neither to break free from the Treasury's influence nor to set a course for monetary policy designed to promote economic stability. In its first seven years, all the Fed had been able to do was engineer an inflation and a contraction-deflation of historic proportions—a not-very-auspicious debut for centralized policymaking.

3

Illusion of Stability: 1921–1930

WITH THE END OF WORLD WAR I, AMERICA set off into the Roaring Twenties, a decade full of change. While the decade may have been revolutionary in terms of changing social, cultural, and economic standards and practices, the 1920s was a period of relative calm in terms of the performance of the economy—particularly when compared with the decades that came before and after. Once the 1920–21 recession was over, as Table 3 indicates, the 1920s were prosperous times for the economy as a whole, if not for all its participants. From the trough of activity in 1921 to the peak in 1929, output rose at an average compounded rate of more than 4% a year. The unemployment rate, which reached as high as 11.7% in 1921, fell rapidly and averaged no higher than 4% for the rest of the decade. And prices in 1929 were actually slightly lower than in 1921 as the economy experienced incredibly stable prices over an extended period.

Despite what was to come in the fall of 1929 and would follow in the subsequent decade, the economy was healthy during the 1920s. Regardless of the efforts of many pre- and postdepression analysts to point out weaknesses in the fiber of the economy during the 1920s, there was little if any trouble brewing, at least until 1929. Two minor slowdowns in business activity in 1924 and 1927 barely show up in annual GNP figures. What the country had was a nine-year period of virtually uninterrupted prosperity, during which time income per capita

Table 3. Economic Indicators, 1920–1930

	Q	M1	M2	P	GE	GR	Surplus Deficit	UN	Prime Rate
1920	-4.3	-2.3	2.9	14	6.4	6.7	0.3	4	7.5
1921	-8.6	-10.8	-7.5	-16.6	5.1	5.6	0.5	11.9	6.6
1922	15.8	10.7	11.9	-8.1	3.3	4	0.7	7.6	4.5
1923	12.1	0.4	3.9	2.4	3.1	3.9	0.8	3.2	5.1
1924	-0.2	6.6	7.8	0	2.9	3.9	1	5.5	4
1925	8.4	6.9	7.5	1.4	2.9	3.7	0.8	4	4
1926	5.9	-2.7	0	-1.6	2.9	3.8	0.9	1.9	4.3
1927	0	1.2	4.6	-2.2	2.8	4	1.2	4.1	4.1
1928	0.6	2.7	3.6	1.6	2.9	3.9	1	4.4	4.8
1929	6.7	0	-1.6	-0.4	3.1	3.9	0.8	3.2	5.8
1930	-9.8	-5.7	-3.9	-2.6	3.3	4.1	0.8	8.7	3.6

Q = Percent change in real GNP (output)
M1 = Percent change in M1 (currency plus checking account deposits)
M2 = Percent change in M2 (currency plus checking and savings accounts)
P = Percent change in GNP Implicit Price Deflator
GE = Federal government expenditures (billions of dollars)
GR = Federal government revenues (billions of dollars)
Surplus/Deficit = GR minus GE
UN = Average unemployment rate (percent)
Prime Rate = Average prime rate of interest (percent)

Sources: See Bibliographic Essay.

rose at a clip of 2% a year. The economy was not roaring; it was purring, with only minor mechanical flaws.

Through it all, the Federal Reserve was gaining in stature and public confidence by leaps and bounds. Its apparent smooth handling of the minirecessions in 1924 and 1927 gave many people the impression that monetary policy was making the economy depression-proof. This is exactly what the creators of the Fed had hoped for, even though the Fed in practice developed into something a bit different from what had been intended. The view of many observers was that although the Fed bungled policy during the 1920–21 recession, lessons were learned, and the Fed became a source of stability in a prosperous economy. Unfortunately, much of the Fed's stabilizing policy achievements were the result of coincidence, and its policymaking skills and understanding of the influence of monetary policy on the economy were more illusion than fact. And even the members of the Federal Reserve Board were caught up in the illusion of their stabilizing skills. They decided the Fed could neutralize the stock market as a source of instability. It may very well be that had the Federal Reserve left well enough alone and not tried to delve into controlling the stock market, the economy could have purred right into the 1930s. Instead, the Fed expanded its role well beyond its skills and understanding and in so doing brought the stability and prosperity of the decade to a grinding halt.

☐ Policy Standards

As the economy settled into postwar stability in 1921 and the government no longer had to contend with financing the wartime deficits in the federal budget, it was time for the makers of both fiscal and monetary policies to choose a path to follow. The election of Warren Harding brought with it, in his own words, a "return to normalcy." In terms of fiscal policy, that meant a return to balanced budgets and the conservative ways of pay-as-you-go government operations that had to be suspended during the war and for a short period thereafter. Little in the way of innovation was to occur in the field of fiscal policy.

On the other hand, the Federal Reserve was now free from the responsibilities of wartime financing and could begin to establish a system of operations of its own. With the international gold standard system still in a shambles after the war, the people at the Fed were forced to find a new set of rules to follow, at least until the rest of the world could find its way back to the gold standard.

☐ **Fiscal "Normalcy"**   With the election of Harding, the country began a 12-year period of Republican control over the White House. These leaders brought with them an economic philosophy that was decidedly probusiness and pro–free enterprise. While the federal government did a commendable job of taking over a major portion of the American economy in 1917 and handing it back over after the war, government control of the wartime economy and the inflation and explosion of the federal debt that had accompanied it left a bad impression on many critics. That is why there was such an emphasis on returning the country to normal operating procedures, whereby the government was limited in size and paid for its programs out of current taxes.

In one respect, there was no genuine return to what was normal before the war. Annual government expenditures had shot up from below $1 billion before the war to more than $10 billion in 1918, but they never again fell below $2.9 billion. In real terms, government expenditures were three times greater in the 1920s than before World War I. The size of the government had grown and could not be completely reversed. If they could not return expenditures to their prewar level, the Republicans were determined to hold the line on government spending and ensure that tax revenues more than covered the costs. The federal budget showed 11 straight surpluses from 1920 to 1930, and the federal debt was reduced from $25 billion to $17 billion by the end of the decade. Thus, in spite of the permanent expansion in government spending that came with the war, postwar policymakers were able to scale back spending to a level that income taxes could easily finance.

The surpluses in 1924 and 1927 are of particular note for their relative size and timing. In those two years tax revenues exceeded expenditures by $1 billion. While the absolute size of the surpluses may not look so striking, in relative terms those surpluses were quite substantial when compared with the levels of expenditures and GNP. Tax revenues exceeded expenditures by more than one-third. At $1 billion, the surpluses were equal to 1.1% of GNP, which would translate to close to $60 billion in 1991. Fiscal policy was strikingly conservative during the entire decade but was especially so in 1924 and 1927.

That fiscal policy should be so conservative in these two years is problematical because the economy suffered mild recessions in both years. As we will see, the Federal Reserve's policy was involved significantly with both the recessions and the subsequent recoveries. Quite independently, however, fiscal policy appears to have been slowing aggregate demand by withdrawing more funds from disposable income than it was returning in government expenditures. From the viewpoint of Keynesian fiscal policy operating rules, the surpluses of 1924 and 1927 dampened aggregate demand. The correct countercyclical policy would have been tax cuts or spending increases that would have resulted in budget deficits in those years. Viewed from that perspective, fiscal policy may have had a hand in at least worsening the minirecessions. Nonetheless, it is noteworthy that the policy followed during this decade contrasts sharply with that followed by Eisenhower in the 1950s—after the Keynesian revolution—even though the broad goals of reducing spending and the federal debt were the same in the later administration.

The Republican administrations of the 1920s were also aware of the possible drag that perennial surpluses were having on the economy—at least on the fortunes of business. In addition to running a tight fiscal ship, the Republicans were determined to lower tax rates. The secretary of the treasury under Harding, Andrew Mellon (who happened to be one of the country's richest men), joined with the Republican Congress in an assault on tax rates. Mellon contended that the cause of general economic prosperity would be furthered by changes that reduced the heavy tax load that had been imposed during the war—particularly on the upper income brackets. His arguments were strikingly similar to those of supply-siders in the 1980s; he believed capital formation and employment expansion would be enhanced by lower tax rates that would redirect funds away from unproductive tax-exempt securities and activities into real investments. The Revenue acts of 1921 and 1924, during Harding's term, and 1926 under Calvin Coolidge, spread the benefits of tax rate reductions to all tax brackets, with a special emphasis on the surtax rates on high incomes, gift taxes, and estate taxes, all of which had been levied on the rich between 1915 and 1920.

The results of the tax reductions were certainly consistent with the predictions of a supply-sider today. Even though tax rates were substantially lowered, tax revenues flowing into the Treasury never dropped. Revenues stayed consistently at around $4 billion. Lower tax rates did not produce less tax revenue, because of the increased economic activity that characterized the decade. Inasmuch as GNP climbed for eight straight years, there was more economic activity every year to tap into with the taxes, and this rise in activity made up for the reduction in tax rates. More people were earning more income, and less of that income was flowing into tax dodges. Almost everyone's after-tax income was higher than before, including the Treasury's. It is hard to argue with these results. But it is also difficult to say whether the tax rate changes actually influenced the state of the economy, as these numbers suggest, or whether other forces were more important in contributing to the prosperous expansion.

Not all the results were good, however. The distribution of income and wealth in the United States became more unequal during the 1920s. The top 1% of the nation's wealth holders and income earners grabbed a larger share by 1929 than they had in 1922. It seems apparent that the tax rate changes contributed to that shift. Thus, while after-tax income per capita was rising rapidly for all income brackets, it was rising fastest for the rich. Although the shifts were not enormous by any measure and have often been exaggerated in order to find explanations for the subsequent depression, the fact is that the overhauled tax system was probably made less equitable at the same time it was made more efficient. Furthermore, the shift in tax incidence away from wealth holdings and toward income—a shift that may have triggered the increased inequality—left the government's revenue-generating system far more prone to cyclical swings in economic activity. Income varies more than wealth during typical business cycle swings, and consequently tax revenues vary more when they are tied to income.

☐ **The Fed's New Guidelines**   As we saw in chapter 2, the Federal Reserve was designed to operate under specific conditions: the real bills doctrine and the gold standard. The war brought down the international gold standard as most participants, importantly Great Britain, left the system. Because the Fed could no longer treat changes in the gold stock as permanent results of trade, it no longer felt compelled to maintain a strict proportionality between the money supply and the gold stock. As we also saw, this situation did not stop the Fed from setting off a serious recession in 1920 when it found its gold-to-money ratio falling toward the lower limit. But the Fed had learned its lesson and would not be captive to the rules of the gold system until the rest of the world was back on board.

Another lesson learned during the postwar period was that operating under the real bill rules obviously did not prevent speculative spending on inventories or inflation. It had been presumed that borrowers would seek loans only to finance those activities which would add to output and that therefore money supply growth would never exceed output expansion. The rapid growth of the money supply in 1919–21 had caused aggregate demand to race ahead of output even though most of the loans had passed the test of being for the purchase of real goods. It was clear that the Fed needed a quantitative standard for decision making to go along with its qualitative standard.

The *Tenth Annual Report* of the Federal Reserve, which came out in early 1924, addressed these two standards. It reestablished that loans of reserves by the Fed to banks should still pass the qualitative test: that the purpose of the loans be for productive uses, not speculation on Wall Street or in real estate. But it also stated that it was the Fed's job to be aware of general economic conditions and that it should not be the source of either serious inflation or serious deflation. In other words, the Fed was announcing that it would neither overexpand the money supply in a full-employment economy, as it had immediately following the war, nor allow the money supply to fall so drastically that it set off a rapid and painful deflation, like it had in 1920–21. As it turned out, the Fed was to act out this promise asymmetrically, worrying more about slowing the rise of the money supply as the economy threatened to experience inflation than about halting the decline of the money supply in the middle of the depression.

This report represents an important landmark in the development of monetary policy. The Federal Reserve, now free from its restrictive ties to war debt financing for a long enough time to gain some perspective, was announcing to the world that it was going to take responsibility for guiding the growth rate of aggregate demand. Lacking the explicit rules of the gold standard, the Fed had substituted some of its own quantitative rules for guiding policy decisions, and the state of the economy would have an important impact on these decisions. The Fed was not going so far as John Maynard Keynes was at that time in suggesting political management of the money supply. Most people at the Fed still wanted the state of the economy to drive the money supply rather than the other way around; in addition, they were still holding out hope for a return to the automatic mechanisms of the gold standard. Benjamin Strong, for one, shied away from a managed money supply vis-à-vis the gold standard because the former left too much room for human error. But at least the Fed was saying it would step in when natural forces drove the money supply too far in either direction. As we will see, it was to be the Fed's failure to live up to its own policy standards that dramatically deepened the Great Depression about eight years down the road.

While the Fed was developing this increased sense of responsibility for the state of the economy, it was discovering the policy tool that gave it the power to control the money supply—that is, once the policymakers got the hang of it. Although the Fed was born with the ability to conduct open market operations (as noted in chapter 2), the Federal Reserve Board did not even begin to understand the impact that open market operations could have on bank reserves and the money supply until around 1921 or 1922. In the early years most purchases of government securities had been made simply to add to the Fed's portfolio of interest-earning assets in order to pay its operating costs. The directors began to notice, however, that when the Fed bought T-bills, bank borrowing of reserves at the Fed dropped off, and that when the Fed sold T-bills, the demand for such borrowing went up. The tendency for this demand to move in the opposite direction of Fed securities holdings was dubbed the "scissors effect," and it showed that the Fed could easily affect credit conditions through open market operations.

Signaling their new awareness of the importance of open market operations, the Fed established the Open Market Investment Committee in 1923. The discovery of the influence of open market operations on the relative availability of credit and the establishment of the policy-making advisory arm did not mean that the Fed came anywhere close to realizing the full potentials of this newly found tool. Nevertheless, armed with a new operating philosophy and an efficient tool to carry it out, the Fed seemed ready to shape forces in the credit markets in a manner that would promote the stability its creators had hoped to bring to the economy.

☐ The Fed Takes Over

When it comes to influential policymaking, the 1920s were certainly the decade of the Fed. While fiscal policy was of some consequence, it remained on one steady course from 1922 to the end of the decade. The tax rate changes and tax system reforms discussed earlier were essentially revenue neutral. The succession of Republican administrations kept the philosophy of fiscal policymakers unchanged. Any swings in policy that occurred during the 1920s came from the Federal Reserve and monetary policy. The Fed gets all the blame or credit for policy impacts in this decade. Whether it was counteracting gold flows, trying to help Great Britain return to the gold standard, dealing with recessions, or reining in the stock market, the Fed was busy making policy moves that significantly affected the state of the economy.

☐ **Bucking the Gold Flows**   One topic that was constantly coming up at Federal Reserve meetings was gold. Was it flowing in or out? What was the ratio of gold to money? Did Britain need lower interest rates in the United States to help it return to the gold standard? Oddly, the Fed's leaders longed for a return to the gold standard system even though they recognized its flaws. There was apparently something comforting about the certainties of the gold system. The Fed's policy in this decade and on into the 1930s was influenced by one reaction or another to the gold situation. Unfortunately, these reactions were inconsistent because the Fed suffered from a split personality when it came to gold. At times the Fed was magnanimously trying to help restore the gold standard, but at other times the Fed acted like a possessive child clinging to its toys—in this case, guarding its stock of the precious metal.

In truth, the Fed had rarely followed the rules of the gold standard. It had not allowed the money supply to rise and fall in proportion to the gold stock. Instead, the Fed was constantly manipulating interest rates and conducting open market operations to counteract gold flows into and out of the country. What is perverse about such actions is that a major goal of the Fed, particularly on the part of Benjamin Strong, was to help Great Britain return to the gold standard as its cornerstone. Indeed, as we will see, policy actions taken in 1924 and 1927 were substantially shaped by that goal. But the best way for country A to help country B return to the rules of the system is for country A to follow those rules itself and allow country B to make the necessary adjustments to its money supply, price level, and exchange rate. The United States made a habit of violating the rules by not allowing its money supply to rise and fall with the gold stock. The Fed conducted two-faced monetary policy with respect to gold.

England had left the gold standard during World War I because it was forced to increase its money supply faster than its gold stock warranted. Whenever a country went to war, it had to leave the gold standard, just as the United States did during the Civil War. The departure from the gold standard was the result of massive increases in government expenditures for the war effort. Unable to pay for all these expenditures out of current tax receipts, warring countries were forced to increase their money supply. They did so either by directly paying with newly created money or by following the more subtle route taken by the United States during World War I when the Treasury borrowed the funds, with the Fed helping indirectly by creating them. With its money supply multiplying, a warring country does not have enough gold to maintain the official ratio, and so it ceases to convert its currency into gold. In other words, the country takes leave of the gold standard.

Before such a country can return to the gold standard, it must make a decision about the value of its currency. The wartime expansion of the money supply will have left the value of the country's currency much lower vis-à-vis other countries' currencies as well as gold, the unvarying yardstick. To rejoin the gold club, the country must either announce a permanent devaluation of its currency (raising the price of gold in terms of its currency) or return the relative market value of the currency to its prewar level. The first choice is traditionally humiliating and raises the price of all imports, but at least it is over with shortly. The second choice requires that the country reverse the money supply increases and inflation of the war period and experience an extended period of money supply contraction and deflation. The United States chose the second path after the Civil War, and it took 14 years of often-painful deflation before the country could return to the gold standard in 1879.

Great Britain faced these same choices, and it, too, took the second route. The prestige of the country that had promoted the gold standard was on the line. It could not take the first choice and retain international stature; its leaders felt compelled to return the pound to its prewar value. Doing so required British policymakers to shrink its money supply, bring down its prices, and increase its gold stock as a prerequisite for a return to gold. Presiding over this approach as chancellor of the exchequer was Winston Churchill. This was not to be his "finest hour." He needed help from the United States, since that is where most of the gold had accumulated. That gold would automatically begin returning to England as long as the U.S. money supply increased in proportion to the gold inflow and the resulting American inflation made British goods cheaper to U.S. consumers—that is, as long as the United States followed the rules.

What the Fed did was *sterilize* changes in the U.S. gold stock. Every time the gold stock rose, the Fed reduced its credit supply to the banking system, and every time the gold stock fell, the Fed injected credit into the system. The Fed had taken control over the domestic money supply away from the vagaries of international trade and gold flows. The rationale was then what it would be today: to keep the growth rate of the money supply on a more stable course. Although this goal is commendable, it is not consistent with an avowed desire to return to the gold standard, and it certainly did not make Churchill's job any easier. The Fed could not maintain control over the domestic money supply and help Great Britain at the same time. As a result, the Fed swung back and forth between the two goals of domestic monetary control and a speedy return to the discipline of the gold standard. Consequently M2 growth experienced some ups and downs as a look back at Figure 1 will show.

☐ **The Minirecessions**   From early 1922 to early 1923, the money supply rose rapidly. This rise was fueled entirely by gold inflows. For a year the Fed played by the rules because doing so was convenient. The economy was recovering from the 1920–21 recession-deflation. As long as output was rising, the Fed was comfortable with allowing the money supply to rise. At the beginning of 1923, however, Strong and others at the Fed became concerned that the economy was showing signs of reaching full employment. It was time to apply the newly crafted quantitative test to determine policy. Further rapid money supply growth would simply fuel inflation, not output expansion. The Fed raised the discount rate and began extracting reserves from the banking system. At the same time, the Fed began its policy of sterilizing gold inflows, at least partially. The gold stock continued to increase rapidly, but the U.S. money supply was held back, much to England's disappointment.

By today's standards, the restrictive policy chosen by the Fed would no doubt receive high marks because it avoided the risk of excessive demand-pull inflation and was not harsh enough to cause a severe recession. The Fed was trying for a "soft landing," in the parlance of 1988–90 Fed watchers. But this policy certainly did not come out of the gold standard playbook. Regardless, an economic slowdown began in the middle of 1923. Industrial production began to sink, and unemployment started to rise.

In the face of this recession the Fed did nothing for almost a year, in spite of an increase in unemployment from 3.2% to 5.5%. The reaction, or lack of one, shows how the Fed intended to apply its quantitative guideline. It slowed the money supply growth rate when inflation was a perceived danger but did nothing to accelerate money growth when recession was an actuality. Board member Adolph Miller's view is telling. He contended that the Fed could not stop a recession; it could only speed a recovery once it began and slow the expansion as it reached full employment. This asymmetrical application of the quantitative guideline was to reappear in 1927 and most dramatically during the contraction of 1929 to 1933.

Federal Reserve policy was finally swung in favor of expansionary action in May 1924, when a series of three discount rate reductions was begun and was accompanied by open market purchases beginning in June. This was just the kind of policy the stagnant economy needed, and a recovery began in September. One can wonder why the Fed waited so long before making an expansionary move, but it is clear why the Fed finally reacted. Great Britain was calling for help, and Benjamin Strong heard the cry. Expansionary monetary policy in the United States would drive interest rates down and prices up in this country, which would tend to send gold flowing toward Great Britain, where prices were lower and interest rates higher. These changes would help America's closest ally build up its stock of gold. Ever a supporter of reestablishing the gold standard, Strong pushed for expansionary policy and the board agreed. That the domestic economy was in need of exactly the same policy was a handy coincidence. Whether domestic recovery or international considerations was more important to the Fed is debatable, but there can be no question that the Fed would not have moved when it did were it not for concern over the gold standard and the plight of Great Britain. All the better that the results benefited the domestic economy.

The economic expansion that began in the fall of 1924 plodded along quite slowly through 1925. By the end of that year, output was no higher than it had been at the beginning, and by early 1926, signs of a recession were beginning to appear. One of those signs was a decline in stock market prices in March 1926. Strong suggested to his colleagues at the Fed that a recession might be nearing and that open market purchases might soon be needed to stimulate economic activity. But monetary policy became progressively more restraining in the latter part of 1926; the discount rate was increased, and the Fed reduced the amount of credit available in the banking system. The recession Strong cautioned against began in the last quarter of the year. The Fed responded to this recession as it did to the previous one: it did nothing for a while. No one at the Fed, including Strong, pushed for expansionary policy. By June 1927, it was apparent to all at the Fed that a recession was in progress, but again the Fed did not move to head off the decline in a countercyclical fashion.

What brought about a policy change for the better was once again consideration for international conditions. Great Britain had returned to the gold standard in 1925, declaring the official value of the pound to be at its prewar level, even though the international markets said it was still worth far less. By overvaluing the pound, Churchill and the British government were guaranteeing that imports would be artificially attractive to British buyers and British exports would be just as artificially unattractive to the rest of the world. The result was a natural flow of gold out of Britain, an outflow that was sure to sentence the British economy to a smaller money supply, less aggregate demand, and more deflation and unemployment—all for the sake of upholding the value of the pound and supposedly England's pride as well. By 1927, the stagnant British economy needed help from the United States and the rest of Europe. Easy money and low interest rates in these countries would stimulate local demand and send gold back in England's direction.

In the summer of 1927, Benjamin Strong met with economic ministers from England and the Continent in a sort of economic summit. From this meeting came a promise from Strong for easier monetary policy in the United States. True to his word, the Fed lowered the discount rate and made open market purchases in July and August. The switch to expansionary policy was followed in November by the beginning of the recovery. Just as had been the case in 1924, monetary policy was shifted to an expansionary program in an effort to aid Great Britain's struggles to return to the gold standard. Once again, the timing was most propitious for the sake of the domestic economy, because the policy helped bring an end to a recession and set off a recovery.

The five-year period 1923–27 was a learning experience for all. Regardless of the motives for the Fed's policy changes in each case, what was apparent was the connection between monetary policy and the state of the economy. Twice policy moves taken to moderately restrain the availability of credit as full employment was reached were followed in short order by mild recessions. Those recessions showed no signs of ending until policy was reversed and replaced by expansionary actions.

The Fed was discovering it had an influence over the economy that had heretofore been unrealized. Meanwhile, the public was beginning to believe that the Fed knew what it was doing and had taken control.

Adding to the sense of confidence in the Fed's abilities to stabilize the economy was the policymakers' use of the newfound tool of open market operations. The Fed had seemingly dipped the economy into two minirecessions and pulled it out while keeping the economy on a generally prosperous road. This all looked like a very promising performance and was certainly an improvement over the postwar mistakes that had produced two violent swings in aggregate demand and economic activity. Unfortunately, this recent success may have bred overconfidence; the people at the Fed felt compelled to broaden their realm of influence to include the stock market.

☐ **Meddling with the Stock Market**   At the same time the Fed was doing its best to help steer the economy in the right direction, it was monitoring developments in the stock market. The Fed's interest in Wall Street can be traced to two fundamental concerns, neither of which stands up to scrutiny. First, the Fed's officers continued to cling to some form of the real bills doctrine; they believed bank loans should be confined to the purchase of tangible merchandise, not speculative assets such as real estate or stocks. The inflationary bubble following World War I had persuaded them to abandon their belief that bank lending would automatically expand and contract with the real needs of trade without causing inflation. As a result, it was necessary to be ever vigilant about where increases in bank loans were going. To be more precise, they wanted to cut off the loans before too many borrowed funds went into speculative areas like the stock market. Money supply increases that flowed into the stock market were seen as clear evidence that the money supply was overflowing relative to the real needs of trade. Again it was not just the quantity of lending that concerned the Fed but also the quality of bank loans.

The second reason for the Fed's wariness of stock market activity was the belief that swings in stock prices endangered the state of the economy. One does not have to get more sophisticated than to turn to the old adage that what goes up must come down. The previous history of the stock market was that stock prices rose rapidly during prosperous times but peaked and fell drastically on the eve of economic contractions. The stock market downturns tended to anticipate the economy's contraction because investors could foresee changing conditions, like rising interest rates and high prices, that would soon choke off the expansion. This order of occurrence—stock market reversal followed by output reversal—tended to fix a cause-and-effect relationship in people's minds. They believed the stock market reversal caused the economic reversal. Therefore, if stock market reversals could be minimized, economic reversals could also be reduced in severity. Thus, it became the Fed's goal to hold down the advance of stock prices in the 1920s because if the stock prices were prevented from rising too far, they could not fall enough to set off a serious economic contraction.

Concern on the part of the Fed over too much money finding its way into the stock market began to mount to an influential level in 1925. Banks were using their excess reserves to finance loans for stock purchases whenever the rates of return on those loans climbed above the rates earned by depositing excess reserves in other banks (the equivalent of today's important federal funds rate, the interest rate paid by banks when they borrow reserves from other banks). The Fed observed that the supply of credit was not growing too rapidly, since the economy was still short of full employment and the general price level was stable. In quantitative terms, monetary policy could have afforded to be more accommodating, particularly since the gold stock was rising. But it was from the qualitative viewpoint that the Fed had qualms. The board did not want the Fed to become an accomplice in fueling an excessive stock market rally that would later crash and bring the economy down with it. As a result, policy followed a restrained course during 1925. It was not until stock prices fell quietly in 1926 that the Fed began considering easier money policies. Indeed, this very fall in stock prices prompted Strong to predict an impending recession.

Stock market worries began to resurface as the expansionary monetary policy of late 1927 led to a flow of funds into stock market loans once again. At the end of the year, policy was switched back to that of restraint as the Fed began selling securities in the open market. When that action did not dry up so-called call loans in the stock market, the discount rate was raised in three shifts, from 3.5% to 5%, in the summer of 1928. These increases did not work, either. Even though banks were no longer supplying funds to stock buyers as they had done earlier, there was no shortage of borrowed money in the market. Non-bank financial institutions and nonfinancial corporations continued to supply loans to prospective stock buyers because the rate of return on the loans was attractively high. Meanwhile, stock buyers continued to use these borrowed funds to buy stocks because the gains in stock prices more than paid the cost of borrowing money.

At this juncture in 1928, a debate began to heat up at the Fed. Policymakers were divided into two camps. One camp, led by Adolph Miller and Charles Hamlin, believed the way to slow rampant speculation in the stock market was to apply qualitative controls, or credit rationing. They argued for "direct pressure" on banks to stop them from making loans to customers for stock purchases. They feared a general rise in interest rates would lead to a business contraction and unemployment. The other camp, led by Benjamin Strong and his successor, George Harrison (Strong died in October 1928), were against credit rationing. They called for discount rate increases as soon as possible to slow the growth of credit in general. They believed it was impossible for the Fed to control the direction of credit; the Fed could control only the total amount of credit available. The "direct pressure" backers were correct in believing general monetary constraint would slow the economic expansion, while those in the Strong camp were correct in their perception that credit rationing would fail to work because the Fed had no explicit power to act as a traffic cop, directing money supply increases only into certain preferred channels and discriminating against others.

What could the Fed do to slow the stock market's ascent? A successful move was likely to stagnate the economy. Any plan that left the economy unharmed was likely to leave the stock market undaunted in its ascent. The two camps argued nonstop throughout 1928 and for more than half of 1929. While they did, a little bit of both approaches was applied—that is, credit rationing was implemented while money supply growth was restrained. But this strategy failed to slow the market's advance. By the time a majority of board members was ready to abandon the rationing approach in favor of a discount rate increase in the late summer of 1929, the original supporters of the rate increase now feared it was too late. The market had reached such dizzying heights that they cringed at the thought of tightening and causing the drastic drop all had been trying to prevent.

Much has been written about this internal conflict in the Fed and the relative merits of the two positions. Neither side was able to come up with a satisfactory solution that would rein in the stock market but leave the economy unscathed, because the Fed did not have the proper tools to control the stock market. Both sides should have paused to consider why there were no such tools. The answer is a simple one that escaped them at the time and continues to escape most historians who study this period: the reason there were no tools is that the Fed's creator did not envision the Fed's expanding its empire to include control over the stock market. In retrospect, the Federal Reserve had no business meddling with the stock market, even indirectly. Policymakers like Strong had rejected such policy guidelines as targeting the economy's general price level, yet they essentially went about targeting the general level of stock prices.

What is so perverse about the Fed's and everybody else's compulsive attention to the activity in the stock market is that despite what has been written by many who know little about the true role of the stock market in the economy, the level of stock prices never reached an unusually high level by historical standards. Calvin Coolidge's 1928 statement that he saw nothing alarming about the stock market situation is often quoted derisively by historians as a sign of how little he knew, when in fact Coolidge was absolutely right. An excellent gauge for determining whether the price of a single stock or the average level of stock prices is justifiable, given economic conditions, is the price-to-earnings ratio, or *PE ratio* (the ratio of stock prices to company profits per share of stock). The average stock market PE ratio spends the overwhelming majority of its time varying between 10 and 20. This translates into an average rate of return on the stocks varying between 10% and 5%, respectively. Average stock prices are insupportably high only when the rates of return on bonds, typically a safer investment, significantly exceed the rates of return on stocks. Historically, this situation has occurred when the average of stock PE ratios has pushed above the level of 20.

It was not until the summer of 1929 that the market PE ratio cracked the 20 barrier. From 1926 to 1929, the ratio climbed from a level near 10—which suggests a rate of return of 10% and is consistent with a major stock rally—until it peaked in 1929. That means the rate of return an investor in the market could expect, even without excessive speculative activity, was above 5% throughout this five-year rally. Interest rates on corporate bonds at 3–4% could not offer such a high rate of return. It was perfectly rational for people to be buying stocks. The earnings of American businesses were rising fast enough to support this bull market until the summer of 1929. Those who write about the excesses of speculation in the stock market point to individual stories of irrational miscalculations. Had these kinds of investors been the rule rather than the exception, the market average PE ratio would have soared well past 20, but it never did. Indeed, had earnings continued to rise for American businesses into 1930 at the average rate of the 1920s, the stock market could easily have added another 25% gain in 1930 while keeping the rate of return on stocks above that on bonds. No crash, not even a hard landing, would have occurred in 1929 had the economic expansion of the 1920s continued.

What ended the economic contraction and subsequently set off the reversal of stock prices in the fall of 1929 was the Fed's restrained monetary policy throughout 1928 and right up to the crash in 1929. The people at the Fed may have never reached agreement on the proper method of restricting stock market speculation—qualitative or quantitative controls—but in the meantime they did produce a highly influential monetary policy. While they debated for almost two years, they did not allow the money supply to grow. Federal Reserve credit outstanding slowly shrank from early 1928 onward. By August 1929, the money supply was lower than it had been 16 months earlier. This period was too extended for the Fed to hold down the money supply. Aggregate demand ceased to grow and deflation worsened. Not surprisingly, by the summer of 1929 a recession had begun as industrial production and output began to fall.

The Fed engineered the beginning of a recession in 1929, as it had in 1923 and 1926. In both those two previous cases, the recession was relatively mild and short-lived, and the Fed brought each to an end by increasing the money supply. In doing so, the Fed had gained stature and the confidence of the business world. And so when the latest recession began, many in business and financial circles expected a similar scenario for 1929. They believed that output and profits would return to their expansion paths, making it unnecessary to sell stocks and possibly making it smart, albeit risky, to acquire even more. Consequently, stock prices continued to rise until August 1929, but the rally was running out of gas. With company earnings and aggregate demand turning downward and interest rates rising in the face of the stagnant money supply, it was no longer wise to continue buying stocks.

Whereas the Fed had been so unsuccessful at slowing the stock rally by using selective credit rationing, policymakers decided in August to lean heavier on restricting aggregate credit growth, and the discount rate was increased. By that time, however, it was too late to halt the rally with an increase in interest rates. The rally had already occurred and was in fact at an end. Nevertheless, this ill-timed move was the last nail in the stock market rally's coffin. The stock sell-off began in spurts in August and September, and turned into an avalanche in October. The Fed finally got what it had been working for—an end to the stock market rally—and what an end.

As hectic as the selling of stocks got, however, the results were not irrational. The market PE ratio fell from its peak of 20 to just below 13, a level implying a 7% rate of return on stocks, which was just above the interest rate on corporate bonds. Though it may not have been orderly, the stock market crash was simply a readjustment or correction of stock prices to new economic conditions, such as lower earnings and higher interest rates. These new conditions were the product of Federal Reserve policy. From this point of view, it is not difficult to determine what caused the economic contraction that began in 1929 or the stock market sell-off that accompanied it. One needs to look no farther than the Fed. By clamping down on the growth of the money supply in 1928 and 1929, the Fed set off its fourth recession of the decade, and this recession brought with it conditions that led stock owners to sell and switch their funds to safer, interest-earning assets.

Many people have written about the crash of 1929, its cause and consequences. The Fed is often still blamed for allowing stock prices to rise too fast, particularly in 1927, when monetary policy was relatively expansionary. It has been argued that more restrained policy then, as well as in the next two years, could have slowed the speculative bubble. As we have seen, however, monetary policy was downright contractionary from December 1927 to the fall of 1929. The falling money supply and general deflation confirm that fact. The money supply never grew too rapidly during the final stages of the stock market rally. As long as the economy stayed healthy, the rally continued, because robust economies fuel such rallies better than money supply increases do. The ends of both the stock market rally and the economic expansion were the products of the Fed's persistent tight money policy in 1928–29, not any so-called inflationary policy in any preceding time period.

Furthermore, the rally itself was not an irrational speculative orgy; nor was the crash such an irrational sell-off. When stock prices fell, they did not bring the economy down with them, as is often surmised. The crash of 1987 should have convinced doubters that the stock market (and movements of prices therein) may be an indicator of future expectations but is seldom a force in shaping the economic future unless policymakers are obsessed with the market, as they were in the 1920s. The stock market crash of 1929 was one manifestation of the recession of 1929. While the crash was historically significant, its negative repercussions on the economy were minor. It no more caused the depression of the 1930s than the crash of 1987 caused one.

Although the 1920s ended with the economy in the middle of a recession, there was no indication of what was to come in the next four years. Industrial production had leveled off after falling from mid-1929 to the end of the year. The Great Depression had really not yet begun. Economic activity had fallen to a lower plateau, but it was not plunging downward. What could be expected in December 1929? Given the Fed's track record during the first several months of the two previous recessions it had caused, one could expect little in the way of policy changes in the following few months. The Adolph Miller philosophy—namely that the Fed should do little to arrest contractions that were in progress—still held sway. The economy could only wait for another well-timed call from Great Britain to convince the Fed to push the money supply upward soon. The call never came, and the Fed did nothing.

4

The Great Contraction: 1930–1933

FROM THE FALL OF 1929 TO THE SPRING OF 1933, the economy sank progressively deeper into the great contraction; Table 4 traces that decline. More has been written about this period and the rest of the 1930s than any other era in U.S. economic history. One would think that with all these efforts, economic historians would have the era nailed down by now. Yet the sheer volume of scholarly material is a clue that a clear-cut explanation for the depression and a consensus assessment of the public policies during this decade have been difficult to obtain.

One reason is that those who analyzed the depression as it was occurring or immediately afterward suffered from the same failings as the policymakers: they lacked the modern aggregate demand/aggregate supply model that could have provided them with a far better understanding of what determines the levels of output, employment, interest rates, and prices. In addition, they lacked insight into how government policies can influence aggregate demand and aggregate supply. The interpretations of these early writers laid down a faulty foundation on which many other, more recent efforts have been built. As a result, we have produced at least three generations of Americans, ranging from students to policymakers, who have entirely the wrong impression about this most important decade.

Table 4. Economic Indicators, 1930–1933

	Q	M1	M2	P	GE	GR	Surplus Deficit	UN	Prime Rate
1930	−9.8	−5.7	−3.9	−2.6	3.3	4.1	0.8	8.7	3.6
1931	−7.6	−12	−15.4	−9.1	3.6	3.1	0.5	15.9	2.6
1932	−14.7	−7.3	−8.8	−10.3	4.7	1.9	−2.8	23.6	2.7
1933	−1.8	−2.7	−9.4	−2.2	4.6	2	−2.6	24.9	1.7

Q = Percent change in real GNP (output)
M1 = Percent change in M1 (currency plus checking account deposits)
M2 = Percent change in M2 (currency plus checking and savings accounts)
  P = Percent change in GNP Implicit Price Deflator
GE = Federal government expenditures (billions of dollars)
GR = Federal government revenues (billions of dollars)
Surplus/Deficit = GR minus GE
UN = Average unemployment rate (percent)
Prime Rate = Average prime rate of interest (percent)

Sources: See Bibliographic Essay.

☐ The Monetary Collapse

From 1929 to the spring of 1933, the money supply fell by close to one-third, and 40% of the nation's banks closed their doors, never to open them again. The three and a half years of monetary collapse ended with the entire banking system closed down in a bank holiday that was ordered by the new president but was precipitated by the Federal Reserve's consistent failure to do its job and arrest the rapid decline of the money supply. To what degree the Fed can be blamed for the depth of the depression is still a matter of debate, but one is extremely hard-pressed to find any other single cause that could have been nearly so influential. As one writer puts it, to explain the worse depression in American history one must find something that was horribly wrong—not just moderately wrong. Monetary policy during this period was cataclysmically bad, as a glance back at Figure 1 emphasizes.

☐ **Charting the Plunge**   The Fed—thanks to the actions of the New York Federal Reserve Bank and its president, George Harrison—reacted well to the stock market crash in October 1929. The discount rate was lowered, and the Fed bought securities in the open market to increase liquidity when it was dangerously scarce. The result was that the money supply was temporarily increased, and there was virtually no hint of a bank panic. Unfortunately, the upward surge in liquidity was reversed soon thereafter, and by December the money supply was lower than it had been in August.

The economy continued to slide deeper into a serious recession during the first half of 1930 as output and prices continued to fall. Many people believed this recession was similar to previous reversals, such as those in 1924 and 1927, and looked for the economy to soon level off and begin a recovery. Indeed, President Hoover predicted just that outcome in May 1930 as the decline appeared to level off. The Fed assumed the same stance it took in the early stages of previous recessions, doing nothing to try to reverse the decline in economic activity. Most members of the Federal Reserve Board still clung to Adolph Miller's view that there was little the Fed could or should do to arrest the contraction. The Fed was inclined to await the beginning of a recovery before it moved to increase the availability of credit. Miller even argued against reductions in the discount rate for fear they would set off a new surge in stock market speculation. Some lessons were apparently very hard to learn.

The Fed's policy in 1930 cannot be described as simply benign neglect. In spite of lowering the discount rate four times by a half-point each time, it followed a generally contractionary course right into the fall of 1930. The money supply fell 2.6% during the first 10 months of the year. This drop came even though the nation's gold stock was in the middle of a climb that extended back to 1929 and would continue until September 1931. The Fed insisted on continuing to violate the rules of the gold standard by refusing to increase the money supply in proportion to the growth in the gold stock. Federal Reserve credit outstanding actually fell by more than one-third from the stock market crash to the fall of 1930. This tightening more than counteracted the gold inflow and caused the money supply to fall to a level as low as that at the end of 1927. With the money supply and velocity both falling, it is not surprising that aggregate demand and output in 1930 were lower than in 1927.

As bad as the economy was performing in September 1930, a recovery was still conceivably around the corner. But what began in October was destined to turn this recession into a record-breaking depression. A series of bank failures, primarily in agricultural areas, set off a full-scale, nationwide bank panic. Throughout the country, depositors scurried to their banks to withdraw their funds before their banks closed and all their money was lost. When the Bank of the United States (a large but otherwise normal commercial bank in New York City that happened to have given itself a rather impressive name) failed, the headlines on the front page of the *New York Times* could hardly have been reassuring to the average American.

The scramble to acquire liquidity by depositors, and by the banks themselves, sent bank deposits and loans tumbling. As a result, the money supply dropped 3% in three months, putting it 6.5% lower in January 1931 than it was in September 1929. The sharp decline in the money supply tells us what the Fed did in the face of the bank crisis: nothing. Because most of the banks that failed were small and not members of the Federal Reserve system, the board did not feel responsible. It believed that the failures were the result of bad management, not a sign of anything fundamentally wrong with conditions in the financial markets.

The effects of the bank panic that led to the closing of more than 600 banks in just two months did not at the time appear to be lasting. As winter was giving way to spring in early 1931, it looked like the recession might be showing the first sprouts of recovery. Industrial production was on the rise, and the descent of all other measures of economic activity had slowed markedly—a sign of the economy's resilience. But just when many customers thought it was safe to go to the bank again, a second banking crisis began in March 1931. This crisis was worse than the preceding year's; bank deposits fell rapidly, dragging the money supply down another 5.5% by the end of August. Even though the gold stock was still rising, the Fed stood by as major portions of the money supply and the banking system disappeared.

While the United States was in the midst of this second banking crisis, Great Britain decided once again to leave the gold standard. One can hardly blame the British, since gold continued to flow out of Great Britain to America, where the Fed kept it locked out of the national and world economy. The British had an excuse for the decline in their money supply: their gold stock was shrinking. The United States had no such excuse. At this point, the Fed decided to begin following normal gold standard procedures. To prevent gold from escaping toward Britain, where it could now fetch an unrestricted price in pounds sterling, the Fed followed its gold standard manual and increased the discount rate in two steps from 1.5% to 3.5%.

Thus, in the middle of a nationwide bank panic characterized by an insatiable demand for liquidity, the Fed made money more scarce and more expensive, the rationale being that gold tends to flow toward the highest interest rate. That may have been routine gold standard procedure, but it caused a worsening of the banking crisis and an acceleration in the drop of the money supply. From August 1931 to January 1932, the money supply fell an additional 12%. By this time, the money supply was at a level comparable to that in 1923. Banks were faced with a swift drain of reserves from both domestic and foreign sources. Unable to meet these demands for currency, record numbers of banks had to close their doors. Contributing to the closures was the rise in long-term interest rates, which drove down the prices of bonds and thereby the value of many bank assets until banks were insolvent as well as illiquid. More than 1,800 banks closed during the final months of 1931.

A change of atmosphere came in 1932. The rash of bank failures eased by the end of January. At about the same time, Congress created the Reconstruction Finance Corporation (RFC), which was endorsed by President Hoover and designed to lend money to troubled firms. Most of those loans went to banks and other financial institutions. By the end of the year, the RFC had injected almost $1 billion in loans into the financial system. In addition, Congress passed the Banking Act of 1932, which loosened the Fed's collateral requirements for issuing currency and banks' collateral requirements for borrowing reserves from the Fed. The Fed was definitely getting strong signals from Congress to increase the money supply.

When Congress began suggesting it might do something radical and take money matters into its own hands, the Fed began moving in April 1932 to buy Treasury securities in the open market. At first the purchases were made slowly and reluctantly. By the summer, however, the Open Market Investment Committee picked up the pace until $1 billion worth of securities had been purchased by August. The purchase program ended just after Congress adjourned, leaving the Fed, which was never enthusiastic about the purchases, without any continuing pressure to add to the money supply.

The timidity with which the Fed approached the purchases (a stance we will discuss a little later) certainly was not consistent with the apparent response of the economy to the increase in bank reserves. The combination of two forces—a slowing of the bank failure epidemic and the injection of new funds by the Fed and the RFC—helped slow the decline of the money supply to the point that it almost leveled off. Industrial production bottomed out in May and climbed into the fall months. Interest rates, which had shot up in late 1932, fell in both the long-term and the short-term markets. Even the stock market reached its lowest point and began to recover ground. Some economists make a strong argument for dating the ultimate trough of the great contraction in the summer of 1932. But in fact the economy had one more major crisis to withstand before the contraction phase of the depression came to an end.

By July 1932, the Fed had purchased as many Treasury securities as it believed appropriate. Excess reserves had reached a level considered more than plentiful by Governor Harrison, usually the main supporter for purchases. For the rest of the year, the Fed allowed its credit outstanding to fall back to the level of early 1932. In other words, it abandoned the brief experiment in expansionary policy, despite the apparent stirrings of a recovery, and returned to a stance of inaction.

A third and final banking crisis began to form during the last three months of 1932. The money supply, which had stopped falling and leveled off during the second half of 1932, fell drastically in January. During the first quarter of 1933, the final three months of the great money supply contraction, 13% more of the money supply ceased to exist. The public's efforts to withdraw funds from banks pushed many more banks over the brink as depositors began to demand not just currency but gold. The latter new demand arose based on speculation that the newly elected Franklin Roosevelt might take some action that would result in a devaluation of the dollar and thereby drive up the dollar price of gold.

In the face of all this hoarding, rising bank indebtedness, and plummeting money supply, what did the Fed do? Once again, nothing. The Fed had already reached a self-imposed ceiling on holdings of Treasury securities and preferred not to breach it. The banking system was crying out for more liquidity, but the Fed would not supply any more. In fact, the Fed moved in the opposite direction. The speculation about Roosevelt's plans for the gold standard had touched off a rather heavy outflow of gold. The Fed's response was exactly the same as it had been in the fall of 1931. The board raised the discount rate in February 1933. That did not stop the gold drain, however, and the Fed found that its stock of gold had fallen below the legal limit, given the size of the money supply. Panic had now reached inside the walls of the Federal Reserve.

The Fed had painted itself and the banking system into a corner. It was now seemingly powerless to save the banks or its own dignity. The Fed suspended its gold reserve requirement and began discussing a bank holiday, a day when all banks would not open for business. That idea was rejected on 3 March. Several state governors went ahead and declared bank holidays in their states on 4 March, and the Fed decided to keep its doors closed on that day as well. Two days later, on 6 March, Roosevelt declared a national bank holiday that in some areas lasted until 15 March. This was not a suspension of payment, such as commonly occurred during financial panics in the days before the Fed. While some banks did fail during those periods of suspension, banks in general did not close their doors. They stayed open, and banking business proceeded except for the payout of currency or specie. The bank holiday of 1933 was a complete shutdown, and it took with it 5,000 more banks, which never reopened. The Fed, created in 1913 to prevent the need for a suspension of payments, precipitated through its policy actions and inaction something far worse and vastly more damaging.

☐ **The Fed Misreads the Signs**   Throughout the three and a half years of monetary decline that we just charted, the Federal Reserve moved in ways that defy logic by the standards of today's understanding of macroeconomics. It is easy to criticize the Fed from that perspective; we necessarily end up painting a picture of the people at the Fed as a group of complete incompetents. That certainly was not the case, since many of the people involved were leaders in the fields of finance and financial legislation. Much of what the Fed did was consistent with the economic orthodoxy of the time and with the ideas of at least a substantial number of economists. The view that a contraction must be allowed to run its course—although today it sounds like the equivalent of the centuries-ago medical practice of bleeding a patient—was widely held. Many policymakers and their advisers, solicited and unsolicited, believed it would be a mistake to try to tinker artificially with the credit markets by applying expansionary monetary policies. The Fed's policies were founded on that belief.

Nevertheless, even though the Fed's actions were in keeping with the theories of many contemporaries, these experts in the field of banking and finance failed to see some very clear handwriting on the wall. They misread strong and clear signals. Alarms were sounding all around them, but they interpreted them as false alarms. Once again, lest we appear to come down too hard on the Fed, it must be remembered that some historians and economic historians continue today to misread the same signs in the same manner after almost 60 years of experience. As mentioned in the previous chapter, some continue today to characterize monetary policy in the latter 1920s as inflationary despite the fact that the money supply grew so slowly (and at times not at all) and prices fell throughout the period. Similarly, some continue to cling to the view held by the Fed during the entire period of 1929 to 1933—namely that the Fed followed a course of monetary ease. This perspective is in spite of overwhelming evidence to the contrary in the form of the rapid decline of the money supply and the thousands of bank failures.

The most obvious signal the Fed misread was the significance of the bank panics. Until the first of three major panic periods began in October 1930, the recession that had started a little over a year earlier was serious but not unusual. No one can really say exactly what set off the first or the other two panics. Given the states where the first bank failures were concentrated, it is probably safe to argue that it started in the rural banks that became insolvent because of a bad harvest or some other agricultural dislocation that caused farmers to default on their loans. The small and undiversified rural banks found the value of their assets falling below that of their liabilities, and they were declared insolvent. Depositors often lost portions of or all their funds. Fearing the same thing might happen to them, depositors in other banks rushed to withdraw their funds. If enough depositors lined up at any one bank, it might be forced to close its doors because of a lack of cash to meet the depositors' demands. Many perfectly healthy banks failed because of a lack of liquidity rather than because of bad loans leading to insolvency.

Regardless of where the panics began, the results were clear. Starting in October 1930, the public demonstrated its preference for currency over maintaining bank deposits, and that preference became progressively more pronounced during the subsequent panics. Basic money and banking mechanics tells us that, all else equal, such withdrawals will drive down the money supply as bankers rebuild their reserves by reducing loans. A dollar in a bank account and a dollar in an individual's pocket are both counted as part of the money supply. But every dollar deposited in a bank is the basis for several dollars of created deposits throughout the banking system. Take one dollar out of a bank and keep it out, and the money supply will eventually shrink by several dollars. This multiplier effect occurs in all fractional reserve banking systems. In the period under discussion, bank panics, which brought depositors rushing to their banks to withdraw funds, drove the money supply down rapidly even in areas where banks were not failing.

The reactions of the nation's bankers to these circumstances made matters worse. To keep their banks liquid enough to satisfy depositors' demands, bank managers were forced to increase their holdings of liquid assets. That meant a rise in excess reserves and a reduction in the number of dollars banks would lend out of any deposit. That reluctance to lend worked to further reduce the money supply. Add onto that the deposits that were destroyed when banks could not meet their depositors' demands and closed their doors (there was no government bailout and depositor payoff), and it is easy to see why the money supply fell by more than one-third during the monetary contraction. Furthermore, in their desperate scramble to find liquidity, bank managers had to sell long-term securities at losses. The fire sale of these securities drove their prices downward and in turn lowered the value of all banks' assets. Thus, even the actions of well-managed banks were contributing to their own demise.

During the first of the bank panic episodes in 1930, the Fed observed that the overwhelming majority of failing banks were relatively small banks in small communities and were not members of the Fed system (and officially out of its jurisdiction). Furthermore, these bank closures were interpreted as signs of bad management rather than an indication of a fundamental problem in the banking system. What the Fed failed to realize was that in an escalating liquidity crisis, it is logical for the relatively small and less efficient banks to fail first. Because the banking system was indeed in the middle of a massive liquidity crisis, the longer the Fed failed to act, the worse the crisis got and the more it threatened previously efficient banks.

The Fed had been invented to provide the banking system with an elastic supply of currency so that just such a scenario would not occur. Its governors' charter assignment was to nip bank panics in the bud, but they failed to see the seriousness of the situation in 1930 or, incredibly, in the later episodes in 1931 and late 1932. Admittedly, many of the banks that failed in the early months were smaller banks born during the first two decades of the century when the number of small nonmember banks swelled. Many were in rural areas and began failing in the 1920s as agriculture prices fell dramatically after the war. But as long as the Fed was watching over a system made up of more than 25,000 banks, its responsibility was to provide liquidity to all banks, not just member banks. If the Fed did not want its member banks infected with the same virus that was befalling nonmember banks, it should have treated the infection before it spread to the whole system. That is just common sense, not fancy economics. The Federal Reserve Board thought differently, however. It is amazing that the same people who in 1928 had deemed it appropriate for the Fed to stray well outside its province and take responsibility over the movement of stock market prices would feel no obligation to ensure the survival of thousands of banks that clearly were its responsibility.

One of the reasons the Fed did not do a better job of coming to the aid of struggling banks was that board members believed they were conducting a policy of monetary ease. From that misconception sprouted the view that a bank in trouble in circumstances of monetary ease was probably unworthy of aid. Even though the money supply was falling at a record pace, the Fed felt credit was readily available because of its faulty interpretation of the quantity of excess reserves in the banking system. When occasions arose to decide whether to conduct open market purchases of government securities in order to add to the supply of reserves in the banking system and thereby add to the supply of credit, policymakers at the Fed looked to the level of excess reserves. They often found large quantities. In fact, when the Fed did make purchases to add to reserves, they were surprised to see banks use those newly created reserves to increase their excess reserves rather than to make loans. The Fed took that as a sign that the banks had an excess of excess reserves—in other words, that money was more than readily available in the banking system and that much more of it was there than was necessary.

What the Fed failed to see at this time, and would again miss later in the decade, was that banks had a great *demand* for excess reserves. If an open market purchase produced only a rise in excess reserves, not an increase in loans, it was a sign that the bank managers believed they needed even more excess reserves. In the middle of a liquidity crisis such as this one, bankers, like everyone else, felt safe only when they had built a wall of protective liquidity around themselves. Had the Fed properly interpreted the rise in excess reserves, they would have realized that the demand for excess reserves was rising faster than the supply—that there was a shortage of reserves. The small additions the Fed made to the total stock of liquidity were trifling compared with what the system needed. The only way to encourage bankers to make more loans was to create more excess reserves than the bankers needed, not to create less—as board members were often inclined to do. The buildup of reserves was interpreted as a sign that monetary policy was already too "inflationary."

That anyone could possibly believe there was too much money in an economy in which the money supply was plummeting and bank failures were numbering in the thousands may seem incomprehensible. The key indicator of the relationship between the supply of and demand for funds is the level of interest rates, and interest rates told the Fed there was a surplus of reserves and money. But the level of interest rates was the sign the Fed misread the most. Throughout the monetary decline, most interest rates were dramatically low. The discount rate was reduced to a low point of 1.5% just before Britain left the gold standard in 1931. Yields on Treasury bonds spent most of the period around 3%, while rates on Treasury bills dropped below 1%. Commercial paper rates fell as low as 3% in 1931 and below 2% in 1933. And rates on short-term commercial loans sank as low as 2.5% in 1931 and 1% in 1933. Compared with past experience, these interest rates were unusually low. With excess reserves rising and interest rates falling, the Fed concluded that money was more than plentiful.

The Fed was not alone in that assessment. Many observers pointed to the low interest rates as a sign that the Fed was really doing all it could to stimulate the economy, but it was all to no avail. In fact, the view that monetary policy was expansionary but impotent during the monetary contraction arose from the combined interpretation of the levels of excess reserves and interest rates. The old saying "You can lead a horse to water, but you can't make it drink" is often evoked as an analogy for the supposed inability of the Fed to translate excess reserves into increases in loans and aggregate demand. Even today, economic historians who do not accept the monetary explanation for the Great Depression—that the economy's main problem during the great contraction was the collapse of the banking system and the plunge of the money supply—point to these low interest rates as proof that money was neither scarce nor dear. As further support, some emphasize that the real money supply (the money supply adjusted for changes in the price level) hardly fell at all, since prices fell as rapidly as the money supply. And if the real money supply was not falling, then money should not be blamed for the drop in aggregate demand.

The mistake made here is to look at market interest rates instead of real interest rates, which equal market rates minus the inflation rate or plus the deflation rate. While interest rates may have looked low in nominal terms during the contraction, they were exceptionally high in real terms. Prices were falling at an average annual rate of 10% during much of this period. The money people were paying back on loans was worth a lot more in terms of purchasing power than the money they borrowed, and that made the true cost of borrowing exorbitantly high. While market rates were below 3% and as low as a fraction of 1%, real interest rates were in the teens. Capital investors cannot afford to pay such interest rates, because very few business projects have rates of return that are so high. Not surprisingly, private capital investment plummeted as real interest rates soared. In fact, capital investment dropped by 100% and took about 16% of aggregate demand with it. The remainder of the drop in aggregate demand came from the decline in consumption set off by the drop in income and employment that resulted from the scarcity of money.

A decline in prices is the mechanism by which the marketplace adjusts to a major drop in the money supply and aggregate demand. Conceivably, if prices fall as fast as the money supply, the real purchasing power of the remaining money and the level of aggregate demand can be maintained. But the financial markets have no way of adjusting interest rates to deal with rapid rates of deflation. If prices are falling at an annual rate of 10%, there is no way of lowering an interest rate that starts out at 5% to a level low enough to accommodate the deflation. For example, charging a 1% market rate while prices are falling at a 10% rate results in a real interest rate of 11%. Real rates in the teens are extremely unusual and have occurred in U.S. economic history only during severe contractions. Thus, even when prices are falling as fast as the money supply, if both are falling too fast the financial market will be unable to find an interest rate that keeps capital investment and aggregate demand from falling. And since the cause of the falling prices reverts back to the falling money supply, the drop in aggregate demand is the result of the money supply's drop—and the blame for this situation rests squarely on the Federal Reserve.

It is understandable that the Fed would not have made the distinction between real and market interest rates in this earlier era. That lesson was to be pounded into the heads of Fed board members during the 1960s and 1970s, when rapid inflation caused major divergences between real and market rates. Again policymakers misread the signs, only in the later period it led to overly expansionary monetary policy. The level of real interest rates is always the true measure of the relative availability of credit. With real interest rates in the teens during the period 1930 to 1933, the real signs were telling the Fed that money was extremely scarce and expensive. But the Fed looked at market rates instead and got the opposite impression.

Unfortunately, the distinction between real versus market interest rates continues to escape many modern policymakers, as well as interpreters of past policy. Thus, to expect the Fed to make that distinction in 1930 is probably asking too much. Nevertheless, the limited experiences of the Fed could have shown the board that it needed to reverse the decline in the money supply. Prices may be able to fall as fast as the money supply, but interest rates cannot. As a result, the economy cannot withstand rapid deflation without a significant drop in real activity. The 1920–21 recession certainly provided the Fed with guidance on that front. It should not have allowed the bank crises to persist in the 1930s, because they were the cause of the rapid drop in the money supply. Regardless of what the Fed thought about the banks that were failing, it should have provided the banking system with ample liquidity to keep banks from closing and adding fuel to the panic. Had the Fed done so, neither the money supply nor prices would have fallen so rapidly, and market interest rates could have sunk low enough to keep real rates at a reasonable level. That would have prevented a major drop in aggregate demand and would have taken the "Great" out of the "Great Depression." To follow such a course, however, the Fed would have had to read the signs better.

When one considers the effect of the monetary contraction on real interest rates, investment, and aggregate demand, it is difficult to escape the conclusion that the Fed deserves most of the blame for the severity of the Great Depression. Those who still cling to the "underconsumptionist theory"—that is, that a major unexplained drop in consumption triggered the drop in aggregate demand—have failed to consider the correct evidence. The drop in consumption and investment that accounted for the drop in demand was caused by the vanishing money supply and the incredibly high real interest rates. Consumers and businesspeople are not complex economic animals; they spend more when money is cheap and less when it is expensive. The reason capital investment and consumption fell so dramatically during the contraction is that money was more scarce and more expensive than in any other time in U.S. history.

□ Balance the Budget or Bust

In much the same way that the contraction was testing the knowledge and skills of the people in charge of monetary policy at the Federal Reserve, the makers of fiscal policy in Congress and the White House were faced with difficult choices. The tax law changes of the 1920s had made the budget much more sensitive to swings in economic activity because taxes tied to incomes and sales had taken over for those tied to wealth and property as the federal government's primary sources of revenue. Consequently, tax revenues rose and fell with the level of GNP. As the economy sank deeper into the depression, the federal budget swung from a surplus to a major deficit. Running a budget deficit during peacetime was simply against the rules for sound fiscal management in this period. In 1932 Congress met the deficit head-on and passed a record tax increase. Any economics student today would recognize this move as a profound policy mistake because it would tend to reduce aggregate demand; however, it was not viewed that way then. The only way to understand such policy is to look back at the fiscal philosophy of the time and the steps taken to operate within that outlook.

□ **Fiscal Philosophy**   Although Moses did not come down from the mountain with an eleventh commandment that said "Thou shalt balance the budget," he may as well have done so, considering the stance policymakers took as the economy entered the Great Depression. This simple axiom was essentially the extent of the rules of fiscal policy—that is, the budget should be in balance annually. Government entities from the smallest boroughs right on up through the states and the federal government all followed the same rule: current revenues should pay for current expenditures. Exceptions were allowed, but they were few and the rules were restrictive in peacetime. Borrowing could be done to finance capital expenditure projects that would be paid off out of future tax revenues. And borrowing was also permitted during a war, when it was recognized that expenditures would have to exceed tax revenues out of necessity; even then, however, postwar surpluses would be prescribed to pay off the debt. These are exactly the rules that were followed by the federal government throughout the 1920s. World War I deficits had boosted the national debt above the $25 billion level, but 11 straight surplus budgets (from 1920 through 1930) had reduced the debt by more than $8 billion.

The Republican administrations of Harding, Coolidge, and Hoover certainly followed these rules to the letter, but the economic contraction changed everything. As GNP sank rapidly, tax revenues flowing into the Treasury fell off sharply. Without any discretionary change in taxing or spending laws on the part of the president or Congress, the budget surplus turned into a deficit. Today, such automatic changes in the budget are referred to as *automatic fiscal policy*, as opposed to explicit changes in policy, which go under the title of *discretionary fiscal policy*. Whether they like it or not, fiscal policymakers must face the fact that during an economic contraction, the automatic drop in tax revenues will push the federal budget into a deficit or deepen an already-existing deficit. Because many economists now believe that a budget deficit tends to add at least a little to aggregate demand, an automatic deficit that appears during a recession is appreciated as beneficial. The deficit, it is thought, slows the decline in aggregate demand and thereby acts as an automatic stabilizer. What "sound fiscal management" was supposed to do in the face of a deficit born out of a depression became a point of theoretical and practical debate.

Given that the comprehensive model of aggregate demand and supply was developed in the years after the depression, policymakers in the 1930s could not refer to it for guidance. Instead, they relied on the orthodoxies of the time, and the consensus said deficits were dangerous. The overriding fear was that by running a deficit and adding to the national debt, the government would be undermining the confidence that Americans and foreigners alike held in the U.S. economy, its government, and the value of the dollar. It was feared that if the government did not at least make an effort to hold down the deficit, confidence in its ability to pay its bills and remain solvent would deteriorate. And if the government's credit rating declined, the ability of all Americans to acquire credit would be eroded. In short, a financial crisis was envisioned if taxes did not cover current expenditures. Pictured in this crisis scenario were further drops in consumption and capital investment spending, events that would send aggregate demand even lower. Moreover, the drop in confidence abroad would set off a sale of dollars and a flow of gold out of the United States, making it necessary for the country to renounce the gold standard.

Efforts to hold down the deficit or balance the budget were seen by policymakers as moves that would prevent the deficit from making the depression worse. Even those economists who believed that running a deficit in a recession was probably a good idea conceded that relatively large deficits could set off an erosion in confidence. Under those circumstances, whatever gain in aggregate demand the deficit itself might create would be canceled out by the losses attributable to the crisis in financial confidence. Thus, as long as most people believed deficits were harmful and acted as if they were, the forecasts were self-fulfilling. Consequently, economists further argued that, to benefit from the expansionary effects of a budget deficit, it would be necessary first to reduce the deficit to a level that did not undermine confidence. At least, that is how most policymakers and their advisers saw it. Confidence and expectations are tricky variables to try to predict and control, but in the absence of a dependable model of output determination, this is exactly what policymakers tried to do.

□ **Taxes versus Deficits**   With the budget showing a $700 million surplus in 1929 (in spite of the downturn in economic activity), Secretary of the Treasury Andrew Mellon implemented a tax rate reduction for 1930. This was a progressive step with which Hoover was comfortable because the budget surplus allowed room for a reduction without throwing the budget into a deficit. This move shows that given a choice between tax increases and decreases, the Hoover administration would have preferred tax cuts. By mid-1930, however, as the depression continued to worsen, Mellon projected that a deficit would appear for the first time in 12 years. He was right; as tax revenues fell by one-quarter and expenditures rose, the surplus was replaced by a $500 million deficit in 1931. Once the deficit appeared, Hoover believed he no longer had a choice. Given the fiscal philosophy of the time, another tax cut was out of the question. The issue was how soon should taxes be increased and by how much.

Hoover, to his credit, was in no hurry to raise taxes in 1931. He clung to the belief that the contraction would not last too much longer. Under such a scenario, a small deficit could be tolerated because most likely it would disappear during the impending recovery. That Hoover should be so confident in 1931 may seem blindly unwarranted in retrospect, given how much the depression worsened in ensuing months. On the other hand, our earlier examination of monetary policy during the same period revealed that lots of people expected economic rebounds in early 1930 and 1931, when the economy did show some positive stirrings. Furthermore, had the Fed moved to halt the decline of the money supply and prevent the second bank crisis in 1931, the rebound could very well have become a reality. Under those circumstances, history would have painted a much more favorable picture of Hoover as the president who cut taxes and held off efforts to raise them in the face of the impending depression. Historians would have declared him a person ahead of his time, rather than an inept conservative.

Unfortunately, the economic slide worsened in mid-1931, and it dragged down tax revenues with it. In 1932 tax receipts, at $1.9 billion, were less than half those in 1930, while expenditures had climbed to their highest level since 1921, at $4.7 billion. The deficit in excess of $2.5 billion—equal to almost 3% of GNP—that began to appear in 1932 sent everyone at the Treasury and in Congress scurrying to devise a proper tax increase for restoring a balanced budget. A wide range of modest increases in excise taxes and tariffs, as well as a national sales tax, was considered. Many of the excise tax and tariff increases were passed along with some hikes in estate taxes, but the brunt of the tax increase came in the form of increases in individual and corporate income tax rates. The Revenue Act of 1932 "soaked the rich," but it also doused the middle class; tax rates were raised, and exemptions were lowered. The result—as all students of the period have come to know— was the greatest peacetime tax increase in the country's history up to that date.

The tax increase was a fiscal failure. Despite the higher tax rates, tax revenues in 1933 were barely higher than in 1932. The continued decline of output and income prevented tax receipts from rising. Indeed, it can be argued that the tax increase itself contributed to that output decline by further slowing consumer spending and thereby further reducing aggregate demand. As a matter of fact, the 1932 tax increase is often used by economists as the best example of bad fiscal policy. In their effort to reduce the budget deficit, congressional leaders probably deepened the depression while making no headway with the deficit. We now recognize that efforts to balance the budget during a depression require the enactment of such contractionary fiscal policies as tax increases or spending decreases, both of which are likely to work to lower aggregate demand and output and exacerbate the problem.

As the presidential election campaign heated up in 1932, Hoover's fiscal policy became one of Franklin Roosevelt's favorite targets. Given what we have just discussed, we would expect some criticism, and it would seem reasonable to expect Hoover's opponent to call for spending increases or tax cuts. But that is not the position Roosevelt took. To the contrary, he criticized Hoover for failing to balance the budget. He even claimed that Hoover's deficits—not his tax increases—were contributing to the depression. He spoke poetically about fiscal ships wrecking on the jagged rocks of loose government spending. Roosevelt promised to balance the budget better than Hoover. In doing so, he was promising to make fiscal policy even more depressing. While the economy was starving for more spending, the 1932 tax increase gave it less, and Roosevelt promised an even stricter diet based on the goal of a balanced budget. The American voters followed the orthodoxy of the time and voted for a balanced budget, but they were also voting for more bad fiscal policy medicine. As it turned out, Roosevelt never did balance the budget, but not for lack of trying. As we will see in the next chapter, the deficit paranoia that characterized fiscal policy in the 1930s helped prolong the agony of the depression throughout the decade. It is abundantly clear that government policy was the biggest contributor to the contraction phase of the Great Depression. The government also had much to do with delaying a complete recovery.

5

The Long Climb Back: 1933–1940

AFTER A FEW FALSE STARTS, THE WORST contraction in U.S. history finally ended in the spring of 1933, and the economy began the long climb back to full employment. The ascent was protracted, since recovery was not complete until after the country had entered World War II. Thus, while the contraction lasted four years, the recovery took close to nine years. This nine-year period was the country's most turbulent since the Civil War; the prolonged suffering tested the economy's resiliency and the people's resolve to retain the free-market system.

This period was also marked by the incredible storm of government activity associated with the New Deal. Never before or since has there been en era in which the federal government was so busy implementing such a variety of programs to revamp and revive the economy. The consensus at the time was that before the economy could hope for a complete recovery the numerous faults in its structure and workings needed to be addressed. It was from this viewpoint that the flurry of legislation called the New Deal was born. We now recognize that most governmental restructuring was inconsequential with respect to the level of economic activity, and the impact of economic policy on the level of output and employment was usually negative. Discretionary fiscal and monetary policy moves were quite limited during the recovery period; nevertheless, the economy's ascent back to full employment took so long partly because it was handicapped by those moves.

The pace and pattern of the recovery are our immediate focus, because they have much to say about how ill-advised was the course taken by policymakers. Next we examine monetary policy, because the recovery, such as it was, was primarily fueled by the growth of the money supply—an expansion that came about despite rather than because of Fed policy. Moreover, fiscal policy, as manifested in the New Deal, probably did more harm than good. Under the circumstances, the nation was fortunate that events turned out as well as they did from 1933 to 1940.

☐   The Long Recovery

Anyone who assesses the recovery phase of the Great Depression is struck by the fact that despite some years with impressive rates of output expansion, the economy had not come close to returning to full employment by the end of the 1930s. With the unemployment rate above 14% in 1940, obviously the long climb back to prosperity would have taken several years had it not been for the intervention of World War II. As cynical and unpatriotic as it may sound, the policies of the German and Japanese governments were probably more instrumental in the recovery of the American economy than any actions taken in Washington.

Table 5 provides a summary of the telling statistics of the 1930s. Four years of output expansion began in 1933. By 1937, the level of output had risen 35% and returned to its predepression, 1929 level. But that was not nearly good enough, because it was no longer 1929. During those eight years, the country's population and labor force had continued to grow, and technological change did not halt. The net results were that (a) output fell well below the economy's full-employment potential; (b) the unemployment rate was still above 14%; and (c) output per capita was substantially below the 1929 level. At this stage, the recovery was only half-complete.

Whereas the labor force and its production capacity do not stop growing during a contraction, it was not good enough merely to return to the precontraction level of output. The full-employment level of output continued to rise at close to 3% annually throughout the contraction and recovery phases of the depression. While the economy was sliding down the hill and climbing back up, the hill was getting bigger. As a result, one could have expected the climb back up to the top of the hill to take significantly longer than the preceding slide down. Such had been the case in contractions before the 1930s episode, and it has been

Table 5. Economic Indicators, 1933–1940

	Q	M1	M2	P	GE	GR	Surplus Deficit	UN	Prime Rate
1933	−1.8	−2.7	−9.4	−2.2	4.6	2	−2.6	24.9	1.7
1934	9.1	15.2	14	8.9	6.7	3	−3.7	21.7	1
1935	9.9	18.4	14.8	3.3	6.5	3.7	−2.8	20.1	0.75
1936	13.9	14.1	11.4	0	8.5	4	−4.5	16.9	0.75
1937	5.3	−5.5	−2	4	7.8	5	−2.8	14.3	0.9
1938	−5	8.9	5.9	−1.5	6.8	5.6	−1.2	19	0.8
1939	8.6	13.5	10.1	−1.6	8.9	5	−3.9	17.2	0.6
1940	7.8	16.3	12.5	2	9.5	6.5	−3	14.6	0.6

Q = Percent change in real GNP (output)
M1 = Percent change in M1 (currency plus checking account deposits)
M2 = Percent change in M2 (currency plus checking and savings accounts)
P = Percent change in GNP Implicit Price Deflator
GE = Federal government expenditures (billions of dollars)
GR = Federal government revenues (billions of dollars)
Surplus/Deficit = GR minus GE
UN = Average unemployment rate (percent)
Prime Rate = Average prime rate of interest (percent)

Sources: See Bibliographic Essay.

the case ever since. That the contraction phase was so long and severe from 1929 to 1933 guaranteed that an unaided recovery to full employment would take well over four years. Never had the economy sunk so far below full employment.

Beyond these considerations, the recovery was even more disappointing from two perspectives. First, in spite of those impressive overall output expansion figures for 1933 to 1937, the recovery got off to a rather halting start. Historically, the steeper and deeper the contraction, the stronger has been the rebound, particularly in its earliest stages. Examples, such as the 1920–21 and 1981–82 recessions, show that when the unemployment rate soars into the double-digit range, the first year or two of the recovery brings that rate down swiftly from its lofty peak to a level that is still too high but is manageable. Such was certainly not the case in 1934 and 1935. The best the economy could accomplish was a reduction in the unemployment rate from 25% to 20%. Industrial production followed a path echoing that of the unemployment rate. Its rapid climb from the trough in the spring of 1933 was typical, but it stalled in the fall of 1933. For the next two years, factory output leveled off and followed a zigzag course. Only in the latter part of 1935 did industrial production crack the 1933 level and set off on a somewhat steady upward path.

The second disappointing aspect of the recovery was the recession the economy suffered from the spring of 1937 to the spring of 1938. Output fell back down to below the 1929 level, unemployment swelled back up to 19% of the labor force, and industrial production once again dropped below the level in the fall of 1933. The economy had lost its footing and slid back down that hill it had been clawing up for four years. And once again the hill continued to grow even as output slipped lower. It took two years to bring industrial production back up to the 1937 level; it was not until 1940 that the unemployment rate was back to the 14% range it had reached in 1937. The recession of 1937 delayed the recovery by at least two years and, but for the war, would probably have added four years to the long climb back to full employment. Without this relapse, the recovery—had it remained on its pre-relapse course and had it not been interrupted by the war—might have been completed by 1941.

The disappointing performance of the economy during the recovery phase of the Great Depression raises obvious questions about why the recovery apparently got off to such a slow start and why, once the recovery had finally locked on to a robust pace, it was suddenly derailed by a recession. Neither of these patterns fits the historically established scenario for a recovery. It all makes one very suspicious about what influences government policy might have had on the economy during this period.

□ Money Fuels the Recovery

An examination of the evidence shows that the recovery phase of the Great Depression began in the spring of 1933. All indices bottomed out and turned upward at the same time. The turnaround for the economy began when the banking system reopened; it certainly could not have started before that date, given the financial chaos reigning during the first months of 1933, when banks were closing and the money supply was plummeting. But the recovery started in earnest the day the bank holiday was over, and it was born out of the reforms that allowed the banks to reopen. The money supply, too, began a four-year advance that lasted until the spring of 1937.

☐ **Financial Reforms**   The contraction could not be halted as long as the banking system was hemorrhaging, as it was in early 1933. A recovery could not begin until confidence was restored in the banking system. The most constructive work anyone in Washington did during the 1930s was probably in the area of banking reform. Once the banking system got itself back on its feet, it pulled the entire economy up with it.

One of the first moves Roosevelt made after being sworn into office was to shut down the banking system. He declared a bank holiday by invoking an emergency law left over from World War I. The holiday lasted for one week, beginning 6 March 1933. During that busy week, particularly over the weekend, the banking system was partially repaired. The Emergency Banking Act of 1933 was hastily passed by Congress. The only historically significant provision was the extra power given to the executive branch to temporarily take over the banking system until the banks were reopened. FDR used that power to entrust the secretary of the treasury with the responsibility of determining which banks were in "satisfactory condition" and could be licensed to reopen. While the secretary was eager to get a large number of banks back in operation, he had to be choosy enough to prevent a new outbreak of bank failures from setting off another crippling panic. During the ensuing week in a step-by-step process, 75% of Fed member banks and 71% of nonmember banks were reopened.

The president assured the public that these banks would be able to meet people's needs. Americans must have been impressed with these actions, because currency immediately began to flow back into the banking system, reversing the trend that had brought the money supply down for the previous three years and paving the way for the money supply to begin to grow.

That was only the beginning of the building of confidence in the banking system through legislative reform and executive action. The next step was the Banking Act of 1933, which came three months after the reopening of the banks. Included was an amendment calling for the establishment of federal deposit insurance. This was by no means a new idea. Deposit insurance had been tried by a variety of states over the preceding century and had never fully succeeded. It had been often proposed, only to be beaten back in Congress by its poor track record and the opposition of the banking community. Well-run banks did not want to operate under a system in which they subsidized their inefficiently run competitors. In spite of bankers' opposition and Roosevelt's initial resistance as well, deposit insurance was temporarily erected on 1 January 1934 and permanently installed by 1935.

The fledgling Federal Deposit Insurance Corporation (FDIC) covered deposits up to $2,500 at first and $5,000 as of July 1934. The impact of the insurance exceeded anyone's expectations, except those of Rep. Henry Steagall and a handful of persistent sponsors. Within the year, more than 90% of the nation's banks with more than 97% of the nation's deposits had joined the corporation. The number of bank failures, which averaged close to 600 annually during the 1920s and was in the thousands during the monetary contraction, shrank immediately to 61 in 1934, and the annual rate did not again reach the triple-digit level until the 1980s. The public's faith in the deposit insurance pushed the ratio of deposits to currency further along the upward path that had started with the reopening of sound banks in 1933.

FDIC succeeded where the Fed had failed miserably—in preventing bank panics. Had the Fed done its job of supplying liquidity to the banking system during the monetary contraction, we might have never resorted to deposit insurance. A central bank that does its job can make federal deposit insurance unnecessary and, given its drawbacks, possibly unwanted. On the other hand, had the FDIC been in existence in 1930 the bank panics would probably never have happened and the money supply would probably never have gone through its catastrophic decline. In short, the worse of the depression could have been avoided had the FDIC been in place four years earlier. It was not until the 1980s, when deregulation came into conflict with the existence of government-insured, risk-free deposits, that the wisdom of deposit insurance was once again questioned.

The deposit insurance provision was not the only plank of the New Deal financial reforms that lasted until the deregulation movement of the 1980s. The Banking Act of 1933 also endorsed the prohibition on interstate banking, separated the banking business from stock brokerage and investment banking, and placed ceilings on interest rates banks could pay depositors on checking (0%) and savings accounts. All three provisions were designed to lessen the likelihood that intense competition among banks and various speculative activities would lead to bank failures. The assumption here was that bank failures during the monetary contraction period were the result of ill-advised banking practices, as opposed to the shortage of liquidity in the banking system. The creation of the FDIC probably made these provisions unnecessary as well as unwarranted—at least, that is what many deregulators came to believe by the 1980s. But in 1933 Congress was not sure about the sources of banking problems, and so it tried to reform anything that looked even remotely suspicious.

Another reform designed to avoid a depression replay was the Securities and Exchange Act of 1934. It included a provision that gave the Fed some control over bank lending for stock purchases. The Fed could set margin requirements, the minimum down payment on a loan for the purpose of buying stocks. This was a tool missing from the Fed's toolbox in the 1920s, when it wanted to rein in stock market speculation. It allowed the Fed to limit the amount of lending for stock purchases without having to reduce the total availability of funds throughout the financial markets.

Further enhancement of the Fed's power and organization came with the Banking Act of 1935. It finalized the reorganization of the Fed power structure by centralizing the control in the hands of the seven-member Board of Governors and the Federal Open Market Committee. The latter was composed of the seven governors plus five Federal Reserve bank presidents. Clearly the power was in the hands of the seven governors and their chair. In addition, the governors were given the power to change reserve requirements on bank deposits within a range from the 1935 level (13%) to twice that level. It was hoped that by delineating the power structure more clearly and adding a potent tool for controlling the money supply, the Fed would be better prepared to deal with future crises. Yet this tool never became what Congress had in mind. And to make matters worse, its first use caused, or at least greatly contributed to, the 1937 relapse.

Arguably, some of these financial reforms—and only the most prominent or relevant are mentioned here—may, in the long run, have been unnecessary or even mistakes. Nevertheless, the vigor with which reform was carried out benefited the economy's recovery by instilling confidence in the public's mind about the operations of banks and other financial institutions. Given that the bank panics and the withdrawal of funds from the banking system arose from a loss of confidence, anything that built trust in the financial system enhanced the recovery. As far as monetary policymaking was concerned, the only reforms that had significant effects on monetary policy during the 1930s were the establishment of the FDIC, which drastically reduced the likelihood of a panic, and the grant to the Fed of the power to change reserve requirements. More important in the recovery phase, however, was an inflow of gold between 1933 and 1941 that caused the money supply to rise rapidly. This "golden avalanche," as it is often called, is best understood in light of the changes in U.S. participation in the gold standard system.

□ **The Golden Avalanche**   One provision of the Emergency Banking Act of 1933 gave President Roosevelt the power to take the United States off the gold standard, and he did so in March 1933.

Gold was no longer allowed to circulate in the economy or between countries, and the value of the dollar on world currency markets was free to fluctuate. At first there was little movement, but in May the value of the dollar began a serious downward march. This was exactly what Roosevelt and others had in mind. Many people in Congress contended the economy needed a policy that was decidedly inflationary. Some of this sentiment arose from the naive belief that because prices fell during the contraction phase of the depression, anything that pushed them upward would spur a recovery.

This idea led to the reflation policies of the New Deal. It was presumed that a devaluation of the dollar would stimulate exports and slow imports. But more important, devaluation was expected to push domestic prices for agricultural goods and other basic commodities upward. This inflation was not envisioned to result from any increase in the money supply or aggregate demand, as one might predict today; instead, the reasoning was that if the price of gold in dollars was increased by the devaluation, then the price of all other goods would rise proportionately. The reflationists had their causes and effects confused. Usually the value of the dollar falls and the price of gold rises because the money supply has increased so rapidly as to cause inflation, which drives down the purchasing power of money. Because the dollar is worth less in all domestic markets, it naturally takes more dollars to buy an ounce of gold or a unit of another country's currency. The dollar depreciation results from inflation. An artificial devaluation of the dollar will not result in inflation (or reflation) unless an inflationary increase in the money supply accompanies it. In that sense, the rationale for devaluation raises serious questions about whether its effects were understood during the New Deal.

What is certain, however, is that Roosevelt declared to the world that America's money supply was no longer going to remain captive to the rules of the gold standard or the desires of other governments. Actually, being on the gold standard had not been such a serious problem. In fact, had the Fed followed the rules and kept the money supply growing in proportion to the gold stock, the money supply would have risen throughout most of the contraction (except for the one-year period starting in the fall of 1931 when Britain left the standard), since gold flowed to the United States most of the time. The gold standard had not been the problem; rather, the problem had been the Fed's failure to use gold inflows to increase the money supply. Nevertheless, devaluation was the official policy in 1933 because Roosevelt wanted a "managed currency."

Throughout the remainder of 1933, the Treasury and Reconstruction Finance Corporation were busy buying gold in order to drive up its price and thereby drive down the value of the dollar. By January 1934, the value of the dollar had fallen approximately 40% as the price for an ounce of gold rose from $20.67 (where it had been since the turn of the century) to almost $35. Deciding that the devaluation had gone far enough and had probably reached its limit, Roosevelt and Congress enacted the Gold Reserve Act of 1934, which fixed the price of gold at $35 an ounce and permanently ended the use of gold as a medium of exchange in domestic transactions.

The strategy in 1934 to buy gold in order to drive up gold prices triggered an accumulation of gold in the United States that continued uninterrupted until 1941. Some of the gold came from American mines, which celebrated the government policy of pushing up gold prices by producing more gold and selling it to the Treasury. But most of the gold came from Europe, drawn to the United States first by the dollar devaluation and then by a massive flight of capital as war progressively became more likely.

During that eight-year period, the nation's gold stock rose by $16 billion, and the monetary base (or high-powered money) climbed by almost precisely the same amount. That in turn provided the basis for a $35 billion increase in the money supply—an average rate of increase in excess of 16% per year. The upward march of the money supply paused for a year, from the spring of 1937 to the spring of 1938, at exactly the same time as the economy experienced the one-year relapse in its recovery. Except for that temporary detour, the growth of the money supply and that of the gold stock paralleled each other. This was no mere coincidence; the money supply grew because of the inflow of gold into the Treasury and its conversion into reserves in the banking system.

What did the Fed have to do with this rapid growth in money supply? Absolutely nothing. After a brief period of open market purchases that gave a timely boost to the money supply during the middle of 1933, the Fed settled into a posture of open market inaction until the outbreak of World War II. Federal Reserve credit outstanding was remarkably steady from 1934 to 1940. And after a few reductions of the discount rate in 1933, the rate was changed only once more for the rest of the decade. With respect to these two policy tools, the Fed took a stance of "passive monetary ease." At least it did not sterilize the gold inflows, as it had done in the 1920s and in the first two years of the decade. It allowed the money supply to grow. In this case, doing nothing was the right program.

Except during the 1937 relapse, the burgeoning gold stock was allowed to propel the money supply upward at a vigorous pace. As can be expected in this case, the growth of the money supply was mirrored by the growth in aggregate demand, industrial output, and real GNP. A 16% annual rate of increase in the money supply would be too fast for an economy near full employment, since output would never be able to keep up with the growth in aggregate demand—double-digit inflation would result. But with the level of output so far below capacity in the 1930s, most of this growth in the money supply and aggregate demand translated into increases in output, which rose at an average annual rate of close to 13%. The net result was rather modest inflation—certainly preferable to the 10% deflation rates of the contraction phase.

Thus, while active monetary policy contributed little to the recovery, the growth of the money supply did contribute to it. Inaction at the Fed was just fine in this case so long as gold continued to flow in and the money supply automatically grew proportionally. The Treasury, with its active purchasing of gold and silver (the effect of the latter being relatively minor), actually did more to boost the growth of the money supply than the Fed did. But most of the gold avalanche was the product of forces outside the influence of government policy at either the Treasury or the Fed. Of course, a defender of the Fed could argue that the Fed performed correctly when it did nothing to sterilize the gold avalanche. That may be true. Nevertheless, it is not wise to give the Fed much credit for the proper intentions when we consider the rationale for Fed policy during the first recovery phase and the 1937 relapse.

☐ **The Reserve Requirement Relapse**   The Fed's relative inaction during the pre-1937 recovery phase was out of necessity rather than choice. The governors were actually quite uncomfortable with the rapid growth rate of the money supply, but there was little they could do with such tools as discount rate changes or open market operations. The vigorous inflow of gold provided an ample supply of reserves to the banking system. Reminiscent of the 1914–17 period of gold inflow, banks had little or no need to borrow additional reserves from the Fed. Hence, changes in the discount rate would have little effect. An increase in the discount rate that was designed to slow the growth of the money supply would have merely drawn more gold toward America and, in turn, increased reserves and spurred money supply growth. Sales of securities on the open market to soak up the ever-growing stock of reserves were out of the question because the Fed did not own enough Treasury securities to soak up the reserves. Moreover, had the Fed sold all its securities, it would have been left with no source of income to pay for its operations.

The Fed was in a very uncomfortable position. On one hand, the governors were not opposed to monetary ease, but on the other, they were concerned that they were losing control. When the time came to slow the growth of the money supply—that is, when the recovery was more nearly complete and monetary inflation became a danger—the Fed would be unable to wield either of its commonly used tools. The focus of the Fed's worries was the quantity of excess reserves held by the banks throughout the system. Since the banking system was reopened in 1933, the average bank had built up a substantial holding of excess reserves. By 1936, the volume of excess reserves was in the $2.5–3 billion range—as great as required reserves and greater than the value of the Fed's portfolio of securities at $2.4 billion. As long as the stock of excess reserves stood at this relatively high level, the Fed would be unable to rein in money supply growth with open market security sales.

Once again, just like before the bank holiday, the people at the Fed assumed the high level of excess reserve holdings was a sign that the banks had surplus excess reserves. The governors were determined to take up some of the slack in excess reserves. They debated the idea of conducting some open market sales to soak up at least a portion of the reserves slack, but they were afraid such a policy move would be interpreted as contractionary and might damage the psychology of recovery. Finally, in 1936 they came on a plan that would use their new tool, reserve requirement changes. The governors decided that a hike in the reserve requirement could turn a portion of the excess reserves into required reserves without causing the banks to cut back their lending. They hoped that excess reserves would shrink, the money supply would be only marginally affected, and they could regain the ability to use open market operations as their primary tool for controlling money supply. Still, they were not sure what would actually happen, since this was the first time they had tried a reserve requirement change.

The 50% increase in reserve requirement implemented in August 1936 was only slightly and temporarily successful. Excess reserves did shrink by $1 billion, to just under $2 billion. This brought their level below that of the Fed's security holdings, thereby raising the prospect that the Fed had been successful. The growth of the money supply did slow, but the excess reserve problem would not go away. By October, propelled by continued inflows of gold and by the banks' continued desire to maintain a high level of liquidity, excess reserves were again on the rise. This situation put more self-imposed pressure on the Fed to halt the trend with more restraining policy, even while the money supply growth rate was falling rapidly.

By the end of 1936, the Treasury joined the battle. It began a program of sterilizing gold inflows. Until this time, whenever gold came into the country's financial or commodity markets it was presented to the Treasury, which bought it with a check. That check cleared through the banking system to the Fed, which credited the reserve account of the bank in which the check was deposited. The Treasury gave the Fed a gold certificate, a kind of IOU, in exchange for the check. The result was an increase in bank reserves and the money supply. It was as if the Treasury, rather than the Fed, was conducting open market operations— buying gold instead of securities. For about nine months, until the fall of 1937, the Treasury changed that procedure and paid for the gold out of its own funds. The gold seller's bank account went up, but the Treasury's went down—hence, no net change in reserves or the money supply.

The Treasury's actions helped stop the growth of excess reserves but did nothing to bring their level down. And that level was still too high to satisfy the Fed. At more than $2 billion, the excess reserves were almost as great as the Fed's security holdings. The governors estimated that as much as three-fourths of those reserves were "superfluous." That meant they would have to sell more than 60% of their securities before they would begin to exert any control over bank lending. They could not afford to do that. The presumption that most excess reserves were essentially unnecessary shows that most of the governors still did not understand the banks' demand for reserves as liquidity insurance. After being hurt by illiquidity during the monetary contraction, bank managers were not comfortable unless they had a nice cushion of cash. The drive for liquidity had pushed down interest rates on short-term securities—attractive because of their easy marketability—so low that there was little opportunity cost in holding extra excess reserves with no risk rather than the short-term securities. Any effort to reduce or soak up those excess reserves would be met by actions to rebuild them, a process that always results in less lending and a smaller money supply.

The Board of Governors decided in January 1937 to raise the reserve requirement all the way to the legal limit in two steps occurring in March and May. After the latter increase, the requirement was twice as high as the level before the first increase in 1936. The effect was striking: excess reserves plummeted to as low as $750 million by August. That drop may have been exactly what the Fed had in mind, but the banks' reaction was not. They immediately began to rebuild their excess reserves by lending less money. As deposits and loan repayments flowed into the banks, they set them aside in reserves instead of lending them out. As a result, the money supply fell 6.5% from March 1937 to May 1938 (see Figure 1). The Fed (with a little help from the Treasury and its sterilization program) did not just slow the rapid growth of the money supply; it put the money supply into reverse. The economy went along for the ride and sank into the relapse of 1937.

That downturn set the recovery back a few years. Industrial production sank to the 1933 level, unemployment climbed to more than 19%, and total output fell by 5%. The one major policy move taken by the Fed during the recovery phase produced a nasty recession on a par with the more recent recession of 1974. Unfortunately, the 1937 recession started with unemployment at 14% rather than 5%. As usual, the Fed was slow to recognize the downturn in economic activity. It did not move to ease its policy stance until late 1937, when it lowered the discount rate (its only change from 1934 through the war years), and early 1938, when it retracted the May 1937 reserve requirement increase. With the Treasury no longer sterilizing gold inflows, the money supply began to rise again in May 1938. The recovery resumed, but the damage was done.

Remarkable as it may seem, the people at the Fed pleaded innocent to charges that they had been responsible for the relapse. The chair of the Board of Governors, Marriner Eccles, and his associate, economist Lauchlin Currie, certainly were not monetarists. In fact, these two men were the most staunch supporters in Washington of the view that the Roosevelt administration needed to increase government spending to stimulate the recovery. In short, they were fiscalists. Their advice for the president is discussed later in this chapter. What is particularly telling was their belief that the 1937 relapse was caused by a shift in fiscal policy in 1936 and 1937. They defended Fed policy to critics by arguing that the drop in the money supply in 1937 and 1938 was the result rather than the cause of the downturn in economic activity. That was also their analysis of the monetary contraction of 1929 to 1933. No wonder the Fed continued to be so passive throughout the 1930s. Monetary policy was being determined by people who placed little importance on movements of the money supply. Incredibly, atheists were running the church.

The resumption of the recovery occurred in the spring of 1938 at the same time that the decline in the money supply was reversed. One could debate with Eccles the root cause, but the facts are clear. As mentioned earlier, the Fed lowered the reserve requirement in April, reversing the May 1937 increase. That change immediately turned $750 million of required reserves into excess reserves. At about the same time, the Treasury also reversed its 1937 policy and desterilized more than $1 billion in gold that had piled up in the 16 months, since the beginning of 1937, in its inactive gold stock. The quantity of high-powered money surged, and by the end of 1938 the money supply had risen 9%.

The recovery got back on track as the money supply returned to its growth path, fueled by the continued inflow of gold from Europe. Between the spring of 1938 and the end of 1941, the gold stock and high-powered money rose by about $10 billion; the money supply expanded by almost $20 billion, at an average annual growth rate in excess of 12%. With aggregate demand back on the rise, industrial production almost doubled during these three and a half years, and unemployment finally fell below 10% for the first time in 10 years. It is difficult to understand how anyone could look at the record and not conclude that the 1937 relapse was the product of the temporary but sharp about-face in monetary policy conducted by both the Fed and the Treasury from late 1936 to early 1938. For more than a year, the monetary authorities deprived the economy of what was fueling the recovery, the growing money supply. Predictably, the recovery collapsed until the gold and money supply valves were reopened in 1938, sending aggregate demand and output back on the growth path toward full employment.

The Fed's effort to control excess reserves proved a costly mistake. The banks' reaction confirmed there was no surplus of excess reserves. When the decade ended, excess reserves had once again ballooned to a value greater than that of the Fed's securities portfolio. But this time the Fed, apparently embarrassed by the recession it supposedly did not cause, hesitated to touch the reserve requirements. Still, revealing that some lessons are hard to learn, the Fed, in an unprecedented move, asked Congress in December 1940 to double the minimum and maximum reserve requirements. That step would have left the new minimum equal to the old maximum (26%) and the new maximum at a whopping 52%. When one considers that the modern requirement is just 12%, the Fed's request was extraordinary. The Fed ended the decade as it had begun, misreading the financial markets' indicators. Fortunately, most of the time in between, the Fed was generally passive, and passivity was much more beneficial during the recovery than it had been during the monetary contraction.

☐　The New Deal

In terms of economic history in general, there was no more active decade in this century than the 1930s, because of the many programs implemented as part of the New Deal—the title generally given to virtually all legislation passed that decade after 1933. While many of these programs would have lasting significance to society, the economy, and the relationship of the government to the marketplace, most had little if any impact on the level of economic activity in the 1930s. That is, they had little influence over the levels of aggregate demand and aggregate supply.

After we have narrowed the New Deal programs down to those which had an effect on output and employment, it becomes apparent that even these programs were not very significant in terms of their impact on economic recovery. What becomes clear is that the New Deal definitely did not bring the economy out of the depression. Many policy moves actually worked to retard the recovery, and those which had a positive effect were not of great enough quantitative magnitude to be consequential. The protracted nature of the recovery phase is a clue that whatever was done was not very successful. Certainly it can be safely said that while the Roosevelt administration did many things to fight the depression, it never committed itself to a policy program designed to lift the level of aggregate demand back up to its 1929 level and beyond.

☐ **The Reflation Strategy** A popular theory in the 1930s held that what the economy needed was higher prices. Again, since it had been observed that prices fall during a contraction and rise during a recovery, many believed what was needed to spur recovery was virtually any policy program that would raise prices. That would not have been such a bad idea, had the first step taken been to determine what had caused prices to fall during the contraction and to reverse that force. Price movements are symptoms of underlying changes in the level of aggregate demand and aggregate supply. Of course, as discussed in the preceding chapter, policymakers did not have a clear picture at all of what determined output and price levels. They lacked the tools of analysis available to us today. Thus, instead of attacking the disease of falling aggregate demand, they attacked the symptom of falling prices.

The classic example of this error was the National Industrial Recovery Act, which was passed in June 1933 and survived until May 1935, when it was declared unconstitutional by the Supreme Court. The act was designed to pull the economy out of the depression through planning and cooperation on the part of businesses. Legislators, business leaders, and labor leaders all agreed that unbridled competition among producers was forcing them to take such actions as lowering prices, cutting production, and laying off workers. Under the legislation, hundreds of industries were "codified" by the National Recovery Administration (NRA). Through negotiations among producers and between producers and labor leaders, the codes established "fair" levels of wages and prices. Fair meant higher. In other words, the government sanctioned and organized collusion, in spite of the existing antitrust legislation.

Studies have indicated that the efforts of the NRA and other reflation programs had a significant upward impact on prices and wages, particularly early in the recovery. One very uncharacteristic element of the recovery phase of the Great Depression is how fast wages and prices rose during the first four years (especially the first two) after the economy bottomed out in 1933. Even though the level of aggregate demand had never been so far below full-employment output, wholesale prices rose by 21% from 1933 to 1935 and by an additional 10% by the spring of 1937. From there, they fell below the 1935 level, and stayed low until 1940. When the shortfall of aggregate demand was at its greatest, prices rose the fastest. That contradicts the laws of supply and demand. In a labor market in which unemployment stayed above 20% throughout the period 1933 to 1935, hourly earnings rose 25%. More than one-fifth of the labor force was not working, yet wages were rising at a rate of 12% per year. That too makes no sense unless wages and prices are being artificially raised.

One might question what harm such reflationary policy could do: Wasn't it better than doing nothing? Definitely not. Deflation is the way the markets deal with a decline in demand, much as a rise in a person's temperature is how the body deals with fighting infections. To artificially raise prices without increasing the level of aggregate demand is like putting someone suffering from malaria in the refrigerator to get his or her temperature down without giving the person any quinine. Both approaches only make the patient worse off. It may sound all right to raise wages and prices, but doing so increases the gap between aggregate demand and full-employment output. Higher prices cause the quantity of goods and services purchased to fall, while higher wages cause the number of workers employed to shrink. Reflation legislates a reduction in the level of aggregate supply, which results in higher prices and lower output. Had the money supply not been growing and pushing the level of aggregate demand upward, as it was during 1933 to 1937, the reflation policies manifested in the NRA, the agricultural programs, the National Labor Relations Act, the minimum wage, and other measures would have caused output to fall and unemployment to rise. As it happened, these programs merely slowed the recovery without actually preventing it. That net capital investment was negative until 1936 should have been a signal that the reflation policy was not good for the economy, even if some individual businesses or labor leaders believed it was good for them and their constituencies.

☐ **The Fiscal Debate**   From the time Roosevelt took office in 1933 until the United States joined World War II, Washington was the scene of a continuous dispute over the proper course for fiscal policy. There were a multitude of theories about the cause of the depression and an even larger number of policy suggestions to promote recovery and reform. Some of the reform proposals were based on the idea that fundamental flaws in the system caused the depression and that the recovery could begin in earnest only when those flaws were corrected. Other reform recommendations were aimed at supposed flaws that predated the depression, but their champions were eager to take advantage of the reform climate to push through their programs. This was particularly the case with efforts to redistribute wealth, income, and tax burdens.

Beyond the many reform disputes was the question of whether deficit spending could encourage recovery by raising demand, sales, and income, thereby stimulating consumer and investment spending. As mentioned earlier, Marriner Eccles and Lauchlin Currie at the Fed were disciples of the "underconsumptionist" explanation of shortfalls of aggregate demand relative to full-employment output. This view, dating back to Thomas Malthus, called for major tax cuts or increases in government spending to boost aggregate demand when consumer and investment spending came up short. In fact, in 1933 (a year before he was appointed to the Federal Reserve Board) Eccles, while testifying before a Senate committee, called for a program of deficit spending rather than budget balancing to promote recovery. By this time, the idea of an income multiplier—whereby an increase in investment or government spending sets off further increases in spending on the part of consumers and capital investors—was being considered in economic circles as a supporting argument for the theory that an increase in government spending would have far-reaching stimulative effects.

Of course, most prominent in this theoretical debate were the ideas of John Maynard Keynes, who took some of the underconsumptionist and multiplier ideas and incorporated them into his model of the macroeconomy. Keynes asserted that autonomous drops in portions of aggregate expenditures—his components of aggregate demand: consumption expenditures, investment expenditures, government expenditures, and net foreign expenditures—set off contractions in output and that the contractions could be reversed by increases in these expenditures. Keynes's recovery program called for an accommodating monetary policy but emphasized a new weapon: increases in government expenditures and tax reductions as the route back to full employment. In other words, Keynes was calling for major deficit spending as the appropriate fiscal policy for economic recovery.

He advanced these ideas in a short book, *The Means to Prosperity* (1933); in a famous open letter to Roosevelt in the *New York Times* on New Year's Eve 1933; in a face-to-face conversation with the president and his staff in 1934; and in a private letter in 1936. Finally, with the publication of *The General Theory of Employment, Interest, and Money* (1936)—arguably this century's most important economics book— Keynes laid out the battle plan for abandoning the program of balanced budgets and replacing it in times of depression with *compensatory fiscal policy*. This approach, which made it the government's responsibility to compensate for shortfalls in private spending with increases in government spending, was embraced by a large number of young academicians, and they joined in the effort to promote these ideas in Washington. The seeds of the Keynesian revolution had been planted, but it took a long time for the overthrow of old ideas to occur.

It is useful to look at what the economy needed and what fiscal policy actually did. Then we might determine how influential changes in government spending and taxes were on output and unemployment. The first step is to establish the size of the full-employment gap—that is, how far below full employment actual output was during the 1930s. From 1929 to 1933, output fell by about $32 billion (measured in 1929 dollars), as investment and consumption fell by almost $16 billion each. By 1933, full-employment GNP had climbed to close to $117 billion. That put the full-employment gap at close to $50 billion dollars at its widest. Just before the relapse of 1937, output was back to its 1929 level, but it was still almost $25 billion short of full employment.

Given those measures of the gap, what increase in autonomous expenditures would have been necessary to push output back to full employment? Most estimates (including Keynes's) of the American income multiplier placed it near two. The fact that investment fell by $16 billion and GNP fell by $32 billion during the contraction supports an estimate of the multiplier at close to two. In 1933 the economy needed an increase in government expenditures of as much as $25 billion to compensate for the loss of investment expenditures and the continued growth of capacity. By 1934, government expenditures had gone up only $2 billion over their 1933 level, and they were lower in 1935. By 1937, with output $25 billion below full employment, expenditures peaked at $4 billion above the 1933 level. The economy would still have needed an additional boost of more than $12 billion in expenditures to push GNP up by the $25 billion needed to reach full employment. It never got it from FDR.

Roosevelt did raise spending levels and did run deficits, but they were drops in the bucket compared to what the economy needed and

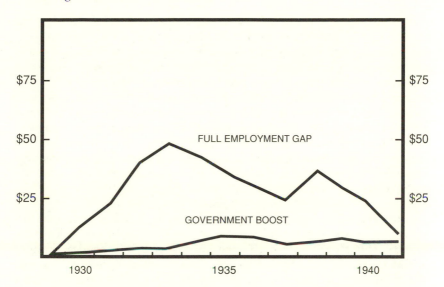

Figure 2. Impact of U.S. government expenditures, 1929–1942 (**in billions of 1929 dollars**). Calculated from *Historical Statistics of the United States: Colonial Times to 1970* (Washington, D.C.: U.S. Department of Commerce, 1975).

what people like Keynes were recommending. Figure 2 depicts the gap between actual and full employment output as well as the income-generating impact of government expenditures increases. Fiscal policy never came close to filling the gap in the 1930s. Furthermore, expenditures and the deficit shrank in 1937 and 1938 even as the economy sank into the relapse. Fiscal policy was contractionary in those two years compared with 1936, and policy was hardly expansionary in 1936 as it was. By 1939, when the full-employment gap was up to $31 billion, government expenditures were once again above $8 billion, or just over $4 billion higher than in 1933. The economy needed a boost of about $15 billion in expenditures, and all it got from Washington was a net injection of $4.5 billion. The story is the same until 1941, when armament expenditures began pushing government spending up by amounts that could truly put a dent into the full-employment gap.

The question of whether the Roosevelt administration ever adopted the Keynesian approach—using increased government expenditures to push the economy back to full employment—has been much debated in history books over the past 50 years. Although the debate often gets quite involved concerning what Roosevelt knew or believed and when, the facts outlined in the foregoing discussion answer the question in short order. Fiscal policy was never used to raise aggregate demand anywhere near enough to push the economy back to full employment. The Keynesian revolution may have been discussed in Washington and there may even have been Keynesian infiltrators in the administration, but the Keynesian prescription was never filled. Indeed, empirical studies have shown that despite the annual deficits and the relief programs, the net effect of fiscal policy (federal, state, and local) most of the time between 1933 and World War II was at best somewhat contractionary. That should be no surprise, for Roosevelt continually maintained efforts to minimize the budget deficit—that is, to hold nonrelief spending to no greater than tax revenues. One economic historian put it best when he declared that the reason fiscal policy was not successful in conquering the depression is that it was never tried.

Roosevelt's lack of commitment to using fiscal policy to achieve full employment is underscored by policy in 1937. With the unemployment rate still above 14%, Roosevelt apparently gave up on the idea of pump priming. That is, he had lost what little faith he had in the government's ability to stimulate increases in private spending with increases in government spending. In addition, he indicated that it was probably not the government's job to try to guarantee full employment anyway. Had the pump been primed during the period 1933 to 1937 with a lot more conviction and several billion dollars more in spending, Roosevelt might have had a better picture of what fiscal policy could do to stimulate aggregate demand during a depression. As it was, spending increases were minimal, and so were the results.

Unimpressed by these results, Roosevelt decided it was time to return to the less revolutionary doctrine of balancing the budget. Projections for 1937 held out the possibility of a balanced budget if spending was held down. Shooting for that ever-elusive balanced budget, the Roosevelt administration held government spending down as best it could in 1937 and 1938. Combining the spending cuts with the contractionary impact of the new social security tax (imposed in 1936 to finance the program to supplement elderly income), the result was a fiscal policy that contributed to a drop in aggregate demand. Meanwhile, the reserve requirement increase at the Fed was stifling aggregate demand. In short, Roosevelt joined with the Fed to cause the relapse of 1937, all for the sake of another misguided attempt to balance the budget. In keeping with the tradition of the infamous tax increase of 1932, fiscal policy in 1937 and 1938 looked like something some cantankerous government official had designed just to make Keynes angry and the depression deeper.

The standard reaction of most anyone who is old enough to have lived through the depression or who has been educated in American history over the past 50 years to this assessment of New Deal recovery programs is bewilderment. Generations have come to believe that the public works spending programs of the 1930s did much to reemploy America's labor force and to spur the recovery. "What about TVA," they ask, "or the PWA or the CCC or all the other jobs and relief programs? Didn't they prime the pump?" No, not much. First, the amount spent on all these programs together took only a small nibble out of the full-employment gap. Second, these programs were financed as much as possible out of tax revenues rather than borrowing. Taxing Peter to employ Paul does not add demand to the economy; it only relocates it. Peter spends less and Paul spends more, but total spending is unchanged. As long as that is the case, output and employment are probably unchanged as well. Thus, even though the government employed as many as 3 million workers in these new programs at their peak, that was not good enough, because (a) the number of unemployed workers in the country was almost 12 million in 1933 and still more than 8 million in 1940, and (b) every time the government used tax revenues to employ one more worker, other jobs generated by consumer spending declined because of the higher taxes.

Beyond considerations about the absolute levels of government spending and the amounts of spending relative to government taxes, most of the government's energy in the field of fiscal policy went into annual revisions of the taxing structure. Somewhere along the line, it was noticed that the distribution of income had become a bit less equal during the 1920s. As we saw two chapters back, populists had been battling this trend all along, and now this inequality was raised as a contributing factor to the depression. To them, curing the depression called for a movement toward an equalization of wealth and income. Year after year during the New Deal era, tax reform bills were passed by Congress with various plans to "soak the rich." By the end of the 1930s, the success of these efforts to equalize the distribution of income was rather small. Certainly the imposition of the new, highly regressive social security tax did not help.

Whether a goal of equalization is right or wrong is wide open to debate, and one's position on this matter must be regarded as purely a value judgment. Some people gain, and others lose. Whether or not society gains from such policies can be neither proved nor disproved. What is more clear, however, is that the distribution of income in the early 1930s probably did little to deepen the contraction, and the efforts to revamp the tax schedule probably did just as little to speed the recovery. Actually, a good case can be made that the incessant tinkering with the tax system and the struggle to raise taxes on business profits—especially the fixation on undistributed corporate profits—help explain the pitifully low levels of capital investment during the recovery. By 1937, gross private investment was just three-fourths of its 1929 level, and investment topped the 1929 figure only in 1941. There are good and bad ways of increasing the tax bite on the rich, and Congress may have picked some of the bad ways by creating disincentives for businesses to plow back earnings into capital purchases. The tinkering alone was enough to discourage investment by increasing uncertainty and risk. The lower was aggregate investment, the bigger was the aggregate demand shortfall.

Ultimately, the levels of aggregate income and aggregate spending were far more important to the state of the economy than the distribution of income. Nevertheless, Congress, the president, and public attention concentrated on the distribution of income because it was a far hotter political issue. And as we will see often in the pages to follow, good politics is not necessarily good economics. Therein lies an important point. The New Deal contained some programs that helped the recovery—particularly in the area of financial reform—but it contained far more that hurt the recovery or at best did nothing to help it. With its relief programs, government did help many people to cope with the depression, and the many areas of activity did generate a feeling of confidence where otherwise there would have been only despair. In that respect, the New Deal had some social and political successes. But the New Deal was a resounding economic failure in that it prolonged the depression by acting like a ball and chain on the recovery. It is difficult to praise a program that slightly softens the blow of unemployment while it simultaneously prolongs that unemployment for years.

The 1937 recession added urgency to the fiscal policy debate. This recession was Roosevelt's, not Hoover's, and it appeared to have been set off by efforts to shrink the deficit. Such a conclusion brought forth a variety of reactions. The obvious one came from Eccles and other supporters of increased deficit spending: the reduction of the deficit caused the recession, and an increase in government expenditures was needed more than ever to spur the recovery. Another reaction was that of FDR, who feared not only that Eccles was perhaps right but that a *permanent* deficit was necessary to restore and maintain full employment. It was one thing to accept a temporary emergency deficit during the deepest part of the depression, but quite another to contemplate that deficits would always be necessary. The latter was an ominous notion; it tended to underscore the suspicion many held all along that there was something fundamentally wrong with the economy if full employment now required constant artificial injections of government demand.

Some of the suggestions for recovery were frighteningly similar to those espoused in 1933: push for a balanced budget; restore the NRA; redistribute income; attack monopoly power with trust-busting and regulations. These were the views of the older New Deal liberals. Others concentrated on calls for more spending using borrowed funds, an approach backed by the younger Keynesians. Ultimately, the approach taken satisfied neither of the two camps. The days of radical reform were past, but the commitment to bring the economy back to full employment through deficit spending was not there either. Nevertheless, the pump-primers were gaining strength, and policy leaned in their direction until armament spending imposed their prescription on the economy.

6

Return to Prosperity: 1940–1950

WHILE ECONOMISTS AND LAWMAKERS were wondering whether stagnation was a permanent malady facing the American economy, World War II began in Europe and eventually spread to the United States. With it came a rapid end to the depression and unemployment, as well as the suspension of a good portion of the New Deal. All attention turned to winning the war. Fiscal and monetary policymakers did their part by figuring out how to pay for this all-out effort. Since the costs were enormous, that was a large assignment. But they did not have to worry about the depression anymore—at least, not so long as the war continued.

☐ Boom Replaces Depression

One of the most striking aspects of World War II was how quickly it rid the economy of the lingering depression. The 1930s ended with unemployment near 15% and output 18% below the full-employment level. Spurred by huge increases in aggregate demand, output climbed swiftly and the unemployment rate dropped to as low as it probably could go in a market economy. Table 6 shows how the economy returned to full employment. In 1942 the unemployment rate sank below the 5% level for the first time since 1929. Later, in 1944, production pushed capacity to the limit, as the unemployment rate fell to 1.2% and the labor

Table 6. Economic Indicators, 1940–1950

	Q	M1	M2	P	GE	GR	Surplus Deficit	UN	Prime Rate
1940	7.8	16.3	12.5	2	9.5	6.5	−3	14.6	0.6
1941	17.7	15	11.1	6.2	13.7	8.7	−5	9.9	0.5
1942	18.8	29.8	23.1	6.6	35	15	−20	4.7	0.7
1943	18.1	27.4	25.5	2.6	79	24	−55	1.9	0.7
1944	8.2	13.6	16.1	1.4	91	44	−47	1.2	0.7
1945	−1.9	12.9	15.4	2.9	93	45	−48	1.9	0.8
1946	−19	5.1	6.7	22.9	55	39	−16	3.9	0.8
1947	−2.8	4.2	4.2	13.9	34	38	4	3.9	1.4
1948	3.9	−1.4	−0.7	7	30	42	12	3.8	1.5
1949	0	−0.5	−0.2	−0.5	39	39	0	5.9	1.5
1950	8.5	4.7	3.7	2.0	43	39	−4	5.3	1.5

Q = Percent change in real GNP (output)
M1 = Percent change in M1 (currency plus checking account deposits)
M2 = Percent change in M2 (currency plus checking and savings accounts)
P = Percent change in GNP Implicit Price Deflator
GE = Federal government expenditures (billions of dollars)
GR = Federal government revenues (billions of dollars)
Surplus/Deficit = GR minus GE
UN = Average unemployment rate (percent)
Prime Rate = Average prime rate of interest (percent)

Sources: See Bibliographic Essay.

participation rate reached record levels. From 1940 to 1944, output climbed by just over 50%, and virtually everybody's living standard (even farmers') jumped significantly. Furthermore, the distribution of income became more equal. Of course, not all was rosy, for war brings shortages, sacrifices, suffering, and deaths, but nothing solves economic woes like prosperity. And this war brought prosperity to an economy that many were beginning to suspect was incapable of ever rebounding in full force.

☐ **Paying for the War**   There is no mystery about what propelled aggregate demand and output up to full employment and beyond: it was the enormous increases in government military expenditures and the accompanying increases in money supply. From 1940 to

1942, military expenditures jumped by more than $20 billion, from a mere $1.8 billion to $22.9 billion. Recalling our discussion in chapter 5, that is exactly the kind of boost in expenditures that the economy had needed throughout the 1930s to bring output up to full employment. The government hesitated to make such a commitment, fearing that it either would not work or would become a permanent responsibility. By 1942, doubts about the efficacy of such a boost in spending were dispelled; however, concerns remained about long-term, postwar policy implications, a topic to be explored later in the chapter.

The surge in government expenditures was just warming up in 1942. Led by the vast military expenses, expenditures soared to almost $100 billion annually in 1944 and 1945, more than 10 times the highest annual levels reached in the 1930s. To put the spending in perspective, one need only compare it with GNP figures. Government expenditures at their peak in 1945 were equal to or greater than the economy's total output in any year up to 1936. The grand total of more than $380 billion in expenditures from 1940 to 1946 dwarfed any measure of government spending in the country's history. For example, total government expenditures since the country's birth had not reached half that amount, and the bill for World War I was only one-tenth as high.

The big problem facing the government was how to finance all this spending. Secretary of the Treasury Henry Morganthau wanted to use tax revenues as much as possible. Anyone in his position would, and he was a determined budget-balancer. But it soon became apparent that the tax increases necessary to avoid heavy debt might prove too great a burden for current taxpayers. The early war expenditures were already bringing individuals improved living standards over those of the 1930s. To tax away most of those gains might deflate civilian enthusiasm for the war effort, an aspect that was almost as important as the morale of the soldiers in the field. As a result, taxes were raised significantly but carefully.

In the end, 45% of the more than $380 billion in wartime expenditures was paid for out of tax revenues, compared with only 33% during World War I. By 1945, annual tax revenues were almost $45 billion, nine times as great as revenues in 1940. Heated debates in Congress centered on where most of the tax burden should fall. Marginal tax rates on upper income brackets escalated, and the practice of withholding taxes from paychecks was begun (the Revenue Act of 1943). At the same time, exemptions were lowered so that more people had to pay taxes at lower levels of income. And on top of these changes, numerous excise taxes were raised, along with corporate profits taxes. In general, the tax base was greatly broadened, and the level of tax rates was raised to pay for as much of the war as was reasonable. Personal income tax became increasingly important as a revenue generator, with the percentage of revenues derived from the "pay as you earn" tax more than doubling, up to 43% from 1940 to 1945.

Despite all these taxes, it was still necessary to finance 55% of the wartime expenditures through borrowing. Some hoped that by issuing war bonds for a major portion of the war expenditures, individuals could be persuaded to voluntarily save significant portions of their income and buy bonds. That way, the average person could be adding to his or her wealth by saving while at the same time providing funds to pay the government's bills. Buying bonds became the patriotic thing to do, as it had been during World War I. To make such purchases more accessible to the public, the Treasury offered a far broader range of securities than was the case with the previous war, when only longer-term bonds were issued. This time, short-term securities were available for those who desired more liquidity than the old Liberty Bonds had provided, and small-denomination savings bonds were born with simple rules so that even children could get aboard the government's saving bandwagon.

The federal debt skyrocketed from $43 billion in 1940 to $269 billion in 1946, which tells us that more than $220 billion had to be borrowed during the war. From 1943 to 1945, the annual budget deficits were more than $50 billion, one-fourth the size of GNP. By 1946, the federal debt exceeded GNP by about 25%. But even with this unprecedented level of borrowing, the $220 billion of new securities were absorbed by the economy relatively smoothly. Of that amount, 28% of the bonds were bought by banks, 25% by individuals, 23% by private institutions, 11% by other government agencies, 10% by the Federal Reserve, and 3% by state and local governments (and absolutely none by Japanese investors).

The economy's ability to absorb these massive injections of debt was greatly enhanced by the policy of the Fed. As it had done during World War I, the Fed—beginning in April 1942—took on the responsibility of helping the Treasury issue so many bonds by holding down interest rates. The Fed pegged the interest rates on government securities. It was always willing to buy securities anytime the short-term rates climbed as high as $\frac{3}{8}$% and the long-term rates pressed $2\frac{1}{2}$%. Whenever securities buyers became a little scarce and interest rates threatened to rise above their targets, the Fed simply became the buyer, thereby increasing the demand for securities and the supply of funds at the same time. Where the Fed had used discount loans of bank reserves to lubricate the purchases of Liberty Bonds during World War I, in the 1940s the Fed bought bonds for its own account on the open market.

Of course, purchases of bonds in the open market create bank reserves and lead to increases in the money supply. From April 1942 to April 1946, the money supply doubled. That monetary expansion came on top of the two preceding years when American neutrality caused major gold inflows. Given that neither the Fed nor the Treasury took steps to neutralize those gold inflows, the money supply had already been racing upward for two years before the Fed began its policy of supporting the bond market. All told, the money supply ballooned by 160% from 1940 to 1946. Those high money supply growth rates look like a mountain in Figure 1.

Except for a one-year period from mid-1941 to mid-1942 when it raised reserve requirements once again in a final effort to reduce excess reserves, the Fed maintained a stance of complete accommodation throughout the war and for a year after it ended. By purchasing more than $20 billion of securities itself and helping M2 (currency plus most bank deposits) grow by more than $80 billion, the Fed certainly did its part in ensuring that the economy could absorb the $220 billion in securities issued by the Treasury. Indeed, it can be argued that the Fed did a better job than during World War I, because it was able to hold interest rates lower on the federal debt during the 1940s. At least by the end of the war, the Fed would never again have to worry about aggregate excess reserves being greater than its stockpile of government securities. Unfortunately, everyone at the Treasury and the Fed knew that when the two agencies resorted to money supply growth to finance a major portion of government expenditures, they were sentencing the economy to some fairly potent inflationary pressures.

☐ **Coping with Inflation**   There is no doubt that the monetization of a large portion of wartime expenditures resulted in inflation. The pattern of price changes, however, does make us pause before linking the price increases to the money supply growth. From 1940 to 1948, prices climbed by more than 80%. The fastest increases came during the two years before and the three years after U.S. participation in the war. The slowdown of inflation during the actual fighting is partly attributable to wage and price controls, which were imposed in 1942 and lasted until mid-1946. The surge in prices after those controls were lifted showed that the controls did not really prevent inflation; they simply delayed it until after the war.

Over the eight-year period, M2 grew by 168%, prices rose by 82%, and output climbed by 43%. In 1948 velocity was about 3% below its 1940 level. These numbers can be displayed in the format of the quantity of money equation, where 1940 figures are expressed as base-year figures:

	Money Supply (M2)	×	Velocity	=	GNP	=	Output	×	Prices
1940	100	×	1.00	=	100	=	100	×	1.00
1948	268	×	.97	=	260	=	143	×	1.82

The left-hand side of the equation shows the growth of aggregate demand, which is matched by the growth of aggregate supply in money terms on the right-hand side. Excesses in the growth of aggregate demand over output translate into increases in prices. Over a period as long as eight years, variations in M2 velocity tend to cancel themselves out, as they did in this case. That leaves the growth rate of aggregate demand explained almost entirely by the rate of growth in the money supply. With the money supply growth more than three times as great as output, it was just a matter of time until this excess demand turned into inflation.

Even without the wage and price controls, the wartime inflation rate would have been slower. Over the five-year period from 1940 to 1945, M2 grew by 133%, and prices rose by only 34%. Part of that difference is explained by the decrease in velocity, but most of that void was filled by increased output. Although the economy reached full employment in 1942, output continued to grow rapidly as the labor participation rate rose to record levels and labor productivity raced upward. The gap between aggregate demand and output was actually not all that great until war production was scaled back after 1945.

As the economy adjusted to the postwar world, output fell from 1945 to 1948. Meanwhile, the money supply continued to rise. Thus, the big gap of more than 100% between the total increase of the money supply and output (which shows up in the preceding equation) was mostly attributable to the two prewar and three postwar years. Even without the delayed-reaction price increases that followed the expiration of controls in June 1946, prices would have surged after the war. Much like the postwar period immediately following World War I, deficit spending continued for an extra year. Since the Fed was still compelled to hold down interest rates, it had to keep buying securities, an action that kept the money supply growing at a brisk, albeit slower, pace until 1947. With the money supply rising and output declining in 1946 and 1947, the gap between demand and output widened, and prices had to rise in a big way to fill that gap. The extra year of price controls after the war ended caused the pressure of excess aggregate demand to build; thus, when controls were lifted, prices shot up fast to make up for lost time.

By the end of 1947, the aftershocks of the war-induced inflation had noticeably subsided. The inflation rate in 1948 tapered off to near 8%, well down from the rate of more than 22% in 1947. A major reason for the inflation slowdown was the deceleration in the growth rate of the money supply. After cruising upward at double-digit annual rates from 1940 to 1945, the money supply rose at a 6% annual average from 1946 to 1948 and did not grow at all in 1948 and 1949. This retardation of money supply growth is interesting. Some people at the Fed, such as Marriner Eccles, had been so concerned about postwar inflation that they argued in favor of retaining wage and price controls well after 1946 and rebuilding them in 1947. They felt helpless to do anything to prevent the inflation, since the Fed was still committed to holding interest rates down. They expected the policy of pegging interest rates would force the Fed to keep the money supply growing at an inflationary pace.

As it turned out, little upward pressure on interest rates occurred in the postwar 1940s. By 1947, the Fed found that it did not take very much to keep interest rates at or below target levels. Equilibrium interest rates were already below the targets. That is surprising, for during a period of rapid inflation we typically expect interest rates to rise with inflationary expectations. Anyone who lived through the 1970s and 1980s, when rising and falling inflationary expectations led to major swings in interest rates, must look back at the 1940s and wonder what on earth held interest rates down. After 1946, it was not the Fed, even though the Fed was poised to do so if necessary.

Interest rates were held down by at least two important forces. First, despite the postwar inflation, inflationary expectations did not exist. In fact, the average American was waiting for prices to fall as they had after the postwar inflationary bubble burst in 1920 and during the depression. The higher that prices soared in 1946 and 1947, the more people were convinced that a major price drop was near. Many Americans were looking around the corner for the return of the economic stagnation of the 1930s. Those expectations helped hold down interest rates; people tended to cling to the many liquid bonds they had accumulated during the war. Because people were not selling bonds, there were no downward pressure on bond prices and no upward pressure on interest rates. The Fed did not have to enter the market as a steady buyer.

The second important force holding down interest rates was the shift in fiscal policy from enormous deficits through 1946 to a balanced budget in 1947 and an $8 billion surplus in 1948. The Treasury went from borrower to saver in two years. By reducing the size of the federal debt in 1947 and 1948, the Treasury was simultaneously reducing the supply of bonds in the market, and this step put downward pressure on interest rates. The combination of changed fiscal policy and deflationary expectations meant the growth rate of the money supply necessary to keep equilibrium interest rates down was relatively low. That was just fine with monetary policymakers; the money supply growth rate was brought down, and down with it came the inflation rate.

In 1948 the Fed was not satisfied with the deceleration of deflation. It was about to make the mistake that policymakers would make a habit of in later years. The inflation rate responds to changes in monetary policy in a fairly reliable but delayed fashion. Changes in the growth rate of the money supply tend to show up in proportional changes in the inflation rate after a lag of several months. As we will see, that lag was close to three years in the 1960s, 1970s, and 1980s, and policymakers neglected to take it into account at the time. It is no surprise that the Fed made the mistake as early as 1948. The money supply slowdown started in late 1946, and the money supply grew less than 5% over the next two years. The rapid rise of prices ended in late 1947, a year after the monetary slowdown began; inflation came to a halt in late 1948, two years after the Fed started hitting the brakes.

Oblivious to the fact that it had already won the bout against inflation—it was just a matter of waiting for the referee to count inflation out—the Fed moved to tighten up on lending in 1948. Throughout the year—in February, June, and September—the Fed raised reserve requirements to their legislative limits. The last increase was made possible only by a special anti-inflation session of Congress that temporarily raised the ceilings on reserve requirements. Obviously, the Fed was not alone in its failure to see that inflation was already under control. The Fed was no longer just slowing the money supply down; it had brought money growth to a standstill. The money supply stopped growing at the end of January 1948, declined for the next 12 months, and did not regain its losses until exactly two years later.

The contraction of the money supply in 1948 and the contractionary swing in fiscal policy (from huge deficits to a sizable surplus) combined to push aggregate demand downward and send the economy into a recession. Industrial production and output fell for about five quarters from mid-1948 to late 1949. Once again, the Fed was slow to react to the existing contraction. It was still worrying about inflation. The Board of Governors waited until May 1949 to begin a series of six reserve requirement reductions that by September 1949 had converted

$4 billion from required to excess reserves. Finally, at the end of the year the monetary base stopped its 14-month descent, and the money supply and output began to rise again just as the decade came to an end. The Fed had been in an extremely awkward position given its commitment to the Treasury, and its efforts to stop inflation were commendable. As we have already seen and will see again in subsequent chapters, however, moderately slowing the growth rate of the money supply can be an excellent strategy, but precipitating a drop in the money supply is invariably a big mistake—almost guaranteed to produce a recession.

□ Full-Employment Policy

The war brought with it exceptional economic prosperity and a return to full employment. That is certainly better than can be said for anything done during the 1930s. Nevertheless, as the war progressed, policy debates continued to thrive. While there was no longer a need to debate the more controversial planks of the New Deal, considerable uncertainty remained about where the economy would head after the war, when the enormous boosts in military spending stopped. Given the lack of consensus about the economy at the end of the 1930s, these qualms were to be expected. While the wartime experience taught important lessons about the economy's responsiveness to fiscal stimulation, doubts still lingered about the underlying health of the private economy. It was obviously capable of reestablishing full employment during a war, but could it do so without massive government expenditures? Even if the economy was deemed capable of reaching full employment on its own, would it be able to maintain that level of activity, or would destabilizing swings in aggregate demand press the government into action with fiscal policy to counteract those swings and ensure full employment? These are the kinds of questions that arose as a broad cast of characters—including the president, his advisers, lawmakers and their advisers, the Federal Reserve staff, business leaders, and academics—tried to hammer out a policymaking consensus for the postwar economy.

□ **Keynesian Lessons**   By 1942, John Maynard Keynes, were he so inclined, could have let out with the loudest "I told you so." This would have been nothing new to the century's most important economist, since failure to heed his advice (outlined in *The Economic Consequences of Peace*) during the peace negotiations following World War I had dire consequences in Germany that contributed to World War II. How the American economy catapulted out of the lingering stagnation of the late 1930s into the overwhelming prosperity of the 1940s stands as compelling prima facie evidence that Keynes had been right all along about what the economy needed to return to full employment: a large boost in government expenditures.

As we saw in the last chapter, Keynes and others were calling for pump priming as early as 1932. Keynes contended that a major drop in aggregate expenditures (consumption and investment) was the cause of the depression. Rather than wait for those private expenditures to rebound, spurred by declines in wages, prices, and interest rates, Keynes called for immediate increases in government expenditures to replace the missing private expenditures. Based on his model of consumption expenditures, he insisted that the increase in government expenditures would set off an income multiplier process whereby the increases in income generated by the boosts in government expenditures would ignite additional increases in consumption. The total rise in income would be significantly larger than the initial increase in government expenditures. In chapter 5 we used that multiplier concept to show the increases in expenditures that would have been necessary to fill Keynes's prescription. Yet the New Deal never came close to delivering the kinds of boosts in expenditures Keynes was talking about and we calculated were necessary. Roosevelt and other policymakers never took Keynes's advice.

The policy of the government and the performance of the economy in the 1940–42 period alone say it all. In 1940 unemployment was still 14.6%; government expenditures were $9.1 billion, just $4.5 billion more than they had been in 1933; and the $3.9 billion deficit was a mere $1.3 billion higher than in 1933. With the gap between actual GNP and full-employment GNP exceeding $26 billion, the Keynesian income-expenditure model tells us that the economy needed as much as $13 billion more in investment or government expenditures to prime the pump—to set off the income multiplier effect and send the economy to full employment. The Roosevelt administration was not committed to such unprecedented increases in expenditures or to the equally unprecedented deficits that would accompany them. The outbreak of the war forced the government to do what it had otherwise been unwilling to do, raise expenditures dramatically—but only after the United States was forced to enter the war itself. Expenditures rose significantly in 1941, but the real boost came in 1942, after war had been declared, when spending jumped by $20 billion. Just as Keynes predicted, unemployment disappeared almost overnight, and the economy actually shot beyond full employment.

What is so frustrating about how quickly and easily the economy leapt back to full employment in 1942 is that the leap could have occurred much sooner. The Roosevelt administration could have increased

government expenditures by the necessary amount—$13–16 billion—
at any time during the preceding nine years. The outbreak of war was
not necessary to justify an increase in expenditures during a depression.
It would have been just as stimulating to the economy had expenditures
increased on public works projects or other domestic programs, and such
expenditures could have started in 1933 instead of 1941. The United
States could have returned to full employment as early as 1936 had bold
increases in government expenditures been executed. Instead, the New
Deal gave the economy bold increases in government planning, artificial
increases in wages and prices, and higher taxes on economic activity—
all of which lengthened the depression.

The economy's recovery in 1942 is the smoking gun in Roosevelt's
hand because it convincingly shows that the Roosevelt administration
delayed the economy's return to full employment by several years with
its insistence on trying to balance the budget and their ill-advised
reflation programs. In all fairness to the policymakers of the 1930s, the
Keynesian prescription was a revolutionary one. One does not have to
be a Keynesian, however, to see that by waiting until 1942 to give the
economy the medicine that was prescribed in 1933, the Roosevelt administration was guilty of at best very conservative doctoring and at worst
malpractice. New Deal measures prolonged the depression by as much
as six years. One has to wonder how much longer Americans would
have had to wait for the return to full employment had the war not
intervened. As we saw in the last chapter, the answer is probably at least
three more years.

The return to full employment in 1942 had an immediate impact
on the philosophy of actual and would-be government policymakers.
Everyone was now persuaded that the economy was capable of operating
at full employment and that the government should devise some way to
ensure that the potential was always fulfilled. Roosevelt, who as late as
1940 was not convinced the government should or could set full employment as a goal, was won over to the full-employment cause. Even his
1944 Republican opponent, Thomas Dewey, and the rest of his party
agreed that full employment would be the "first objective of national
policy" after the war. Republicans and Democrats alike believed that if
the private economy was not capable of generating a sufficient number
of jobs to hold unemployment to a minimum, it was now the government's responsibility to fill the gap in some manner. It was universally
accepted that the government would take on a new role after the war as
the guarantor of full employment. The first steps in the Keynesian
revolution had been taken.

☐ **The Employment Act of 1946** A landmark piece of legislation signifying the government's assumption of at least partial responsibility for maintaining full employment was the Employment Act of 1946. Many call it the Full Employment Act, since that was its original title before Congress watered down both the title and the content of the bill. Even in its toned-down final version the bill is revolutionary because of the expanded role for the government that it mandated.

A similar philosophical transformation was occurring in Great Britain, Keynes's homeland. Policymakers on both sides of the Atlantic began to look ahead to anticipate the needs of the postwar economy. In conjunction with efforts to create the United Nations, Keynes of Britain and Dexter White of the United States, along with financial experts representing other allies, met in July 1944 and devised the Bretton Woods system (named after the New Hampshire resort hotel where the meetings were held), which was the postwar international trade and finance agreement. Among other things, the Bretton Woods agreement established (a) a fixed exchange rate currency system based on the American dollar and (b) a framework for the reduction of trade restrictions among the countries of Western Europe and North America.

The European participants in this agreement were haunted by one major fear—that the United States would suffer a postwar recession or depression and export it to Europe. Because the American economy had become so large and the European economies—either individually or as a group—were so dependent on exports to America, swings in U.S. economic activity were sure to set off ripple effects in Europe. The worst-case scenario was a postwar American relapse into a state of depression like that in the 1930s. In that case, the decline of American income would translate into a decline in American imports of European products, and in turn a reduction in aggregate demand and a recession in Europe as well. Because trade with America made up a substantially larger fraction of each European economy's GNP than European trade affected the American GNP, leaders presumed the direction of causality would always follow the path from the United States to Europe, as had probably occurred in the 1930s. Whatever economic disease America developed would be caught by Europe.

The Europeans insisted on some sort of assurance from American policymakers that they would not allow anything like the Great Depression to develop again. Apparently, all involved believed the wartime experience indicated that the U.S. government had the ability to prevent such a recurrence. Thus, the Bretton Woods negotiations provided extra impetus to the full-employment movement that was already gathering a full head of steam in Washington.

Starting in late 1944, members of Congress set out to draft legislation that would declare full employment a national policy goal. Some senators and their staffs put together the first draft of the Full Employment Act. It called for the preparation of an annual planning report by the president's staff, wherein the level of aggregate demand needed to achieve full employment would be calculated, along with the actual level of private demand and the level of government expenditures needed to make up the difference. The influence of the newly developed "gap" analysis was evident. The government was assigned the task of filling up the gap between private spending and the spending necessary to achieve or maintain full employment.

Much about the original version of the act sparked debate and controversy. Some worried that such legislation doomed the government to running perennial deficits and sentenced the economy to ever-increasing government involvement. Others shied away from putting the government out on a limb and guaranteeing full employment when no complete agreement existed on what exactly full employment meant. Did it mean zero unemployment? Did it mean everyone had to work, whether he or she wanted to or not? Does everyone have a "right" to work? Aside from these concerns, others doubted the government's ability to predict the future and conduct policy accordingly.

Ultimately, the bill went through so many revisions and was so watered down that it makes a rather weak statement. Congress declared that it was the responsibility of the federal government "to promote maximum employment, production, and purchasing power." Gone were the words *full employment,* and nowhere to be found were specific instructions about how full employment was to be promoted. What was left was the creation of the Council of Economic Advisors, the three-member committee designed to study the economy and offer suggestions for achieving an equilibrium between aggregate demand and aggregate supply as close to full employment as possible. The council's annual reports to the president were to be the guidelines for government policymaking.

That the final version of the Employment Act took on this watered-down form says much about public opinion at the time. Although the overwhelming majority of Americans wanted the government to help the economy maintain full employment, there was no clear consensus on how the government was to accomplish that goal in peacetime. Most Americans were unwilling to risk crippling the free-market economy with a rigid program of government planning. Keynesians did not want such an invasion, but their plan for the use of stabilizing fiscal policy was not yet sufficiently clear, even in their own minds, to be set up as a specific national policy. Postwar policy debates within Congress and between the president and Congress underscored that the Keynesian revolution was still in its infancy. Finalization of the Bretton Woods agreement required some commitment to full employment to come out of Congress in 1946, even if policymakers were not yet ready with a specific program. Though what emerged was relatively vague, such a bill would never have been considered just five years earlier. Times were certainly changing.

☐ **The Ascendance of Fiscal Policy**   Even though Congress failed to lay out specific objectives or methods in the Employment Act, one thing was becoming abundantly clear: virtually everyone involved in the debate was talking about fiscal policy; monetary policy was put on the back burner. Whereas in previous years the only appropriate fiscal policy had been a balanced budget, now people of all political persuasions were freely considering such options as compensatory fiscal policy, functional finance, and automatic stabilizers. Fiscal policy had truly become the fashionable policy for discussion, if not yet for exclusive use. While at one level a debate brewed over whether or not to use fiscal policy, at another level practitioners busied themselves with determining exactly how to use it. The concept of manipulating aggregate demand through the adjustments of expenditures and taxes was the center of attention in the 1940s.

The ascent of fiscal policy can be traced to a combination of developments. First, monetary policy as a stabilization tool had fallen out of favor during the depression. That was in sharp contrast to the prematurely lofty perch on which the Fed and its policy mandate were placed in the 1920s. As we saw in chapter 3, the Fed's apparent successful use of open market operations to ward off serious recessions in 1924 and 1927 had given rise to the illusion that the Fed was ready and able to stabilize the economy. The depression changed everyone's mind, but for the wrong reasons. The misinterpretations of monetary signals (such as market interest rates and the quantity of excess reserves) and the Fed's response to those conditions led many to believe wrongly (as discussed in chapter 4) that the depression occurred despite easy-money policies at the Fed. Reinterpretations of the events in the 1930s have since shown that monetary policy was extremely potent and extraordinarily contractionary from 1928 to 1933 and again from 1936 to 1938. Furthermore, it can be seen that the most important force behind the recovery periods of 1933 to 1936 and 1938 to 1941 (and, some would argue, even the war years) was the rapid growth of the money supply The 1930s stand as a

monument to the potency of monetary policy as well as the Fed's unfortunately improper application of that policy. Nevertheless, the common
view in the 1940s was that monetary policy was unreliable, particularly
in stimulating aggregate demand. Fiscal policy arose as an alternative.

Given the many invasive policies attempted during the New Deal
era, fiscal policy stood out as a very attractive alternative. Changes in
the aggregate levels of spending and taxing did relatively little to the
inner workings of the economy. It was not necessary to call business and
labor leaders together in order to make fiscal policy changes; nor was it
necessary to get permission from the Supreme Court—a touchy subject
with Roosevelt. Fiscal policy was seen as fairly evenhanded and noninva-
sive, with very little in its workings to threaten the market system. For
these reasons, both conservatives and liberals found fiscal policy a potentially attractive option.

Finally, the ascent of fiscal policy coincided with the gradual increase in acceptance of Keynesian economics. Keynes was not as strict a
fiscalist as some Keynesians later came to be. After all, his ideas of
monetary reform in the 1920s called for a domestically managed money
supply with an eye toward the very goals laid out in the Employment
Act. Both Benjamin Strong and Roosevelt (when he took the United
States off the gold standard) were influenced by these proposals. Still,
Keynes's theories are principally associated with fiscal policy because he
offered fiscal policy as a new option for dealing with a depression. His
income-expenditure model is the perfect theoretical device for demon-
strating how fiscal policy can be applied, and he used it to show that
government expenditures could be increased to make up for a shortfall
of investment expenditures (business purchases of capital). After all,
Keynes did give us compensatory fiscal policy to replace the balanced
budget rule as a vehicle to reach a stable full-employment equilibrium.
The Keynesian revolution and the fiscal revolution came hand in hand.

The acceptance of fiscal policy as a stabilization tool required abandoning the goal of an annually balanced budget—a goal that was very
hard for most, including Roosevelt and his successor, Harry Truman, to
forswear. Compensatory fiscal policy called for increases in government
expenditures during recessions, without matching increases in taxes.
Deficit spending was Keynes's prescription for a depressed economy.
Economists who came to accept Keynes's model, such as Alvin Hansen
and Abba Lerner, had to step forward and try to convince the public that
it was all right for the government to run a deficit and add to the federal
debt. Here is another area where the war experience contained a
Keynesian lesson in policymaking. That the economy was not just sur-
viving but prospering while shouldering a federal debt in excess of GNP

robbed the national debt of some of its ability to strike terror in the hearts of fiscally conservative Americans. This situation made it easier to convince other Americans that deficits, at the appropriate times, were not just all right but actually preferred.

A major plank in the prodeficits argument was a contention that the size of the federal debt was of little concern. Even Keynes himself needed a bit of persuading on this point. Lerner contended that because the overwhelming majority of the debt was owed by Americans to Americans, it was not a burden on current or future generations. While most economists began to agree at least in part with that appraisal, other people in the White House and Congress did not and would not soon abandon the balanced budget rule. Politicians have continued to use fear of the federal debt as a campaign issue without interruption into the 1990s, even though many of those same public officials have been guilty of adding to the debt at the same time they were haranguing against it.

Hansen and Lerner believed that through a complete business cycle, which might extend over several years, periods would arise when the economy needed a dampening of aggregate demand, in addition to times when a boost in demand would be required. They claimed that compensatory fiscal policy was not just a one-sided antidepression tool but was instead a full-time strategy for smoothing out the peaks and valleys in aggregate expenditures that arise mainly from swings in investment expenditures. Thus, even though there would be times when deficits would be correct, there would also be periods when a balanced budget or a surplus budget would be the right policy. Indeed, this work led to the suggestion that the budget might be balanced in the aggregate over the entire business cycle period, with deficits during recession years being counterbalanced by surpluses during inflationary times. This view made the conservative budget-balancers slightly more comfortable with temporary deficits, for it raised the possibility that the Keynesian approach could be followed without starting an upward trend in the federal debt. Under those circumstances, fiscal policy was poised to take center stage as a stabilization tool. The philosophical ascent of fiscal policy as a full-time stabilization tool was well under way. Practical discretionary applications of the concepts would take a while longer to develop.

☐ The Postwar Policy Puzzle

No sooner had the economy reached full employment during the war than people began to worry about what would happen after the war.

Certainly, by 1944 it was apparent that the war would have a positive outcome in the not-too-distant future, and postwar planning began in earnest. The Bretton Woods negotiations were one example. Any war-time discussion of economic conditions after the war focused on the question of whether or not the economy would simply return to the stagnation of the thirties, once the massive military expenditures were reduced. Still another wartime Keynesian lesson seemed to be that without substantial government expenditures bolstering aggregate demand, the economy might indeed slip back into a high-unemployment situation. On the other hand, there was ample evidence to support the expectation that prosperity would continue now that the economy had shaken the doldrums of the depression and the failures of the New Deal.

Obviously, the direction stabilization policy took immediately following the war depended on the answer to this question. While the postwar period brought uncertainty, it also presented a challenge. Now that fiscal policy had apparently eclipsed monetary policy as a stabilization tool in the minds of many policymakers, the postwar period would offer the first opportunities to apply the concepts of compensatory fiscal policy and functional finance to the economy.

☐ **Stagnation or Boom?**   The anticipation of renewed post-war stagnation can be greatly blamed on the Keynesians. Late in the 1930s, Hansen, a reluctant but eventually enthusiastic apostle of Keynes's model, warned about the likelihood that the American economy was doomed to experience secular stagnation. To Hansen's way of thinking, the depression was just the beginning. He envisioned the combination of consumption and investment expenditures falling progressively farther behind total output. Part of his theory derived from Keynes's consumption model, which could be used to show that the ratio of consumption to output would decline over time. That would leave an ever-widening gap for investment to fill. The pathetic performance of investment during the 1930s gave Hansen little reason to count on investment filling the gap. Hansen's pessimism was also based on other concerns, such as the fact that population growth was slowing, supposedly further stunting the growth in consumption.

While Hansen's fears were theoretical, the government discovered empirical evidence to support the stagnationist prediction. During the war, the government began calculating GNP and national income for the first time. No wonder policymakers seemed to stumble in the dark in earlier years—they had so little information about the economy to gauge its health. While the government statisticians were at it, they estimated GNP, national income, disposable income (income after taxes), and consumption for the years 1929 to 1942. When they put the disposable income and consumption data together, they found a stable relationship between the two variables, just as Keynes had theorized. This finding gave Keynes's model a boost of empirical support, and it gave policymakers a possible guideline.

The data for 1929 to 1942 indicated a marginal propensity to consume (the ratio of the change in consumption divided by the change in income) of less than 80% and a secular declining ratio of consumption to income. These data seemed to support Hansen's fears. Because the relationship between income and consumption appeared so stable over the test period, some government economists presumed the same ratios would hold after the war. Estimates of postwar income were used to make projections of postwar consumption. Those projections were alarmingly low. When the consumption projections were added to investment predictions, the sum of private aggregate expenditures looked like it would fall drastically short of full-employment output—that is, the dreaded full-employment gap would return unless government expenditures were at least maintained at wartime levels.

The prognosis for the economy was not good. The only apparent way to avoid a return to stagnation after the war was for the government to fill in this gap, the difference between full-employment output and aggregate demand. And what made matters all the more disconcerting was evidence suggesting that the gap would grow every year, requiring the level of government expenditures to rise. The percentage of GNP purchased by the government would have to increase progressively in order to ensure full employment. Such a prospect may have been attractive to some of the more liberal members of Congress but was downright terrifying to their more conservative colleagues.

As it turned out, the predictions of postwar stagnation could not have been farther from reality. The economy did not stray from full employment until the recession of 1948–49. Output did fall from 1945 to 1947, but that was due not to a lack of aggregate demand but to a shrinking of aggregate supply, as the labor force declined when many people, primarily women, returned to their prewar roles outside the labor force. Demand was anything but weak. Both consumption and investment exploded after the war. Consumers had piled up savings in the form of government securities during the war when consumer goods were scarce and buying war bonds was the patriotic thing to do. These surplus funds fueled a 50% surge in consumer spending from 1944 to 1947. Private investment, which had just returned to 1929 levels at $18 billion in 1941, only to be squeezed out by the massive government expenditures during the war, leapt upward to $32 billion by 1947. With this two-pronged surge in private expenditures, the full-employment gap did not appear in 1946 and 1947. We can safely say the gap was nonexistent in 1947 because the economy was easily at full employment, with only a 3.6% unemployment rate, while the budget was balanced. Private demand was able to buy up total full-employment output without any boost in government expenditures.

Secular stagnation was a myth. It turned out that Hansen was wrong, and so were the government economists' projections. The consumption formula used by the economists was based on data from the depression years and was not the least bit applicable to the postwar economy. Simon Kuznets, through his extensive efforts in GNP measurement, discovered that the American long-term ratios between both consumption and income and changes in consumption and income were close to 90%—far higher than the depression figures. He also saw no downward trend in these ratios as Keynes and Hansen theorized and as the depression and wartime data had indicated. The first time government economists were given a chance to make empirical projections and policy suggestions, they were dead wrong. As we will see, it would not be the last time.

☐ **The Postwar Fiscal Tests**   As the economy tested the postwar waters, policymakers within the Truman administration and Congress began the gradual process of incorporating the new fiscal theories into policies. The underlying good health of the economy made their work a lot easier than it would have been a decade earlier. In that respect, all parties were lucky, because fiscal policy moved very tentatively and fortuitously in the Keynesian direction during the peacetime Truman years.

Interestingly enough, the initial postwar application of compensatory fiscal policy was employed to slow aggregate demand rather than boost it. The first problem that had to be dealt with after the war was inflation rather than stagnation—at least, that is what Truman thought—and that required budget tightening. But before Truman could adopt such a policy, he had to face a fiscal revolt by congressional Republicans and southern Democrats who teamed together to cut taxes in an all-out conservative effort to bring the postwar level of government expenditures back under control. The Revenue Act of 1945 lopped more than $5 billion from taxes by 1946. This cut violated Truman's goals of "fiscal responsibility," and ordinarily such a tax cut might have been inflationary; in this case, however, government expenditures fell even more at the same time. The result was a reduction of the federal deficit from almost $54 billion in 1945 to nearly $21 billion in 1946. Thus, the net effect of fiscal policy in 1946 was decidedly contractionary.

The deficit reduction program continued in 1947, when a $21 billion drop in expenditures eliminated the deficit and brought the budget in balance for the first time since 1930. With inflation still identified as the number-one enemy by the White House and government spending the villain in the eyes of conservative members of Congress, further expenditure reductions were accomplished in 1948. Contractionary fiscal policy was easily promoted with the president and Congress coincidentally in favor of spending cuts, even though their rationales were different. The 1948 budget showed an $8 billion surplus. Had monetary policy not turned so contractionary in 1948, we could probably look back at fiscal policy up to early 1948 and say it was well suited to the state of the economy. There can be no doubt that changes in the federal budget fit a prescription for anti-inflation policy in a full-employment economy. As it was, however, with the money supply falling from 1948 to 1949, aggregate demand was dampened too much. The economy entered the first of what in the subsequent 40 years would prove to be several policy-induced recessions set off by government efforts to ward off a surge of inflation, a surge that was also induced by the government's own earlier policy actions.

In early 1948 Truman continued to believe inflation was still endangering economic stability. Congress disagreed. Where Truman might have suggested a tax increase with appeals to "fiscal responsibility," conservative forces in Congress were still pushing for further reductions in both expenditures and taxes. The 1948 surplus and the projected surplus for 1949 persuaded many that a tax cut was needed. Seeking extra support for the latest in their annual crusade to cut taxes, proponents of a tax cut pointed to indications that the inflation surge and the postwar boom were both losing steam. This time the president could not stop these legislators, even with his veto, and the Revenue Act of 1948 was passed in April.

The tax cut made Truman even more convinced that he had to battle inflation. At midyear, he called together a special session of Congress to attack inflation. The only congressional change of consequence was the temporary hike in the ceilings for reserve requirements at the Fed. As discussed earlier in this chapter, the Fed took advantage of this adjustment to raise reserve requirements enough to send the money supply sliding downward. By the fall of 1948, a recession had begun.

Truman was fortunate. The 1948 recession began late and quietly enough so that it did no damage to his reelection miracle in November. Moreover, the tax cut he tried to veto earlier in the year could not have been passed at a better time. Its $4–5 billion reduction in government receipts helped cushion the blow of the shrinking money supply on the level of aggregate demand. Even though it was not passed for reasons associated with compensatory, countercyclical fiscal policy, its timing was precisely what a Keynesian doctor would have ordered. The recession was a rather mild one in spite of the money supply's decline; the 1948 tax cut may be one reason. Once again, as with wartime spending, government policy seems to have accidentally substantiated the Keynesian model.

Policymakers were still not tuned into the Keynesian program, but they were groping increasingly closer. No increase in expenditures or an additional tax cut was passed to boost the economy out of the recession. The relative mildness of the contraction was offered as a reason for not taking such moves, and projected impending increases in cold war military spending was another. Instead, the budget surplus was allowed to turn into small deficits in 1949 and 1950. That may not have been active compensatory policy, but at least no one seriously tried to balance the budget either. That is at least a victory for passive Keynesianism. Fiscal policymakers were inclined to let automatic stabilizers do their job. As we shall see, that theme dominated fiscal policy throughout the 1950s. A total commitment to the Keynesian model was still at least a decade away.

7

Postwar Stability:
1950–1960

IT IS EASY TO PICTURE AN ECONOMIC HIS-
tory professor telling his or her class about a tranquil decade when the
country was led by a strong and revered former military leader, when
the prime rate of interest averaged a mere 3.3%, when budget surpluses were not uncommon and an unusually large budget deficit was
only $13 billion, when prices rose at an average annual rate of just
2.6%, and when unemployment averaged near 5%. "Like, whoa! That
must have been a long time ago, Dude," interjects one of the students.
"There hasn't been a single year during my life when we have, like,
reached such totally excellent numbers." Thinking back to rerun episodes of "Happy Days," the class will probably not be surprised to find
out that this period of economic tranquility was the distant 1950s.
That was the decade when their professor was in Little League and
when policymakers at the Fed and in the Eisenhower administration
managed to steer the economy along what in retrospect was a relatively stable course.

The period 1950 to 1960 sets itself apart in terms of the philosophy
and action of stabilization policies, as well as the economy's performance, which was shaped by those policies. The Federal Reserve declared its independence from the Treasury's war-financing constraints
and developed a countercyclical policy style within a decidedly anti-
inflationary framework. At the same time, President Eisenhower strug-
gled to bring government spending under control and eliminate deficits

while avoiding his predecessors' frequent errors of trying to balance the budget during recession years.

All in all, stabilization policymaking in the 1950s became a bit more enlightened than in the past, and it was decidedly more successful than in the decades that followed. Despite this fact, which in looking back we can now see plainly, policymakers were roundly criticized during the 1950s and for many years thereafter for restraining the economy too much and preventing it from performing to its potential. We will see in chapter 8 that in the ensuing two decades, without the restraint of the 1950s, more active policymakers sent the economy on a highly unstable course that made the quieter times of the 1950s look a lot better in retrospect. This decade truly was a pleasant economic interlude between the instability and uncertainty of the years that preceded and followed it. There was a minimum of policymaking as the economy caught its breath before boarding the policy roller coaster that took off in the 1960s.

☐ Surveying the Fifties

No sooner had the 1950s begun than the Korean War ignited in June 1950. The economy had been on the rebound from the minor recession it had experienced in 1949 and was headed back toward full employment. The surge in demand and the shortages that were expected to accompany the outbreak of the war set off a burst of speculative buying on the part of producers and consumers, all trying to beat the expected price increases. Private sector demand combined with government demand aimed at the war effort quickly pushed aggregate demand and output upward. Before the end of the year, unemployment was well below 5%, and the economy was operating beyond full employment. Nevertheless, aside from a brief acceleration of inflation during the speculative bubble in the first eight months of the war, prices increased at a strikingly slow pace during the Korean War. This was partially attributable to the wage and price controls imposed by the government but must also be credited to the restraint on budget deficits and money supply increases practiced during the war.

Unemployment hovered around 3% as Eisenhower took office in 1953 with promises to bring peace to Korea and to battle excessive government spending and inflation, a barely visible but ever-lurking menace on the domestic front. The war did end soon, in the summer of 1953, and the economy promptly went into a thirteen-month recession. This "rolling adjustment," as the Eisenhower administration liked to call it to avoid use of the R-word, caused the unemployment rate to virtually double; six percent of the labor force could not find jobs by the summer of 1954. The decline in income to nearly 93.5% of potential GNP dashed Eisenhower's hopes of quickly eliminating Truman's budget deficits. Buoyed by some well-timed expansionary monetary policy, however, the economy began a strong recovery at the end of the summer of 1954.

The expansion lasted for three years. Output rose quickly, and unemployment fell rapidly during the first year. For the next two years, the economy settled into a holding pattern at or beyond full employment, with unemployment in the low 4% range and output creeping up at a below-average rate. The relative health of the economy permitted Eisenhower to eliminate the budget deficit and to show surpluses for two and a half years. The only cloud in all this silver lining was the inflation rate. First, prices had continued to rise, albeit more slowly, right on through the just-passed recession. Falling prices had been the norm for recessions until this time. Rising prices in the face of falling aggregate demand was a new phenomenon and one that contradicted the Keynesian model. Then the 1954–57 expansion brought an average inflation rate of close to 3.5%, which further fanned the fears of a new, relentless peacetime inflation.

Federal Reserve efforts to slow the growth of aggregate demand precipitated a downturn in demand and sales, and a recession began in August 1957. This contraction was shorter than the previous one, as the Fed quickly reversed its course and within a few months had set off a surge in the growth rate of the money supply to its fastest pace of the decade. An upturn in activity commenced as early as spring of the next year. During those months of contraction, however, output fell 6% below its potential, the unemployment rate visited the 7% range, and the budget surplus Eisenhower had been so carefully cultivating turned into a deficit exceeding $12 billion. Although this recession was relatively brief, it was at least as bad as the prior one and came far too close on the previous one's heels to satisfy most people. And once again, prices continued their persistent climb right on through the downturn.

The next expansion proved to be shorter than the last. Output climbed for only 24 months before it turned down again in April 1960. During the expansion, output never quite made it back to its potential; the unemployment rate had not even reached 5% before this third recession of Eisenhower's term began. This one was probably the least serious of the three, as output stayed above 95% of its potential and unemployment temporarily returned to the 7% zone; nevertheless, the

recession's timing was not good for the election chances of Richard
Nixon and the Republican party. Nixon learned the harsh lesson that
unemployed workers blame the incumbent party, and they have a lot of
free time to vote for someone who promises more vitality for the economy. Given the exceptionally close results of the 1960 presidential election, the recession that year was an important deciding factor.

Thus, even though the data for the 1950s, on average, give the look
of a prosperous and stable economy, there was room to complain. The
expansions got progressively shorter in duration, and the intervening
unemployment peaks got progressively higher. A comparison of the
data in table 7 with the data for the 1940s or the 1920s shows that by the

Table 7:   Economic Indicators, 1950–60

	Q	M1	M2	P	CPI	GE	GR	Surplus Deficit	UN	Prime Rate
1950	8.5	4.7	3.7	2	5.9	43	39	−4	5.3	2.1
1951	10.3	5.8	5.3	4.8	5	45	52	+7	3.3	2.6
1952	3.9	3.6	4.6	1.5	0.8	68	66	−2	3	3
1953	4	1.4	2.8	1.6	0.7	76	70	−6	2.9	3.2
1954	− 1.3	2.8	4	1.6	−0.7	71	70	−1	5.5	3.1
1955	5.6	2.1	2.3	3.2	0.4	68	65	−3	4.4	3.2
1956	2.1	1.4	2.2	3.4	3	71	75	+4	4.1	3.8
1957	1.7	−0.7	2.2	3.6	2.9	77	80	+3	4.3	4.2
1958	−0.8	3.9	6.6	2.1	1.8	82	80	−2	6.8	3.8
1959	5.8	0.5	1.5	2.4	1.7	92	79	−13	5.5	4.5
1960	2.2	0.5	4.9	1.6	1.4	92	92	0	5.5	4.8

Q   = Percent change in real GNP (output)
M1 = Percent change in M1 (currency plus checking account deposits)
M2 = Percent change in M2 (currency plus checking and savings accounts)
P   = Percent change in GNP Implicit Price Deflator
CPI = Percent change in Consumer Price Index
GE = Federal government expenditures (billions of dollars)
GR = Federal government revenues (billions of dollars)
Surplus/Deficit = GR minus GE
UN = Average unemployment rate (percent)
Prime Rate = Average prime rate of interest (percent)

Sources: See Bibliographic Essay.

end of the decade, unemployment rates were higher, and output growth rates were lower than those to which people had become accustomed. Moveover, prices persistently rose during both expansions and contractions, prompting discussions about "seller's inflation" or "structural inflation," phrases referring to price increases that resulted from the sluggish growth of, or declines in, aggregate supply rather than excessive aggregate demand. A variety of culprits—including unions, big business, slow productivity gains, even Communists—were blamed for the economy's performance, which seemed lackluster compared with Japan, Germany, several Third World countries, and (most important) the Soviet Union. Perhaps we can find some clues to the economy's performance in the conduct of monetary and fiscal policies.

☐ The Fed Asserts Itself

One of the most striking aspects of policy in the 1950s is how slowly the money supply grew throughout the decade. For the 11-year period from the beginning of 1950 to the end of 1960, M2 grew at an average rate of only 3.7% per year. Since the depths of the monetary contraction in 1933, money supply growth had averaged in the double digits. The policy of the 1950s marked an extraordinary change of pace that was in many ways reminiscent of the 1920s. To formulate such a policy approach, the Fed first had to reestablish its independence and free itself of the restrictions of helping the Treasury finance its debt. Then it could set its policy based on its own assessment of market needs.

☐ **Freedom from the Treasury**   The surge in speculative buying that accompanied the outbreak of the Korean War brought to the public eye a dispute between the Treasury and the Fed that had been brewing beneath the surface. The Fed had been committed since early in World War II to a policy of holding down interest rates for the sake of easing the Treasury's efforts to finance the issuance of securities. Even though the large deficits had disappeared with the end of the war, the need to support bond prices continued. It was still believed that bondholders, both current and potential, would not tolerate a rise in interest rates and the fall in bond prices that necessarily goes along. This drop in bond values would, it was argued, hurt bondholders so much that they would no longer be willing to buy newly issued ones. That would spell doom for the Treasury's ability to float new issues of bonds to pay off old ones and would mean an insolvency crisis for the government. Every time the Fed protested its role as the ever-ready buyer of last resort for Treasury securities, the Treasury made it feel guilty by painting the insolvency scenario and asking, "Now you don't want to cause that, do you?"

No, the Fed did not want to set off such a scenario, but its hands were tied by a policy of pegging bond prices, and, as was the case after World War I, it was unable to fight inflation. As wholesale prices shot up in late 1950, the Fed felt powerless. As long as it was forced to hold long-term interest rates below 2.5%, the Fed was not going to be able to slow spending and halt the rapid rise in wholesale prices. Short-term rates began rising, but the 2.5% ceiling on long-term rates became harder and harder to maintain. Although the Fed continued to buy major portions of Treasury issuances of long-term securities, it tried to sell an equal amount from its existing portfolio in an effort to add as little as possible to the supply of reserves in the banking system. Something had to give; the Fed could not continue buying securities with one hand and selling with the other, hoping to hold down bond prices.

The continued rise in wholesale prices could not be tolerated by members of the Board of Governors. By January 1951, it was apparent that efforts to hold long-term interest rates below the 2.5% mark would add too much money to the economy and too much fuel to the inflation fires. The Fed officials protested more loudly, and President Truman was forced to meet with Secretary of the Treasury Carl Snyder and Fed Chair Thomas McCabe. The 2.5% ceiling was retained, but protests from within the Fed, Congress, and the business community grew progressively louder; the independence of the Fed and the stability of prices were at stake.

Finally, on 4 March 1951, the Treasury and Fed, after much debate and posturing, reached an "accord" whereby the Fed agreed to be cooperative in helping the Treasury issue securities but not to the point of unlimited monetization of the debt. In other words, the interest rate ceiling was removed. The Fed was allowed to pursue a policy of moderating the growth of the money supply in order to ward off inflation. The news that interest rates and bond prices were now free to vary was greeted by the financial markets with a collective yawn, rather than panic. Treasury securities were now certainly different, since they were no longer automatically convertible into money at a fixed price at the Fed. Thus, the risk factor associated with owning these securities definitely increased. Nevertheless, in spite of no longer being a sure thing, Treasury securities (old and new) were still attractive, marketable assets. The postaccord scenario proved once again (as was shown in the 1930s and 1940s) that the financial markets could absorb large quantities of government debt without the central bank having resort to money creation.

The Fed was fairly conservative with its newfound freedom. Long-term rates did immediately pop through the 2.5% ceiling, but not by much, as the rates stayed below 3% for at least two years. The Fed allowed the growth rate of the money supply to accelerate a bit, while letting interest rates climb a bit as well. The M2 growth rate rose to more than 5% for 1951 and 4.5% for 1952, still relatively conservative figures for an economy in the middle of a war, limited though it was. When shortages did not accompany the Korean War, speculative buying and inflationary expectations subsided. The accord helped in that respect as well, since it increased public confidence in the Fed's ability to control inflation. Those forces, possibly along with the wage and price controls, kept inflation and inflationary expectations well under control right through 1954, thereby making the Fed's job of walking the narrow path between higher interest rates and inflation relatively easy.

☐ **Slow but a Little Unsteady**   The postaccord policy at the Fed gradually took on the stamp of its conservative new chair, William McChesney Martin, who replaced McCabe in April 1951 and held the post for almost 20 years. During the first half of his term, he was definitely anti-inflation. He was inclined to keep the growth rate of the money supply down and was willing to vary interest rates to levels necessary to keep the economy on a stable course. Unfortunately, this meant the money supply growth rate was prone to variations that created swings in aggregate demand, such swings often conflicting with his goals of stability.

Despite the absence of any concrete signs, the Fed became concerned about an outbreak of inflation beginning in 1953 and signaled its anxiety with an increase in the discount rate and a decided slowdown in the money supply growth that cut the rate in half by midyear. In addition, in March the Federal Open Market Committee officially reaffirmed its independence and declared it would keep its "hands off" the Treasury's latest offerings. Consequently, interest rates climbed and a slight credit crunch occurred in the financial markets. Long-term bond prices sank, long-term rates climbed above 3%, and the Treasury offerings were selling at the initial auction at a discount from their face price.

Meanwhile, the Korean War was winding down to a negotiated end in the summer of 1953. Business activity peaked in July, and the decade's first recession was about to begin. Not really aware that a recession was just getting started, the Fed lowered the reserve requirement in May and July as a defensive action in response to the predicament developing in the financial markets. Nevertheless, M2 grew at a rate of only 2.4% during the first six months of the recession. The Fed started the new year with discount rate and reserve requirement reductions, as well as some open market purchases of government securities. All three monetary policy tools were employed to add to the money supply, and by the latter half of 1954, M2 was back growing at a 4.5% annual rate. These tactics were an excellent example of countercyclical monetary policy, and the economy responded appropriately with a recovery starting in August 1954.

Many sources claim that the Fed pumped too much liquidity into the system during the 1953–54 recession, the expansion period that followed, and the 1957 recession. But the excess reserves and money supply numbers simply do not support this criticism. The M2 growth rates for the six half-year periods during the three-year expansion were, in annual terms, 4.7%, 3.1%, 1.5%, 2.2%, 2.1%, and 3.5%—an average of only 2.5% and slower than output. As in the 1920s, critics were apparently referring qualitatively to government securities transactions rather than quantitatively to amounts of money. The Fed had adopted a "bills only" strategy of buying and selling only short-term Treasury securities (Treasury bills, that is) when it conducted open market operations. Some felt this approach caused a lack of balance between the short- and long-term markets, creating too much liquidity in the former. This criticism arose despite the fact that the quantity of high-powered money did not rise during these years. The growth of the money supply was all due to increases in the ratios of bank deposits to reserves. The Fed was basically in a neutral stance. It did nothing to change high-powered money, and it raised the discount rate six times from the spring of 1956 to the spring of 1957 solely to keep the discount rate in line with climbing short-term interest rates. We should not accuse the Fed of being too generous in its creation of liquidity.

While it is hard to fault the Fed for its actions through the first half of 1957, what it did during the second half had much to do with causing the 1957 recession. The Fed stopped the growth of the money supply. In August the Board of Governors helped to halt the economic expansion by hiking the discount rate from 3% to 3.5% against the protests of the Eisenhower administration. From August to the end of 1957, M2 stood still. Why the Fed stopped money growth is not clear, but the reaction to the consequences of its own policy was swift. The governors pushed the discount rate back down in November and followed that move with three more rate reductions in early 1958. The reserve requirement was lowered four times during the same period, and open market purchases were made from February to September 1958. This was an extraordinarily swift reversal in policy, and, as in 1954, the Fed used all three tools to fight the recession. Monetary policymakers clearly were getting the knack of fighting recessions with expansionary policy. Unfortunately, they were also picking up the habit of setting off those very recessions by applying overly restrictive policies.

The Fed promoted the recovery of 1958 as M2 jumped upward at an 8.2% annual rate for the first half of the year. That was the fastest growth period for the decade. An M2 expansion rate of 4.8% for the remainder of the year resulted in a lofty 6.5% money supply increase for 1958. The Fed understandably started to apply the brakes in early 1959, slowing money supply to an annual rate of 3.9% for the first half of the year. What it did for the next year could be explained by the desire to play a perverse trick on Richard Nixon (although no evidence points to this explanation) or an effort to hike up interest rates so as to correct the balance of payments deficit by attracting foreign financial investors to America. The money supply fell from June 1959 to June 1960, virtually guaranteeing that a recession would occur during the election year. Arthur Burns, formerly on Eisenhower's Council of Economic Advisors but now out of government, warned his friend Nixon of the impending contraction, and Nixon passed this warning on to the administration. Nixon's suggestion of more expansionary fiscal policy was ignored because, as we will shortly see, Eisenhower and his advisers were too busy fighting the demons of inflation and a budget deficit. The downturn began in April 1960 and helped carry the Republicans right out of the White House.

Once again, the Fed recognized a recession after it had hit and applied all its tools against it during the latter half of 1960. But the damage had been done. The state of the economy in the 1950s was one of the biggest issues of the 1960 campaign, and the economic downturn in 1960 was a decisive factor in John Kennedy's narrow election victory. Had the Fed not put the money supply into reverse from August 1959 to June 1960, it stands to reason that the 1960 recession would never have occurred. And it is also likely that with about 700,000 fewer unemployed workers to worry about, Nixon would have been elected instead of Kennedy. One can only speculate how different history would have been under those circumstances. Once again, the Fed shaped more than just a bit of American economic history. Though the 1960 recession may have been a mere blip on the economic history time line, its consequences were no doubt profound in terms of political and social history.

□ Fiscal Evolution

After all the discussion and debate over fiscal policy and the attention given to refining its theoretical principles that seemed to dominate the

1940s, we might have expected to find the "fiscal revolution" in full swing during the 1950s, with Keynesian economics guiding policymakers in a pattern of countercyclical tax and spending changes. While Keynes's influence was certainly spreading among lawmakers in Washington, D.C.—in addition to behind the ivy-covered walls among academics— the White House staff and Congress remained essentially unpersuaded. Truman and Eisenhower, two fiscally conservative presidents, were more interested in paying the bills than in adopting the new economics of functional finance. This does not mean Truman and Eisenhower were oblivious to the ever-growing group of newly converted Keynesians or that they reverted to the mistakes of the 1930s. Some lessons had been learned. Nevertheless, traditional concerns over budget balancing were important to these two administrations. Inflation was consistently seen as the disease most likely to infect the economy, and policy was biased toward preserving price stability rather than minimizing unemployment. Keynesians did not capture the presidential palace until 1961; meanwhile, the fiscal revolution slowed to an evolutionary pace during the 1950s.

☐ **Battling Inflation with the Budget**   The Truman administration had built a reputation for balancing the budget—running up three straight surplus budgets to finish off the 1940s. That came despite a variety of domestic spending programs as part of the Fair Deal. Yet the budget for the first year of the new decade slipped into a deficit. Truman, determined not to tarnish his record of social consciousness combined with fiscal restraint, called for corporate tax increases to offset the 1950 deficit. With the outbreak of the Korean War at midyear, further tax increases became part of his multipronged effort to ward off the expected inflation associated with wartime expenditures.

Congress was more in the mood for domestic spending reductions than tax increases. Republicans and conservative Democrats flexed their political muscles in an arm-wrestling contest with the president. The budget showed a small deficit in 1950 but was back in the black in 1951. By that time, the surge in inflationary expectations that followed the start of the war had begun to subside. The economic boom was driving up tax revenues at a faster rate than the expenditures. As a result, Congress was not so inclined to accept Truman's tax increase plan even if he was seeking more defense expenditures. Increased military appropriations only spurred some in Congress to push harder for spending cuts in domestic programs.

Truman's budget for 1952 requested substantial increases in military expenditures that could not be matched by domestic program cuts.

Total government expenditures jumped by almost 50%. The budget also projected as much as a $16 billion deficit if no adjustment was made in taxes. Truman pushed for tax increases that would yield more than $10 billion in new revenues. Congress met him halfway, with a tax package that brought in just under $6 billion more in revenues, and it tacked on an across-the-boards spending cut of its own. Once again, the robust economic expansion generated additional tax revenues; even though expenditures rose by $22 billion, tax revenues fell less than $2 billion short.

To this point, the combination of Truman's tax hike and the parsimony of Congress had kept the budget from adding much if any excess aggregate demand to the economy. Fiscal policy, along with wage and price controls and Federal Reserve policy, deserves credit for helping to keep inflation under control in a wartime economy that was operating beyond full employment. Once again, the White House showed it was ready to use countercyclical fiscal policy—even if simply in the form of an effort to balance the budget—to slow demand during inflationary times. Nevertheless, policymakers during the Truman presidency still displayed apparent reluctance to apply the Keynesian prescription of expansionary policy to recessions.

Early in his term, Eisenhower would be provided with an opportunity to demonstrate whether the revolution had taken hold. Eisenhower inherited both the war and a budget deficit. During the presidential campaign, he had been somewhat successful at tagging the Democrats with blame for the war, deficits, and inflation. Of course, the Republicans still carried the Hooverian cross: being blamed for the Great Depression. The new president was determined to eliminate the deficit and reduce the national debt while keeping a lid on the inflation rate without the crutch of wage and price controls. And most important, he intended to accomplish these feats of economic daring without setting off a serious recession. He was not always so successful at balancing the budget and avoiding recessions, but there is no doubt that the best way to view fiscal policy during the Eisenhower administration is from the vantage of an inflation fighter whose main weapon was a budget surplus. There were times—during recessions—that Eisenhower and his policymakers had to adjust their assessment of the relative dangers facing the economy and turn their attention more toward unemployment. Nevertheless, the overall program was to balance the budget and run surpluses whenever possible in order to lessen the likelihood of excess aggregate demand contributing to a higher rate of inflation.

Not everyone was in complete agreement with Eisenhower's assessment of the economy's biggest threat. Some leaned more in the direction of slow growth and excessive unemployment (especially toward the end of the decade) as the problems most worthy of fiscal policy attention. Yet a consensus within both the White House and Congress listed inflation as economic public enemy No 1. Indeed, the decade of the 1950s was marked by a veritable obsession with inflation, despite that the inflation rate never exceeded 3.6% after the Korean War. That point is discussed later in this chapter; for now, suffice it to say that Eisenhower's inflation fears were pandemic, and the conservative nature of the fiscal policy during his eight-year term was based on those fears and entirely consistent with them.

The Eisenhower presidency was the last to set budget surpluses as a policy goal and to be somewhat successful at it. If we look at the 32 quarterly data of Eisenhower's eight budget years, we find plus figures appear 15 times. That is slightly below Truman's figures, which showed 16 surplus quarters in a somewhat shorter period. Both of their fiscal records stand in sharp contrast with the deluge of deficits that followed. Only 11 surplus quarters were accomplished in the 1960s, and none at all appeared during the next two decades. Interestingly enough, inflation has plagued the economy to varying degrees since the 1960s. Truman and Eisenhower had different approaches to balanced budgets, with Truman more likely to raise taxes and Eisenhower determined to hold down all forms of government spending. Nonetheless, neither was a Keynesian disciple, and both battled inflation with the same weapon, budget surpluses.

☐ **Recession Concessions**   Three roadblocks stood before Eisenhower in his plan to eliminate the deficit, balance the budget, and begin to reduce the national debt: each of the three recessions that occurred during his presidency. We have already seen that the Federal Reserve probably had a hand in setting off at least the last two downturns with significant money supply slowdowns. Major reductions in defense spending probably contributed to the first as the Korean War came to an end, and possibly to the second. Regardless of the origins of these recessions, all three presented administration policymakers with a challenge. The last thing Eisenhower wanted was to act out the Democratic party's prophecy that the first Republican administration since Hoover's would reenact history and lord over another depression. He could not let these recessions get out of hand. In addition, Eisenhower felt compelled to assure Americans that he would not tear down the government welfare "safety net" that had been constructed during the previous 20 years.

The recessions put the administration in an awkward position because they were accompanied by a decline in tax revenues and a rise in government safety-net transfer payments. While Eisenhower was trying to eliminate deficits, the recessions worked to create or increase them. A glance at the budgetary record for the 1950s shows that the recessions obviously disturbed Eisenhower's plans. That record suggests, however, that fiscal policy followed a very Keynesian countercyclical pattern, with budget deficits during the recessions and surpluses during the prosperous years. Should one take this apparent manifestation of functional finance as a sign that the administration practiced Keynesian fiscal policy? The answer is no. While fiscal policy had improved from the days of the enormous tax increase in 1932, when policymakers tried to cancel the automatic stabilizing effects of the declines in tax revenue, policy had not evolved further than allowing the automatic stabilizers to operate. There is little evidence of active antirecession expansionary fiscal policy being applied during the three Eisenhower-era recessions.

For example, no sooner had Eisenhower settled into the White House and begun taking a carving knife to expenditures than the economy began a contraction in the summer of 1953. Despite the recession, the president continued to push hard for more spending cuts and balked at suggestions of speeding up tax reductions already legislated. As a result, his spending cuts came before and exceeded the previously scheduled tax cuts. Had there been no recession, the budget would have shown a surplus in 1954. In just over a year, the full-employment budget had been swung from a deficit to a surplus. That indicates discretionary fiscal policy was contractionary and became progressively more so throughout the entire recession—no signs of Keynes here. This was the second recession since passage of the Employment Act of 1946 that had produced pro- rather than countercyclical discretionary fiscal policy. Deficits appeared on the budget in spite rather than because of discretionary policy. Balanced budget considerations continued to outweigh stabilization goals.

The emphasis on the budget carried over through the 1954 to 1957 expansion. Eisenhower finally got his balanced budget in 1955, and he refused to consider any policy that would endanger it. Excise and corporate tax reductions scheduled to go into effect in 1955 were delayed for three years. With the inflation rate above 3% during these expansion years, it is wise to remember that fiscal policy was designed to discourage inflation. In that respect, the policy fit the goal—a consensus one—and was moderately restrictive into 1957.

The recession that began in 1957 gave the Eisenhower administration another chance—albeit too soon for anyone's taste—to show whether more than mere rumors of the Keynesian revolution had reached the White House. This time the response was still hesitant but significantly better. The budget was allowed to slide from a surplus to a deficit by the last quarter of 1957. Credit for the budget swing must go entirely to the automatic stabilizers, at least until the trough of the recession had been reached in the spring of 1958. In contrast to the 1953 episode, discretionary fiscal policy did not continue on a contractionary course right through the recession. It moved from neutral—allowing the automatic stabilizers to produce a substantial deficit—during the contraction to mildly expansionary during the recovery phase. An acceleration in already-legislated spending programs boosted government expenditures in late 1958 and early 1959. While policy did not push up the date of the beginning of the recovery, neither did it push it back, and it did spur the expansion slightly. Allowing a deficit of almost $13 billion to form was a major concession on Eisenhower's part. Keynes would have said, "Now, this is a little more like it."

As we saw earlier in the chapter, the expansion was short-lived, with another recession beginning in the spring of 1960. The Federal Reserve deserves most if not all of the blame for starting this recession. It is, however, possible to take the view that a portion of the blame rests with fiscal policy, which was relatively contractionary by 1960. The large budget deficit begot by the 1957 recession had virtually disappeared by the end of 1959 as a result of the expansion's positive effects on tax revenues. That means fiscal policy was essentially neutral up to the end of 1959. But further squeezing of expenditures, particularly military ones, led to a substantial surplus by the first quarter of 1960.

Inasmuch as the economy never made it all the way back to full employment during this recovery, fiscal policy could be judged to have leaned too heavily on the restrictive side in 1960. Be that as it may, had the Fed not put the money supply into reverse in 1959, the fiscal constraints of 1960 alone would not have precipitated a recession. Most likely, what would have occurred was nothing worse than what is now popularly dubbed a "soft landing"—a slowdown in expansion as the economy reaches full employment—plus one more year of budget surpluses for Eisenhower. In a scenario of continued monetary growth, the economic expansion would probably have continued to full employment, and the fiscal policy course taken in 1959 and early 1960 might have been praised as appropriate for avoiding inflation.

With fiscal policymakers just beginning to show signs of experimenting with countercyclical policy, it is asking too much to expect them to have taken a reading of monetary policy, anticipated its imminent contractionary effects, and adjusted the budget accordingly. Given that most forecasts at the beginning of 1960 predicted further expansion (apparently ignoring the declining money supply), the fiscal policy program was fairly wisely chosen under the circumstances. We cannot blame Eisenhower and his advisers for the independent Fed's mistakes; nor can we expect the administration to have counteracted those errors before their effects were known.

Because everyone was slow to recognize a recession was in progress, and the Eisenhower administration even slower to admit the recession's existence after the truth became apparent, fiscal policy did little to battle the recession or speed the recovery. As in the previous recession, nothing was done with discretionary fiscal policy to reverse the contraction before output reached its trough (this time in early 1961). Indeed, as we just established, fiscal policy was rather restrictive through the second quarter of 1960. That this was an election year might lead us to expect more expansionary fiscal policy. But in the tradition it established in 1956—the previous presidential election year—the Eisenhower administration chose to be more restrictive than during the off-election years. One certainly cannot accuse the Republicans of trying to buy votes. When the election results left the president in a lame-duck situation, discretionary expansionary policy was delayed until the new administration took office in 1961. On a positive note, the budget was allowed to slide into a deficit by the last quarter of 1960. That was disappointing for Eisenhower, given his budgetary goals, but it showed his flexibility. He was once again willing to accept a deficit and allow automatic stabilizers to dampen the recession, even though doing so meant he left office with the bitter aftertaste of more red ink.

☐ A Fifties Perspective

The 1950s was a coming-of-age decade for economy watchers. After 20 years of disruption, the economy finally settled back into its postdepression/postwar period of normality. Much to the surprise of many observers, the private sector did very well on its own, with consumption and investment expenditures propelling aggregate demand upward and increases in labor productivity spurring aggregate supply. Income per capita rose at close to the long-run trend rate of 1.6% per year. Unemployment averaged 5.2% after the end of the Korean War, while the average annual inflation rate for the whole decade was only 2.5%. M2 rose at an annual average rate of about 3.5%, and output climbed at an annual rate of 2.8%. Even though the budget record reveals surplus years, the national debt did climb a modest $17 billion during the decade. Yet the economy's rate of growth was far outstripping the growth of the debt. The federal debt, as a percentage of GNP, fell dratmatically, from 89% to 57%.

As suggested at the beginning of this chapter, it is hard to find much fault with the economy's performance in the 1950s, especially when we view it from the perspective of the 1990s. By virtually every current standard, the economy's performance was satisfactory to outstanding. True, we have found minor faults in the conduct and timing of monetary and fiscal policies, but those mistakes were kept within narrow bounds so that their negative consequences were modest. The economy did not stray far from a full-employment/stable-price state. The private economy itself was fundamentally sound and required little intervention. Since policymakers seemed to be developing more skill at counteracting recessions (whether or not they had set them off) the outlook should have been fairly rosy as the 1960s began.

Yet a surprisingly substantial amount of gloom pervaded the 1950s until John Kennedy was able to harness it as a campaign weapon. Many critics were persuaded the economy was underperforming. The cold war contributed to the economic insecurity. Soviet output was growing at rates more than twice that of the United States. *Sputnik* fever and missile-gap paranoia fed anxiety over the economy's performance. And given the realities of politics and the duties established under the Employment Act, the current government had to take responsibility for the economy's supposed shortcomings. Where did these negative perceptions come from, and were they merited?

Obviously, standards of performance in the 1950s were different from those in the 1990s. The biggest differences involved the assessment of unemployment and inflation. Critics of the 1950s were apparently very choosy in selecting their standards. When it came to the appropriate unemployment rate for the economy, the standards of the 1920s and 1940s were applied. As a result, many believed the natural rate of unemployment was as low as 3% and certainly no higher than 4%. Yet in the years after the Korean War, unemployment never dipped below 4%. Therefore, to those who set such demanding standards for low unemployment, the peacetime economy never seemed to reach full employment during Eisenhower's term. Much discussion centered on the rise of structural unemployment—long-term unemployment attributable to a lack of marketable job skills—and portrayed it as a sign of failures in the economy and public policy.

To use the unemployment measures of the 1920s and 1940s as the standard of achievement set impossible goals for the 1950s. Obviously, people had been spoiled by the low unemployment rates of the 1940s, but by and large those rates were of little relevance to the peacetime economy of the 1950s. Moreover, it was not fair to compare the 1950s rates with those of the 1920s. Rural unemployment was poorly measured prior to World War II, and there was more of it than previously thought in the 1920s. Given the depressed conditions in agriculture, chances are that unemployment rates overall were never truly as low as claimed in the 1920s. By the 1950s, with the development of unemployment compensation, the greater urbanization of the labor force, and the better measuring techniques, routine unemployment rates were naturally higher. What had definitely increased was frictional unemployment—the short-term unemployment of people changing jobs and careers—because unemployment was considerably less painful than in the 1920s as a result of government support. More recent estimates of the natural rate of unemployment, approximately 4.5% for the 1920s and between 4.8% and 5.1% for the 1950s, confirm the rise in frictional unemployment. The numbers also show that the unemployment rate during the 1950s was at or below the full-employment rate far more often than critics at the time perceived.

The dissatisfaction with the inflation rate in the 1950s was linked to the overly demanding expectations for the unemployment rate. Because many presumed unemployment was consistently above the full-employment rate, they also believed prices should not be rising at all. In the Keynesian model, inflation is the result of excessive aggregate demand, especially in a full-employment economy. But with the economy supposedly short of full employment and the money supply growing relatively slowly, excess-demand inflation—known as demand-pull inflation—should not have been a problem. Rising prices associated with an unemployment rate of 4.5%—the average rate for the decade—did not make sense when full employment was thought to occur at a 4% rate or less. Of course, if the natural rate of unemployment is nearer to 5%, a 4.5% average rate is clearly inflationary. The source of the moderate inflation of the 1950s is no mystery when one accepts that unemployment was actually pushed below its natural rate during the entire 1954–57 expansion period. It was *demand-pull* inflation, pure and simple.

Because they believed inflation was setting in at inexplicably high rates of unemployment, economists went off in search of causes other than excess aggregate demand. The 1950s was the decade when a variety of supply-side inflation theories were born—for example, "seller's inflation," "structural inflation," and "creeping inflation." All were founded on the idea that imperfections in the factor and product markets were creating an upward bias on prices.

Contributing to the suspicion that the economy faced a new form

of inflation was the fact that prices not only did not fall but continued to
rise during the three recessions occurring in the Eisenhower years. It
was during those recession years that criticism of government policy
was magnified. Even while output was going down and unemployment
was rising, prices continued to rise. This combination is inconsistent
with simply a change in aggregate demand, and it was dissimilar to what
had occurred in previous recessions. Until the 1950s, prices fell at least a
little during all recessions, including the 1949 recession. Falling output
combined with rising prices can result only from a reduction in the level
of aggregate supply. That is *cost-push inflation*, or, as Paul Samuelson
christened it, "stagflation."

Doubtless, the rules had changed by the 1950s. Wages and prices
were much more sticky in the downward direction. Much of that sticki-
ness can be traced to legislation passed during the previous two decades,
such as the minimum wage and the Wagner Act, as well as the increased
involvement of government in the marketplace. Prices were less likely
than in the past to fall in the face of declining demand, and increased
union power made wage cuts a less acceptable response to slack demand.
In addition, the phenomenon of rising prices during recessions was a
manifestation of a force that was to become more and more important in
the years to follow the 1950s.

Inflationary expectations sprouted during this period. Although
prices rose at a modest pace during the expansions periods, participants
in the marketplace began to expect them to continue their climb in the
future. The inflation ate away at the real purchasing power of suppliers
of all factors of production—land, raw material, labor, and capital. To
protect their real standards of living, these suppliers began increasing
the prices of their factor services. These market reactions drove up
production costs, caused the level of aggregate supply to shrink, and
sent prices up farther and faster.

The inflationary expectations—often called adaptive expectations—
did not disappear when aggregate demand dropped and a recession began.
Even as output is falling and factor demand is slacking off during a
recession, factor suppliers are still trying to make up lost ground by
pushing up the factor prices. This fuels a continuation of the inflation
momentum. The recession eventually slows the momentum, brings
down the inflation rate, and dampens expectations of more inflation. But
as we will see in the next chapter, the combination of falling output and no
progress on the inflation front can persist for as much as two years into a
recession. During those times, inflation appears to be the fault of unions
and big business, when in actuality their actions are simply reactions to

and symptoms of an inflation ultimately caused by excessive aggregate demand.

The economy, like stabilization policy, was evolving in the 1950s. The way the markets worked was changing, and the standards by which the economy's performance was measured should have been changing as well. Had policymakers and critics alike simply recognized full employment as somewhere nearer to a 5% than a 3% rate of unemployment, much of the public discontent with policy-making would have evaporated. The compulsion to push unemployment down to levels that turned out to be inflationary would have subsided. The relatively slow rate of output expansion would also have been easily understood, since output cannot rise faster than about 3% per year when the economy is at full employment. Inflation (what there was of it), as well as inflationary fears and expectations, would have been reduced. As a result, the perceived need to clamp down periodically on inflation with restrictive fiscal and monetary policies would never have arisen, and the last two recessions of the decade might not have occurred at all. Replace those years of contraction with just modest expansion, and the talk of stagnation would never have materialized; moreover, invention of the term *stagflation* would have been put off for several years.

We cannot expect policy to be enlightened if the assessment of where the economy stands is off the mark. But it is only through the wisdom of hindsight that we are able to make a better assessment. This was all pretty much new territory for everyone in the 1950s. The American economy was performing fairly well overall, but expectations were too high, an aspect that led naturally to minor—but, in retrospect, unwarranted—disappointments.

8

The Stagflation Era: 1960–1980

IN THE FALL OF 1960 JOHN KENNEDY WAS elected partly because he was able to exploit discontent over the economy's performance during the 1950s and to blame the "stagflation" on the Eisenhower administration. At that time, the unemployment rate stood at 5.5% and the inflation rate at less than 2%. In the jargon of the late 1970s, the *misery index*—the sum of the inflation rate and the unemployment rate—read a mere 7, but that was considered too high by the incoming policymakers. The 20 years that followed were highlighted by the Keynesian experiment in activist government stabilization policy and a journey into more stagflation than anyone could have imagined back in 1960. By 1980, the misery index stood at 20, with no relief in sight.

The differences between where the economy stood in 1960 and where it stood in 1980 were so great that one economic historian speculated about how a modern-day Rip van Winkle might have reacted on waking from a 20-year nap in 1980: if his aches and pains did not keep him in bed, the shock of seeing the poor shape of the economy would surely have prompted him to crawl back under the sheets. In 1980 the economy was a mess, and almost all the blame must be placed on the makers of fiscal and monetary policy. A look at Table 8 pinpoints some of the shocking facts. Prices, which were up 177% since 1960, were rising at a clip of 12% even though unemployment exceeded 7%. The federal budget was more than six times as large as in 1960, and the

Table 8: Economic Indicators, 1960–1980

	Q	M1	M2	P	CPI	GE	GR	Surplus Deficit	UN	Prime Rate
1960	2.2	0.5	4.9	1.6	1.4	92	92	0	5.5	4.8
1961	2.6	3.2	7.4	1	0.7	98	94	−4	6.7	4.5
1962	5.3	1.9	8.1	2.2	1.2	107	100	−7	5.5	4.5
1963	4.1	3.7	8.4	1.6	1.6	111	107	−4	5.7	4.5
1964	5.3	4.6	8	1.5	1.2	118	113	−5	5.2	4.5
1965	5.8	4.7	8.1	2.7	1.9	118	117	−1	4.5	4.5
1966	5.8	2.5	4.5	3.6	3.4	134	131	−3	3.8	5.6
1967	2.9	6.5	9.2	2.6	3	157	149	−8	3.8	5.6
1968	4.1	7.7	8	5	4.7	178	153	− 25	3.6	6.3
1969	2.4	3.3	4.1	5.6	6.1	184	187	3	3.5	8
1970	−0.3	5.1	6.5	5.5	5.5	196	193	−3	4.9	7.9
1971	2.8	6.5	13.5	5.7	3.4	210	187	−13	5.9	5.7
1972	5	9.2	13	4.7	3.4	231	207	−24	5.6	5.3
1973	5.2	5.5	6.9	6.5	8.8	246	231	−15	4.9	8
1974	−0.5	4.3	5.5	9.1	12.2	269	263	−6	5.6	10.8
1975	−1.3	4.8	12.6	9.8	7	332	279	−53	8.5	7.9
1976	4.9	6.6	13.7	6.4	4.8	371	298	−73	7.7	6.8
1977	4.7	8.1	10.6	6.7	6.8	409	356	−53	7.1	6.8
1978	5.3	8.2	8	7.3	9	459	400	−59	6.1	9.1
1979	2.5	7.6	8	8.9	13.3	503	463	−40	5.8	12.7
1980	−0.2	6.8	8.9	9	12.5	591	517	−74	7.1	15.3

Q = Percent change in real GNP (output)
M1 = Percent change in M1 (currency plus checking account deposits)
M2 = Percent change in M2 (currency plus checking and saving accounts)
P = Percent change in GNP Implicit Price Deflator
CPI = Percent change in Consumer Price Index
GE = Federal government expenditures (billions of dollars)
GR = Federal government revenues (billions of dollars)
Surplus/Deficit = GR minus GE
UN = Average unemployment rate (percent)
Prime Rate = Average prime rate of interest (percent)

Sources: See Bibliographic Essay.

national debt had tripled from nearly $300 billion to more than $900 billion. M1 had virtually tripled, while M2 was more than five times greater in 1980 than in 1960. The prime rate of interest, less than 5% in 1960, was in the midteens and on the rise, headed for 20. The news was not all bad, since output was 91% higher as well, but most of those gains came in the 1960s. By 1980, the economy was adrift in the growth doldrums, with labor productivity virtually unchanged in five years and real hourly earnings falling. It was clear that policymakers had led the economy off course, and many feared they had lost control completely.

☐ Part 1: The Monetary Roller Coaster

Most accounts of this 20-year period, particularly the first half, emphasize the fiscal policy of the Kennedy-Johnson administrations. The 1964 tax cut is commonly given credit for boosting the economy to full employment, and the large increases in government spending on the Vietnam War and on Great Society programs are blamed for setting off the inflation that carried on into the 1980s. Monetary policy takes a backseat in the history books because that is exactly where it sat in the minds of economists and policymakers. The Keynesian revolution ruled in Washington, D.C. Most people did not think the money supply mattered very much. Monetarists were few, and they were not taken very seriously. That might explain why it took years for people to notice the dramatic difference between monetary policy in the 1950s and that in the subsequent 20 years. There was a revolution all right, but the most important change occurred at the Federal Reserve; however, 10 years passed before more than a handful of people caught on to what was happening.

When annual money supply growth rates reached the teens in the early 1970s, the contrast with the 1950s, when M2 rose by a total of only 46%, began to make an impression. But it was not until the eve of the 1980s that opinions swung to favor the view that monetary policy—more precisely, excessively rapid money growth—had been the chief source of inflation over the preceding 15 years. Along the way, it also became apparent that wide swings in the growth rate of the money supply were without exception followed by similar waves in economic activity. Money mattered a great deal to output in the short run and to prices in the long run. Even the Fed came around to this view, and in 1979 policymakers embarked on an experiment in monetarism.

☐ **Money and Inflation**   Fiscal policy usually hogs the policy spotlight in accounts of the 1960s and the outbreak of inflation.

Although we certainly want to evaluate those policies, there is something more fundamental to understanding the inflation of this period—that is, an examination of the critical change in monetary policy that began around 1960. The money supply, which had grown so slowly since World War II, set peacetime records for rapid growth during the 1960s and 1970s. That M2 exploded by more than 400% over this period while output expanded by a respectable, albeit much smaller, 91% is our first clue that the inflation was fueled by excessive monetary growth. Indeed, the monetary revolution was far more influential in shaping the inflation era than the fiscal revolution was.

The monetary revolution began in late 1960 when the M2 growth rate, which had averaged 3% annually from 1954 to 1960, jumped to 7.4%—almost three times that year's increase in output. M2 growth then settled in at just over 8% annually for the next five years. Figure 3 shows clearly the high plateau the money growth rate achieved in the first half of the 1960s compared with that of the 1950s up to 1958, when the Fed showed its first signs of breaking out of the conservative mold. While most everyone in Washington was debating the pros and cons of various fiscal policy strategies for stimulating aggregate demand and economic growth, the Fed was taking expansionary matters into its own hands. In just five years, M2 ballooned by 47%, while output managed a 25% gain. With the money supply growing almost twice as fast as output, it is not surprising that Milton Friedman, the consummate monetarist, cautioned that a significant acceleration in inflation was imminent. Because the inflation rate was averaging less than 2% per year, few people listened to his warnings, and when the inflation acceleration did come in 1965 and 1966, fewer still connected it with monetary policy, since fiscal policy was getting all the attention.

So many accounts of this period have associated the acceleration of inflation with the expansionary fiscal policy of the Johnson administration that the link has become locked in our memory. A close look at the data shows this is an obvious mistake. First, as can be seen in Figure 4, the inflation acceleration started in 1964, yet the federal budget showed a surplus as late as the second quarter of 1966. The surge in government expenditures did not come until late in 1966 and 1967, more than two years after the inflation rate started upward. The inflation rate had already risen from 1.5% in 1964 to the 3.5–4% range in 1966 when fiscal policy began to be inflationary as well. The continued attribution of the 1960s inflation acceleration to fiscal policy is like a formula murder mystery of the Perry Mason genre. We enter the room and see a dead body (the economy), a victim of murder (inflation), with the suspect (fiscal policy) standing over it holding the weapon (expansionary

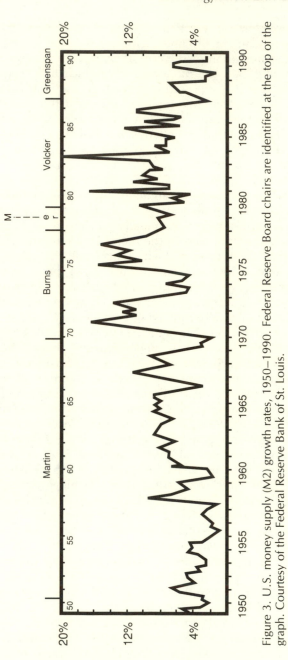

Figure 3. U.S. money supply (M2) growth rates, 1950–1990. Federal Reserve Board chairs are identified at the top of the graph. Courtesy of the Federal Reserve Bank of St. Louis.

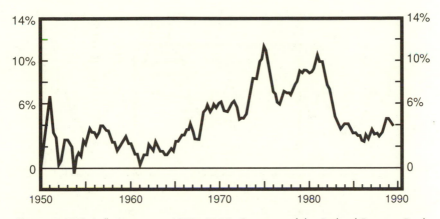

Figure 4. U.S. inflation rates, 1950–1990. Courtesy of the Federal Reserve Bank of St. Louis.

policy). Circumstantial evidence points to the guilt of the suspect, when in actuality the victim was already dead when the suspect came on the body. The true killer (the Fed) meanwhile gets away to commit future crimes. It is about time we locked up the real culprit. Fiscal policy was indeed inflationary in 1966 and 1967, but by the time—to use another analogy—the inflation seed had already been sown by the Fed, and the plant had already begun to grow.

What delayed the inflation upswing and made the money explanation look bad was the movement of velocity. M2 velocity, as Figure 5 shows, has experienced many ups and downs but has tended to average close to 1.6 for decades. It had reached a relatively high level of more than 1.72 in 1960. From there it fell until the end of 1965 to a low point of 1.57, a 9% slide. That helped to dampen the expansionary impact of the excessive money supply growth and to narrow the gap between aggregate demand and output. The net result was that aggregate demand grew by 33%, only 8% faster than output.

But every zig in M2 velocity over the past 35 years has eventually been followed by a zag of equal proportion, and the 1960s were no exception. M2 velocity began a five-year climb during the second half of the decade that essentially erased the decline of the first half. During this five-year rise, with M2 also increasing at an annual rate of 6.5%, the inflation rate accelerated. By the end of the decade, M2 had doubled, while output had grown by 45% and prices had filled in the gap with a 36% increase. Let us display those changes in the quantity of money equation format with 1960 figures expressed as base-year figures:

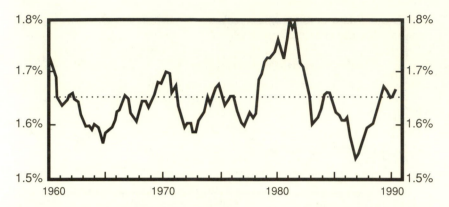

Figure 5. Velocity of money (GNP/M2) in the United States, 1960–1990. Courtesy of the Federal Reserve Bank of St. Louis.

	Money Supply (M2)	× Velocity	= GNP	= Output	× Prices
1960	100	× 1.00	= 100	= 100	× 1.00
1970	201	× .98	= 197	= 145	× 1.36

This, however, was only the beginning. During the 1970s, the money supply and prices rose even faster. M2 grew at an annual compounded rate of 10%, putting the money supply 160% higher in 1980 than in 1970. Output managed to increase by only 32% during the decade, significantly lower than the 45% of the 1960s. The gap between the growth in aggregate demand and that in output widened to a canyon. Naturally, rising prices had once again to fill in the difference, as the following figures show:

	Money Supply (M2)	× Velocity	= GNP	= Output	× Prices
1970	100	× 1.00	= 100	= 100	× 1.00
1980	260	× 1.04	= 270	= 132	× 2.04

M2 growth averaged more than 13% in 1971 and 1972 and more than 12% in 1975 through 1977. That is about four times the average expansion rate for output. Because the economy had not achieved a one-year output expansion of more than 5.8% since the Korean War, no one should have expected output to be able to keep pace with aggregate demand when demand was rising so fast.

There is no mystery as to where the inflation came from when we examine the data about money supply growth rates. Let us look at the numbers for the entire 20-year period:

	Money Supply (M2)	×	Velocity	=	GNP	=	Output	×	Prices
1960	100	×	1.00	=	100	=	100	×	1.00
1980	523	×	1.01	=	529	=	191	×	2.77

Throughout the era, velocity traveled up and down but was essentially the same in 1980 as in 1960. As a result, the gigantic increase in aggregate demand is entirely attributable to the very rapid growth of the money supply. As will be discussed later, however, it was not at all obvious to many who, or what, was to blame for the rapid inflation. Blame was scattered in all directions—OPEC, big business, unions, slow productivity growth. Regardless of the impact these and other variables had, or even of how well or poorly the economy had performed, output never could have come close to keeping pace with such rapid monetary growth. We will presently consider the factors that motivated the Fed, but the fact remains that there was a direct, albeit delayed, link between the money supply growth rate and the inflation rate.

☐ **Interest Rates, Deficits, and Money**   While the Keynesians in the Kennedy administration concentrated on fiscal policy proposals, the Federal Reserve was placed in the background to quietly implement its own approach. The primary concerns of Federal Reserve policymakers for the greater portion of the stagflation era were the unemployment and interest rates. One consistent theme that molded monetary policy was the desire to push or hold down these rates; often, the governors could think of little else when making policy decisions. Ultimately, their obsession led them to disproportionately high money supply growth rates. Unfortunately, the harder they tried to bring interest rates down, the faster they increased the money supply. Doing so led to progressively higher inflation rates, which simply produced even higher interest rates. Like an addict, the Fed got caught on a treadmill that it did not escape until the 1980s. The more money the Fed pumped into the financial markets, the more the markets seemed to need.

In the previous chapter we discussed how unemployment target rates were probably set too ambitiously low in the 1950s. That continued throughout the next two decades. Efforts to hold unemployment below the natural rate with easy-money policy tended to produce accelerating inflation. And then when restrictive policy was applied to slow inflation, unemployment phobia prompted the Fed to return hastily to expansionary policy. While the Kennedy administration was delayed in its application of expansionary fiscal policy—for reasons we will consider shortly—the Fed took the lead in driving down the unemployment rate that had been pushed up by the 1960–61 recession.

Interest rates, which had been in the 3% range throughout the mid-1960s, had cracked 4% in 1957 and 5% in 1959. They were just under 5% when Kennedy took office, and there was concern in the White House and the Fed that high interest rates could slow economic growth. Indeed, Kennedy's economic advisers listed slow monetary growth in the 1950s as one of the causes of the economy's sluggish performance. On the other hand, the balance of payments had been consistently showing a deficit, causing a drain on the gold stock. Higher interest rates would counteract that trend by drawing foreign financial investment into the United States. At the urging of the administration, the Fed attempted a policy strategy that would push short-term interest rates up (to attract foreign policy capital inflows) and long term-rates down (to encourage capital investment). All involved were probably foolish to think the Fed could partition the markets so well as to accomplish this artificial "Operation Twist," as it was called. In the end, investors were not tricked, and all the Fed accomplished was a significantly higher money supply growth rate.

The rapid money growth propelled aggregate demand upward. As long as velocity was falling, however, output was almost able to keep up with aggregate demand. But when velocity headed upward starting at the end of 1964, the increased rate of money circulation began to magnify the gap between the growth rate of the money supply and that of output. M2 climbed at an 8.1% clip and velocity added an additional 3%. Aggregate demand was rising at a rate better than 11%—almost twice as fast as output, even though the economy was having an outstanding year of expansion. That, as noted, was when inflation began to accelerate. Shortly thereafter, interest rates began to rise. Even though the money supply was rising by as much as 9% annually in late 1965, interest rates were nevertheless beginning to rise.

Were interest rates climbing in a violation of the laws of supply and demand? No. What was being witnessed was the rebirth of inflationary expectations in the financial markets. The higher the inflation rate—and hence the expected rate of inflation—the higher interest rates must rise to allow real (adjusted for inflation) rates of return to be maintained. When the expected inflation rate is 10%, market interest rates will be 10% higher than they would be when the expected inflation rate is zero. Interest rates tend to lag behind the inflation rate both when it rises and when it falls, but inflation and high interest rates go together.

The expansionary monetary policy the Fed was following to hold down interest rates was now triggering the exact opposite, in the form of higher market interest rates.

The Fed faced a policy conundrum that would baffle monetary policymakers for the next 15 years. Simple Keynesian money-market mechanics call for a money supply increase to push interest rates down. But in an inflationary economy, that approach only adds fuel to the inflation and eventually sends interest rates even higher.

The Fed's problem was an old one. Its governors still could not distinguish between real versus market interest rates. During the monetary contraction of 1929 to 1933, they interpreted low market interest rates as a sign of monetary ease, when in fact real interest rates exceeded 10%. They failed to take into account the effects of deflation on interest rates. In the inflation era the mistake was in the opposite direction. In the early 1960s the Fed's monetary policy directives spoke of "firm" money-market conditions. Translate that into "monetary restraint." What was their indicator of monetary restraint? As we know, it certainly could not be the growth of the money supply. Instead, their yardstick was the level of market interest rates, which were relatively high and rising. As Figure 6 shows, real interest rates, the true measures of monetary restraint, had peaked in 1960 (when the money supply had been falling). After that, they followed a downward trend throughout the decade. That tells us—and should have told the Fed—that monetary policy was consistently expansionary, not restrained, over those ten years. This midreading of interest rate signals would get far worse in the years to follow.

Before the Fed had a chance even to recognize the puzzle of rising prices and interest rates, another problem arose that made the governors' predicament more complicated. In 1966 the Johnson administration greatly expanded government expenditures on the Vietnam War buildup and the Great Society domestic programs. The result was a budget swing from a small surplus in early 1966 to a large deficit by the end of the year and an even larger one in 1967. Because the economy was at full employment, everyone judged the surge in government spending to be inflationary. Nevertheless, policymakers in the White House and Congress hesitated to raise taxes to head off the deficit. The responsibility for fighting inflation fell on the Fed's shoulders by default. The Fed chair, William McChesney Martin, always happy to "lean against the wind," directed monetary policy toward counteracting the inflationary tendencies of fiscal policy. The discount rate was increased against the White House's wishes at the end of 1965, and the money supply growth rate was cut in half in late 1966 and early 1967.

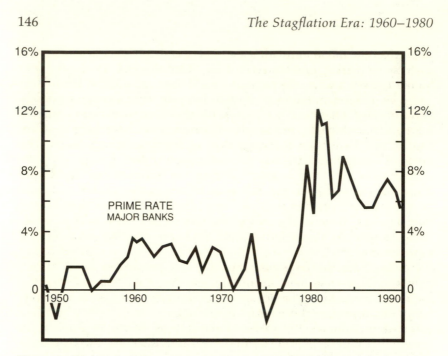

Figure 6. Real U.S. interest rates, 1950–1990. Adapted from the Council of Economic Advisors, *Economic Report of the President* (Washington, D.C.: U.S. Government Printing Office, 1950–90).

Interest rates climbd to the 6% range in 1967. The economy was sujected to what was popularly known as the "credit crunch." In the 1990s we could look back at 6% rates with wistful nostalgia and grumble that those folks back in the 1960s did not know what a real crunch was. Nevertheless, interest rates were relatively high as the Fed cut down on the money supply growth just when inflation was picking up its pace. More important, interest rate ceilings set by the Fed—particularly for savings and loans—were below market rates. This action set off a major withdrawal of funds from these intermediaries in a process called financial disintermediation. A howl arose from the housing and automobile industries, as well as from other credit-sensitive sectors of the economy, because of the shortage of funds. The high rates were cutting into aggregate demand, and the economy's expansion was in danger.

Now we come to another crucial turning point in the monetary history of this period. The Fed had a choice: (a) it could continue with its restrictive policy, which was really only a return to a slower growth rate level typical of the 1950s, or (b) it could respond to popular demand

and return the money growth rate to the precrunch level in an effort to push those market interest rates down. Had the Fed chosen the first course and stuck to it, the economy could have escaped the 1960s with just a short-term inflationary bubble. Interest rates would eventually have subsided. Of course, for a while money would have been tight and the economy sluggish, but serious inflation could have been avoided. That would have been the equivalent of parental "tough love." The easier choice at the time was the expansionary one. By choosing the second route, the Fed guaranteed that the inflation rate would get worse; it ensured that the full inflationary impact of the excessive money supply growth of the first half of the decade would burgeon and be magnified. In so doing, the governors set a precedent that would guide them right through 1980 and send the economy far down the inflation road.

Every time the Fed put the breaks on the growth rate of the money supply in an attempt to slow inflation, the rise in interest rates and the decline in economic activity prompted the Fed to give up its efforts to fight inflation before those efforts could show a positive effect. The Fed would then jump on the accelerator and speed up the money supply growth rate in order to bring down the interest rates and revive aggregate demand. The surge in the money supply would bring a brief respite, as interest rates would temporarily fall. But the money wave would once again send aggregate demand racing ahead of output and send interest rates upward as the effects of more rapid inflation and inflationary expectations worked their way through the financial markets.

☐ **Martin Leaves His Mark** The roller-coaster ride on which the Fed took the money supply in the 1950s was the gentle Kiddie Dips compared with the racing Big Dipper trip for the period from 1965 through 1980. In fact, I suspect that the graph of the M2 growth rate for the 1950–90 period shown in Figure 3 was used by an exercycle company as a model for the pattern of their electronic bike ride that simulates a ride through the hills. The 1950–65 period and the 1980s are perfect for the warm-up and cool-down sections, respectively, while the 1960s and the 1970s provide an ideal paradigm for the hilly, interval-training section.

The M2 growth rate went through large swings from 3% in 1966 to 12% in 1967, from 9% in 1968 to 3% in 1969, from 2% in early 1970 to 16% in 1971, from 12% in 1972 to 5% in 1973, from 5% in 1974 to 15% in 1975, from 14% in 1976 to 8% in 1978, and from 6% in early 1980 to 15% later that year. All through this ride, both the peaks and valleys got progressively higher as the trend in the money supply growth rate rose. By 1980, easy money meant an M2 growth rate in the

teens, and tight money was associated with an M2 growth rate of 6%—
a rate that would have been considered easy money back in 1959. It is
no wonder that the inflation rate was on an upward trend and that the
economy followed such a cyclical course. If we hop on our bikes, we can
continue to retrace the monetary policy course.

Chairman Martin lorded over the first half of the ride. By the end
of 1966, the Fed had completed the warm-up phase and was ready to
enter the hilly section. For the rest of the decade, Martin's Fed took the
money supply and the economy on a fast and unsteady course—in stark
contrast to policy in the 1950s. The money supply growth rate was high
in 1967 and 1968, with M2 rising at an average rate near 8.5%, even
though inflation was considered a worsening problem. The governors
kept waiting for Congress to pass a promised tax increase; thus, they
hesitated to apply monetary restraint, anticipating that fiscal policy
would soon provide the needed constraint. Besides, the Johnson administration lobbied for keeping interest rates lower during the election year.
Right when Nixon was elected, monetary policy changed course, and
the growth rate of the money supply went down drastically. Martin
seemed to have it in for Nixon. Remember, the Fed hit the money
supply brakes in 1959 and 1960 and ruined, with a recession, Nixon's
election chances in 1960. In 1968 the Fed kept the money supply growing rapidly. In fact, the growth rate climbed throughout the year to
more than 9% until the November election, as the Fed hoped easier
money would hold down market interest rates. That policy certainly
benefited the incumbent party, Nixon's opponent.

After Nixon won despite that policy, the Fed decided it was time to
fight inflation with a monetary slowdown. After all, one of Nixon's
main campaign promise was to control inflation. Nixon was surprised
and keenly disappointed to learn he would be unable to replace Martin
as Fed chair until Martin's term expired in January 1970. That gave the
Fed the whole year of 1969 to clamp down on the money supply. The
M2 growth rate sank to as low as 2% by the end of this year. Aggregate
demand stalled, and a recession began in December 1969.

Martin left the Fed after almost two decades. During that time,
monetary policy gradually became more and more inflationary and
destabilizing. A conservative, anti-inflation chair in his early years,
Martin allowed his goal to hold down unemployment and his strategy of
market interest rate targeting (as well as possibly political partisanship)
to turn him into a reed buffeted back and forth by economic and political
winds between easy- and tight-money policies. Though Martin got off
the Fed ride at the very bottom of a big dip before the ride had reached
some of its largest hills and valleys, he had been the one who had

steered the money supply up the big incline and into the first couple of dips. Martin set the precedents that would be followed for the remainder of the ride. One consolation for his place in history was that his successor would make him look better by comparison.

Nixon appointed his old friend from the Eisenhower administration, Arthur Burns (ironically, the man who warned Nixon about the probable adverse effects of the Fed's policies under Martin in 1960), to replace Martin. Burns was a real puzzle. His words indicated he was a conservative monetarist who was constantly working toward a slow and steady growth rate of the money supply. His actions, however, were quite different, as a glance back at Figure 3 clearly demonstrates. Burns fell prey to the same factors that influenced Martin—unemployment, market interest rates, and politics—and he repeated the same mistakes with greater severity. Burns's term was punctuated by two complete cycles of extremely expansionary policy followed by a severe tightening. Money supply growth was as far from slow and steady as one could imagine. The upward trend in the peaks and valleys continued as the average rate of growth in M2 exceeded 10%.

Nixon was not at all comfortable with the recession that had just begun as he moved into the White House, and he used his influence with Burns to push for more expansionary policy. Though how much Burns was swayed by Nixon's preferences is a matter of debate, there is no dispute over the direction in which he steered monetary policy. The M2 growth rate was up to 10% and climbing higher by the end of 1970, and the money supply grew a whopping 28% more over the next two years. Those are numbers to which the Fed under Martin never came close.

The 1970 portion of this surge in the money supply can be partly traced to the Fed's prompt and wise response to the potential financial crisis brought on by the bankruptcy of the Penn Central Railroad, an enormous company with lots of debt outstanding. To avoid a liquidity crisis in the money market, the Fed used its monetary tools to flood the market with reserves. A crisis was averted, and the Fed's actions finally showed that the central bank could do what its designers had in mind when they set it up as the lender of last resort almost 60 years earlier. That may have been the only sign of progress during Burns's term.

Expansionary policy was justifiable in 1970, but it is difficult to justify the excessive money growth of the next two years. As a result of prodding by members of the Council of Economic Advisors and Congress at the end of Martin's term, it was decided to base policy less n money-market conditions, which had (at the bottom line) always really meant interest rates, and more on monetary aggregates. Since Burns took office, the Fed had been expressing its policy with a greater eye toward the growth rate of monetary aggregates like M1. Disputes arising between the president's economic advisers and the Fed over appropriate growth rates confirm the increased emphasis on monetary aggregates. But it is apparent from the Fed's policy that it was not using money supply growth rates as its only or even its primary guide. Alternatively, if the Fed was trying to target money supply growth rates, it was not coming even remotely close to the targets.

Talking about money supply growth rates is one thing; basing policy on them is another. Monetary policy under Burns's stewardship looked at both interest rates and money supply growth rates but continued to use market interest rates and unemployment as the ultimate guides for determining policy. When money demand and inflationary expectations rose and pushed interest rates upward or when unemployment was not cooperative, the Fed responded with faster money supply growth. Had the people at the Fed bothered to look at real interest rates, as can be seen in Figure 6 they would have discovered that those rates were at their lowest level since the Korean War and that they were falling from a peak in 1969 toward zero and below. This is a clear sign that monetary policy was extremely expansionary. Aside from maintaining the long-standing tradition of misreading market versus real interest rates, the Fed's overly expansionary policy of 1971 and 1972 was a response to the economy's sluggish recovery from the trough of the 1970 recession. The unsatisfactorily high unemployment rate was triggering faster money growth at the prompting of people in the White House. The Fed was more concerned with hitting unemployment targets than monetary ones.

☐ **New Economic Policy**   By 1971, with the inflation rate near 6%, Burns had already lost confidence in the Fed's ability to control the inflation rate and to keep the economy expanding. This point is interesting, since the Fed had taken no anti-inflationary measures under Burns. He began to suggest the need for wage and price controls. He was not alone, as other (but by no means all) members of Nixon's economic brain trust were gradually showing more interest in "incomes policy" (the often-used euphemism for controls). The Council of Economic Advisors had set goals for the inflation and unemployment rates (3% and 4.5%, respectively) that were looking farther and farther out of reach as the expansion slowed and inflation did not. It was becoming apparent that orthodox fiscal and monetary policies could not cope with both inflation and unemployment at the same time. Stimulating the recovery was not consistent with fighting inflation.

At the same time that domestic economic problems were weighing on Nixon, international trade and exchange difficulties were worsening. The United States had developed a habitual balance of payments deficit, and that deficit was on the rise. Merchandise trade surpluses were eroding and were unable to outweigh the deficits on capital accounts (investment and foreign aid by Americans in foreign countries). More dollars were flowing out of the country than were coming back in, and these dollars (commonly called Eurodollars today) were piling up in European banks. Dollars were convertible into gold under the Bretton Woods agreement of 1946. France enjoyed doing just that, and the American stock of gold shrank throughout the 1960s. By 1971, the gold stock was down to $12 billion, while the aggregate value of the dollars deposited in foreign banks was more than three times that much. There clearly was an excess supply of dollars in the world currency markets, but exchange rates were fixed, and so was the price of gold, at $35 an ounce. A run on American gold was developing into a panic by August 1971.

This international problem was ultimately the result of the Fed's monetary revolution during the preceding decade. As we saw earlier, the money supply had risen by more than twice as much as output during that period, and prices had made up the difference as the purchasing power of the dollar fell domestically. The laws of the market dictate that the value of the dollar in the world currency markets should have been falling as well, since the American inflation rate exceeded that of many of this country's trading partners. But the Bretton Woods system was one of fixed exchange rates. By the rules of the system, the rest of the world was forced to absorb the excess dollars by purchasing them in the markets with increases in their own money supply. That caused inflation in these countries. In short, the United States was exporting inflation to the rest of the world. The 1946 Employment Act had been an assurance to Europe that America would not export recessions. It turned out the Fed had erred in the opposite direction.

Nixon was in a predicament. He had to act quickly on the international front, and he felt he needed to act just as quickly on the domestic front. Actually, there was little reason to take drastic actions domestically. The economy was expanding, and the inflation rate was not getting any worse. But as we all learned, political paranoia ran deep in the Nixon administration. After a secret meeting of a closed set of advisers, Nixon jolted the economy with the New Economic Policy program on 15 August 1971. Two main planks of the program were wage and price controls and an end to the convertibility of dollars into gold. In one controversial and contradictory stroke, the president imposed increased government power over the domestic economy and set in motion the release of foreign exchange markets from government regulation. Domestic wage and price increases were first prohibited for 90 days and then limited by bureaucratic edict for the next two to three years, while fixed exchange rate policy was being abandoned in favor of floating rates.

There is no doubt that Nixon had to do something on the international front. A crisis had arisen. The official value of the dollar was well above its true market value; the Fed had seen to that. To continue with the Bretton Woods system would first have required a major devaluation of the dollar. Then the Fed would have to discipline itself, drastically slow down the growth rate of the money supply, and act like it was following the rules of the old gold standard. Such an approach would make domestic monetary policy a hostage of the international system. That is always unpalatable when expansionary monetary policy is preferred, and it was particularly unattractive to Nixon at a time when he was concerned with increasing aggregate demand. His only recourse under those self-imposed restrictions was to destroy the Bretton Woods system and let the value of the dollar sink. The end of gold conversion was the first step. Devaluations and the eventual floating of the dollar and other exchange rates followed over the next four years. The 1960s monetary revolution—which in 1944 some conservative economists had predicted would naturally arise from the Bretton Woods agreement—had brought the system to an end.

The wage and price controls were an unnecessary and disruptive example of self-serving economic policy shaped by political considerations. Nixon wanted unemployment to fall as low as possible in 1972, since that was an election year. His memory of the political consequences of high unemployment in 1960 was still vivid. Burns was already busy fueling an expansion with double-digit money supply growth. That policy was likely to cover the unemployment problem. The inflation rate, however, was an embarrassment and a sign of failure. The solution was simple. Nixon made inflation illegal for 90 days and imposed an artificial speed limit after that. Politically, the controls were a success, as the inflation rate was held in check through the election of 1972.

Economically, the controls were an absolute failure. While the inflation rate was temporarily slowed, price increases were merely delayed, not prevented. A casual glance at price index information or back at Figure 4 shows what empirical studies have confirmed: when one allows for the postcontrols inflationary bubble, it is clear that total price increases were not reduced by the controls and may even have been magnified by the shortages that developed while the controls were in place. The gap between aggregate demand and output got progressively larger during the controls period and was filled by a rush of price increases after the controls were lifted.

Crucial to the failure of the controls was the fact that the Fed allowed the money supply to grow in such an inflationary manner coincident with the controls. How inconsistent can government policy be when one arm is fueling the inflation and another is trying to artificially contain it? The Fed's policy widened the gap between demand and output and thereby worsened the shortages brought on by the controls and the inflationary surge that followed them.

One of the reasons policymakers resorted to the controls was their frustration with the ability of conventional policy to reduce inflation. Reminiscent of the 1950s, many observers could not understand why prices continued to rise at a 5.5% clip right on through the 1970 recession and into 1971. That old pest inflationary expectations had been let out of the jar again. Despite the slowdown in aggregate demand and economic activity, prices continued to be pushed upward by adaptive inflationary expectations in the factor markets. Much as the acceleration of inflation had lagged well behind the surge in money supply growth, the deceleration of inflation lagged two to three years behind an imposition of contractionary monetary policy. Output changes tended to lag an average of eight months behind monetary policy changes, but prices trailed behind by another two years. That relationship meant that the deflationary effects of a monetary slowdown would not show up until the economy had first put up with well over a year of recession. Prices would keep climbing as if they were unaffected by the monetary slowdown, even as the unemployment rate climbed. Fighting inflation required patience—lots of patience—and the Fed had precious little of that commodity.

☐ **The Burns Cycle**   The economy got out of the doldrums in 1972, and by the end of the year unemployment was back down below 5%, just in time for the November election. With the election over and controls in their final less restrictive phase, Burns turned his entire attention to the inflationary bubble. Given the two- to three-year lag between monetary policy changes and inflation rate changes, the inflationary impact of the excessive money supply growth of 1971 and 1972 was in 1973 just kicking in. Moreover, the wage and price controls were phasing out in 1973. All that excess aggregate demand and the inflationary expectations built up over the preceding two years ignited an explosion of product and factor price increases. The M2 growth rate was reduced to 6.9% in 1973 and to 5.5% in 1974, less than half the rates of the preceding years. Just as in 1968–69, the money supply growth rate was cut in half. And just as occurred four years before, aggregate demand fell, and a recession began within the year.

Although monetary policy was all that was needed to set off a recession, OPEC gave the economy a supply-side shock that contributed potently to the recession's severity. Oil prices leapt from nearly $1.50 a barrel in 1973 to more than $12 by 1975. The combination of restrictive monetary policy and the oil embargo, which began in October 1973, ensured that a major recession would occur. And major it was, as unemployment reached 8.9% in the spring of 1975, when the recession's trough was finally reached. OPEC oil ministers could not have picked a worse time to set off a reduction in aggregate supply from the viewpoint of the American economy. With aggregate demand growth cut in half, aggregate supply shrinking, and prices racing up at an 8% rate, output had only one direction to go in late 1973: down.

Some accounts of this period blame the recession primarily or even solely on the oil crisis, paying little or no attention to monetary policy. Reports on the 1990 Persian Gulf crisis often cited the 1974 recession as an earlier example of how a big hike in oil prices could affect the economy. While it is difficult to precisely weight the respective impacts on output of the contractionary monetary policy and the rising oil prices, it should be made clear that the 1974–75 recession (which actually started in the last months of 1973) would have happened without an oil shock. The severity of the W-shaped canyon that occurs during the 1973–74 period on the money supply growth rate graph in Figure 3 is striking. This canyon is deeper and wider than the one that preceded the 1970 recession, and it dwarfs the ravines of the 1950s. Fed policy alone was enough to cause a recession.

The Fed stuck to its reduced money growth throughout 1974. One thing making it easier to do so was President Ford's determination to slow inflation. Ford backed the Fed's anti-inflationary stance until the end of the year. When Ford changed his plans, over the 1974 Christmas holiday, and decided to run for the office to which he was appointed, he changed his policy priorities as well. The noble and politically courageous quest to stop inflation was replaced by a more politically expedient aspiration to end the recession and begin an expansion that would bring the unemployment rate down. Significantly, monetary policy did an about-face at the same time. The M2 growth rate was headed off to new heights for the next three years, during which it averaged more than 12% annually. The recovery, which began in March 1975, had not progressed enough to get Ford elected in 1976, for unemployment still lingered at 7.8% at election time. In November 1976 Jimmy Carter used the misery-index reading of 15 against Ford and took his place in the White House. Meanwhile, the inflation rate had subsided in early 1976, exactly three years after Burns hit the money supply brakes and exactly one year after Ford and Burns gave up on fighting inflation.

The Fed continued to keep the money supply growing rapidly in early 1977 in order to further fuel the recovery. Some monetary historians have suggested that Burns was bucking for a reappointment after Carter won the election. Despite his efforts, Burns had many enemies in the Carter administration. They persuaded Carter not to reappoint him in 1978. Burns had lived and died by the political sword. He was seen to have served Republican presidents too closely; this aspect made him too unsavory for the Democrats. During his term, Federal Reserve policy was Burns's policy. No chair before or since has used his clout to such an extent in order to strong-arm the other governors for their support of his policies. Burns's bullying tactics meant that his stamp was firmly placed on Fed policy. As a result, history can safely place most if not all the blame for the Fed's terrible track record during Burns's term on the chair himself. What is ironic about Burns's tenure is that he maintained a posture of being a devout and resolute inflation fighter. He spoke and even looked the part. But underneath that facade of parsimony was the man who gave the United States double-digit inflation. Even though the economy was harmed by Burns's policies, it benefited in the short run from his guise because it helped to hold down inflationary expectations. When Burns and his facade left office, inflationary expectations accelerated. Market interest rates began a three-year, 14% ascent.

☐ **From Miller to Volcker**   Whoever replaced Burns was destined to inherit a lot of inflation. Even though Burns spent his last few months in office toning down the growth rate of the money supply to the 8% range, the damage had already been done. Allowing for the now-predictable three-year lag, the 1975–77 burst of double-digit M2 growth began producing an inflation acceleration right on schedule as 1978 began. Rapid inflation through 1980 was assured. The person with the dubious honor of taking over the Fed in the middle of this inflation surge was G. William Miller. Although he had a strong background in business and banking and was highly respected on his appointment, the markets apparently had little faith in his inflation-fighting skills, as evidenced by the relentless rise of interest rates.

In actuality, Miller did a reasonable job. He held the M2 growth rate to an annual 8.6% for the year and a half he served as chair. This was a significantly less severe slowdown than Burns engineered in 1973 and 1974, and it was slower (and steadier) than any annual rate Paul Volcker would accomplish until 1984. Had the Fed stuck with Miller's pace in a steady fashion for a few more years, the inflation rate would have subsided to the 4% range during his allocated four-year term. He, instead of Volcker, would have been anointed as the great inflation fighter. But image is everything in Washington and on Wall Street, where Miller instead of Burns was being blamed for the inflation of 1979. The mechanics of lags were lost on Miller's critics.

When Miller voted on the losing side of a question about a discount rate increase, the financial and business world had even less faith in his ability to run the Fed and fight inflation. Miller definitely got a bum rap. Of course, guessing what Miller would have done for the rest of his term is impossible. Given the expediencies of politics, he might have leaned more toward faster money supply growth. Indeed, his troubles with holding the money supply growth rate down in the summer of 1979 suggest just that possibility. Nevertheless, Miller did far more to slow inflation and far less to worsen it than most monetary analysts have recognized.

The economy and the Carter administration went through a most unsettling year in 1979. The monetary restraint of 1978 produced an economic slowdown on schedule in 1979. Output increased in only the third quarter and was up by a mere 0.6% at the end of the year. Meanwhile, prices continued to race upward. In addition to the delayed impact of money on demand and prices, OPEC gave oil prices their biggest boost since the embargo period, as oil prices doubled. Gasoline lines reappeared. A climate of hyperactivity was developing in the investment markets. We have already noted the movement of interest rates. Financial assets with negative real rates of return had become such unsafe havens for wealth that people scurried to get into gold, silver, real estate, and other real commodities. A wise strategy was to spend money quickly before prices rose further. That tactic drove the velocity of money upward and exacerbated the inflation surge. The country had lost confidence in Carter, the Fed, and the economy.

In a move to reinstill confidence, the president spoke to the nation on 14 July in what became known as his "malaise speech." He placed the blame for inflation on everyone except the Fed (which he never mentioned), and he called for a general program of individual restraint and abstention in order to dampen the manifestations of inflationary expectations. As a sign of resolve, Carter replaced a major portion of his cabinet and shifted Miller, whose work he admired, from the Fed to the Treasury. Now Carter needed someone at the Fed who would command respect from day one. His eventual choice was Paul Volcker, the head of the New York Federal Reserve Bank and a well-known conservative, anti-inflation Democrat.

☐ **Volcker's Monetarist Gamble**   Volcker knew that to take the wind out of inflation, the economy needed a continuation or a stronger dose of the policy of less money and higher interest rates. With real interest rates below zero, it seemed clear to Volcker that market rates would have to be increased by several percentage points to slow demand. But whereas market interest rates were already cracking the 10% barrier, Volcker found it nearly impossible to sell the kind of interest rate increase he felt was necessary. He hit on the idea of adopting (at least publicly) the monetarist strategy of targeting money supply growth rates. Under such an approach, interest rate movements are de-emphasized in favor of keeping the money supply growing at some fixed rate.

Anyone even slightly aware of the mechanics of supply and demand could recognize that holding down the money supply growth rate was sure to send interest rates rising farther. Volcker hoped his new approach would distract attention from rising interest rates. In October 1979 he managed to convince the other governors to take a monetarist approach in hope that the markets would be convinced of the Fed's resolve to slow inflation. Nevertheless, all the board members knew they were voting for tight money, higher interest rates, and a recession in the near future.

The Fed squeezed down harder on the money supply growth rate over the next six months. The M2 growth rate slowed to 5.8%. During the deceleration, the economy raced onward and upward. The Consumer Price Index (CPI) inflation rate reached 16.8% in January 1980, and interest rates catapulted from the 0% range to more than 18%. That put real interest rates at a still-low 2%, not high enough to yet slow short-term consumer demand but high enough to begin putting a crimp in housing and automobile demand. The combination of stalling aggregate demand and shrinking aggregate supply—another surge in oil prices accompanied the crisis in Iran—was almost sure to bring a recession as it had in 1974, but the Fed could not see it coming just around the bend. All the governors could see in early March was that the markets were apparently not the least bit impressed with its new anti-inflation initiative and that money supply growth had actually accelerated to a rate above 10% in February.

Emergency meetings at the Fed were called to further rein in the money supply and the economy. The main bone of contention in these discussions, as it had been since the October strategy change, was how far to let the federal funds rate (and thereby all other interest rates) rise. Yes, that is right—Fed policy was still, despite its new monetarist banner, obsessed with interest rates. Volcker may have wanted the public to pay less attention to interest rate movements, but the governors certainly were not doing so themselves. Instead of keeping the money supply on a steady course as monetarism called for, the Fed was about to begin a period of interest rate reactions that would send the money supply gyrating as never before. As the economy slipped into a recession in early 1980, the Fed was further tightening the money supply.

In an effort to take some of the inflation-fighting initiative,the Carter administration insisted that the Fed impose credit controls—that is, specific quantity limits on consumer credit, such as through credit cards. Since record market interest rates were not stopping credit-card users, perhaps credit controls would. No one at the Fed wanted to set up such a system, and the Fed was not compelled to do so, but Carter pressed hard. Volcker compromised with a set of credit controls that was designed to sound impressive but to do very little. Carter went before the nation in March 1980 and called for a moratorium on credit spending. While the controls themselves may not have been very potent, the public response was. Americans everywhere destroyed their credit cards, stopped buying on credit, and paid off their loans. Carter's plan worked too well. Aggregate demand plummeted, and the economy dived into a recession. Output fell at a whopping 10% annual rate in the second quarter.

Actually, economic activity had peaked in January, and output was already drifting downward before the credit meltdown. Restrictive monetary policy was having the expected effect on demand and output right on schedule, notwithstanding the Fed's impatience with the output lag. The public's reaction to the credit moratorium, however, drove both the money supply and aggregate demand down sharply. When people pay back loans, the money supply shrinks, and M2 fell slightly in April. The story with M1 was more volatile, and unfortunately the Fed was trying to target M1. It, in the words of one Fed governor, "dropped like a stone," falling by almost $7 billion in April. The drop in M1 was exaggerated by a move from checking accounts into interest-earning assets, such as savings accounts and nonbank assets. Shifting from checking to savings accounts does not really change the amount of spendable money available; nor does it change M2; that is why true monetarists prefer to use M2 rather than M1 as a measure of the money supply. But we already know that the Fed was only operating behind a monetarist facade. A prudent monetarist would have remained calm and noted that M2 had grown at a 5% annual rate so far in 1980 (despite the April dip) and a 5.4% annual rate since October—both a bit below their target ranges—and called for a slight easing.

No prudent monetarists occupied the Fed headquarters in Washington. The M1 free-fall greatly alarmed the governors. The questions they faced were twofold: (a) What should they do to reverse the apparent decline in the money supply? and (b) How far should they allow interest rates to fall in order to accomplish the reversal? Again, market interest rates, which peaked at the 18–20% range in late March and dropped rapidly in April and May, dominated their concerns. The Fed was composed mostly of Keynesian interest rate targeters trying to act like monetarist money-supply targeters. It was like having druids trying to run the Vatican.

Market interest rates were being propelled up and down by the CPI inflation rate, which shot up by over four points to 16% throughout the first three months of 1980 and fell back down below 11% during the second quarter. Instead of easing more reserves into the system to counteract the actual minor shrinkage in money supply, the Fed flooded the market, thereby sending real interest rates toward zero. That action showed monetary policy was exceptionally expansionary in the summer of 1980, a point borne out by the money supply growth rates. M2 exploded at an annual rate of more than 17% in June through August.

The flood of money brought the recession to a rapid halt. Output rose at a 2.4% rate in the third quarter. That was an extraordinarily severe and short recession, and the lag between money supply changes and output changes was unusually short. But one should not be surprised considering the wild swing the Fed was putting the money supply through and the effects of these swings on expectations. By September, the people at the Fed realized their summer splurge had been a huge mistake. They moved to slow the money supply growth rate back down. Essentially, they planned to start all over again from where they had been a year earlier and see whether they could do a better job of stabilizing and slowing the money supply growth rate. That meant another run-up of interest rates just when Carter could least afford it politically.

The Fed wasted a year and made the economy worse off during that time, and Carter was stuck with the results. Carter must have felt as Nixon had in 1960. With interest rates near 15%, the CPI inflation rate over 13%, and unemployment at 7.7% (putting the misery index at 20), Carter's reelection bid was doomed.

The first 16 months of Volcker's reign at the Fed were decidedly not what the doctor ordered. He promised to stabilize the growth rate of the money supply as measured by M1. The growth rate of M1 sunk to

−3% in early 1980 and catapulted to 16% in late 1980. A graph of M1 growth rates in 1980 looks like a serious earthquake on a seismograph— Figure 3 shows the slightly less erratic movements in M2. Volcker had managed to pack a patented, Arthur Burns, four-year monetary cycle into a single year. This was no way to instill confidence or to dampen inflationary expectations. If Volcker lacked the patience to stick by his restrictive policy for more than six months and if he resorted to the same inflationary policy of his predecessors to yank the economy out of a recession as soon as it began, inflation rates in the teens and interest rates in the twenties could be just around the corner.

At the end of 1980, the volatility of the money supply generated little hope that the Fed was going to bring inflation under control any-time soon. Magnified inflationary expectations were manifested in ever-climbing interest rates and a continued rise in velocity. Even though the average rate of growth in M2 had been near 8% for the prior three years, inflation was still in the teens. A look at the quantity of money equation for this three-year period shows that the rapid rise of velocity (from 1.6 to 1.8, well above its long-run average) and the slow growth of output (only a total of 6.8%) were behind this inflationary bubble. If the Fed could reduce the volatility and keep the average money supply growth path in the same ballpark as it had been, the inflation rate was sure to subside. The marketplace held out little hope, however, for such discipline at the Fed because of its track record for producing instability over the preceding 20 years, especially in 1980, the most unstable of all.

☐ Part 2: Keynesian Fiscal Activism, from Stardom to Exile

When Kennedy moved into the White House in 1961, he appointed a group of economic advisers that carried the Keynesian revolution from academia to Washington, from theory to practice. The members of the Council of Economic Advisors (including James Tobin and chairman Walter Heller), as well as other economists (such as Paul Samuelson) inside and outside the adminstration who had the new president's ear, were of a younger generation—like the president. They had been trained during the post–*General Theory* era and were steeped in the ideas of fiscal activism. They came to Washington on a mission of fine-tune aggregate demand through tax and spending changes, to boost the economy to full employment, and to conduct enlightened counter-cyclical policy. This ambitious plan came to be known as the New Economics. Its goal was to make the business cycle obsolete and to direct the American economy on a stronger growth path.

The revolutionaries actually had a rather hesitant banner carrier in Kennedy, whose economic training was decidedly limited and whose natural inclinations were toward fiscal conservatism and balanced budgets. Heller and Samuelson eventually "educated" the president and then turned their attention toward Congress. The tax cut of 1964 was the product of these efforts. It was judged by the consensus to be an unqualified success as the economy reached full employment in 1965, and the revolution appeared complete and permanent. But the glow of success was short-lived.

The Vietnam War deficits that soon followed were precisely what the economy did not need. Fiscal policy became a source of instability. Next, after a two-year wait, an anti-inflation tax increase was passed in 1968, and it had no apparent effect on aggregate demand. The luster of fiscal policy began to dull. When even Nixon declared his allegiance to Keynes and the wisdom of deficit spending, one began to suspect that Keynesian economics may have fallen into the wrong hands—politicians of either party. The balanced budget of 1969 became the last one. A decade of uninterrupted and often ill-advised deficits followed.

Fiscal policy developed a cyclical pattern that echoed the one we found in monetary policy. An anti-inflationary tightening of policy was followed by a recession, which shortly brought on a hasty reversal and a heavy dose of expansionary and inflationary policy. Recession paranoia was such an important motivating factor that fiscal policy took on a heavy expansionary bias, even in periods of full employment. As a result, fiscal policy became a source rather than a cure of inflation. By the end of the 1970s, fiscal policy had taken a backseat to monetary policy as the primary tool of aggregate demand management. Fiscal policy was simply expansionary for virtually the entire decade. Fine-tuning and aggregate demand management to achieve full employment and stable prices gave way to the politics of reelection fiscal policy. While the Keynesian effects on aggregate demand of various budgets continued to be considered throughout the 1970s, it was more of an afterthought. The fiscal revolution was corrupted by politics.

☐ **The 1964 Tax Cut** The dominant theme of these new fiscalists in the Kennedy administration was *fiscal drag*. They believed that what was slowing the economy's growth in the late 1950s and early 1960s was excessive taxes. As the economy expands, tax revenues flowing into the government increase, since virtually all taxes are tied to the level of economic activity. Thus, a growing economy tends to generate increasing amounts of tax revenues. It was theorized that the growing tax burden acts like a drag on the economy, impeding further growth by dampening aggregate demand—hence the term "fiscal drag." The proposed solution to this impairment on growth was to periodically cut tax rates in order to avoid a stagnation of consumer spending. It should be noted that these concerns existed at a time when government spending was under far better control than it would be in later years. As we will see, fiscal drag ceased to be a legitimate concern as early as the late 1960s and was virtually forgotten in the deficit deluge of the 1970s and 1980s.

Such an argument that the economy was suffering from too much taxation was a bit hard to sell when the budget was so prone to showing deficits. Eisenhower had not been persuaded, and Kennedy was a hard sell. But the fiscalists had developed a budgetary gauge in the 1950s that convinced them fiscal policy could actually be contractionary even though the budget was showing a deficit. That gauge was the *full-employment budget* (also called the *structural budget* in more recent years), which measures the surplus or deficit the budget would show were the economy at full employment. Under the Keynesian programs of compensatory fiscal policy and functional finance, the policy manual states that the actual budget should be balanced when the economy is near full employment. Because tax revenues and GNP are positively related, however, the actual budget will be pushed into a deficit when output is below full employment, as during the 1930s.

To determine whether discretionary fiscal policy is expansionary or contractionary, the full-employment budget is estimated. Tax revenues that would be generated were the economy at full employment are compared with full-employment government expenditures. A full-employment budget deficit is said to indicate expansionary fiscal policy, while a full-employment surplus is a sign of contractionary policy—regardless of what the actual budget may read. This concept had been used by Cary Brown in 1956 to demonstrate how contractionary fiscal policy had been during the New Deal. When output is below full employment and the full-employment budget shows a surplus, the economy is said to be suffering from fiscal drag. The proper policy to combat fiscal drag is a tax cut, even if the actual budget reads a deficit.

Even though Eisenhower was concerned about deficits, his fiscal policy can be judged to have been contractionary most of the time, according to the full-employment budget gauge. The reason is that the full-employment budget showed surpluses in the last years of his term, as Figure 7 shows. Kennedy's advisers, before and after the election, pointed to this indicator as a sign that fiscal policy was contributing to

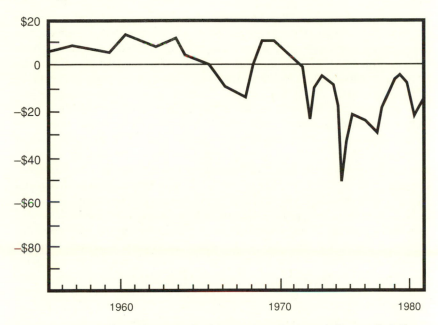

Figure 7. U.S. full-employment budget, 1955–1980 (in billions of dollars). Adapted from the Council of Economic Advisors, *Economic Report of the President* (Washington, D.C.: U.S. Government Printing Office, 1955–80).

the economy's sluggishness. Kennedy the presidential candidate was happy to use this information as background support for his criticisms of the current administration. But Kennedy the new president was not quite so willing to go along with his advisers' plan, which called for a tax cut to eliminate the full-employment budget surplus.

Eliminating a theoretical surplus was one thing, but what about the actual deficit that existed in 1961 and 1962? No matter how hard Heller tried to convince Kennedy and others in Washington that a tax cut would set off such a strong expansion that the deficit would eventually disappear, the idea of cutting taxes in the face of an existing deficit simply did not sit well with lawmakers. The Keynesian revolution had still not won over the president or many influential members of Congress, such as Wilbur Mills of the House Ways and Means Committee and Harry Byrd of the Senate Finance Committee.

Kennedy finally declared his conversion to Keynesian deficit spending in 1962, but he backslid a bit in favor of budget balancing toward the end of the year. In fact, the full-employment budget, which had been pushed into the red in 1961 and 1962, crawled back on the surplus side in 1963—a contractionary swing. But as the expansion slowed and unemployment hovered at more than 5.5%, Kennedy was finally won over completely to the tax cut plan in early 1963. Congressional leaders, more interested in tax reform than tax reduction, would prove to be more stubborn.

Taxes were ultimately cut after Kennedy's death, in February 1964 (a full year after Kennedy's proposal). President Johnson did some arm-twisting and marshaled support on Capitol Hill. The Revenue Act of 1964 reduced personal and corporate income tax rates enough to reduce tax revenues by more than $11 billion, an amount designed to wipe out the full-employment surplus at the time. The actual budget deficit did rise as everyone expected, but to the relief of the Council of Economic Advisors and to the delight of all, the deficit disappeared within a year of the law's passage. That government expenditures were held constant between 1964 and 1965 (as Johnson had promised Congress) helped rising tax revenues catch up to expenditures. Remember this point when we get to the tax cuts in the early 1980s. Regardless, the budget deficit was reduced despite (or because of) a tax cut, and that was an impressive result—impressive to both Keynesian demand-siders and, as we will see in the next chapter, conservative supply-siders.

The tax cut was apparently a great success. Unemployment, which had been lingering near 5.5% for two years, fell below 5% for the first time since 1957 and below 4% within two years of the cut. On closer inspection, however, the picture one gets is not quite so clear. The drop in unemployment in 1964 came so early in the year that it cannot be fairly attributed to the tax cut. That drop was actually the result of a surge in output that antedated the tax cut. In the two years preceding the tax cut, output was rising at an annual rate of more than 5.5%. Expansion then slowed for the final three quarters of 1964 to a 3% annual rate. Output took off in 1965 at a 7.5% clip. The timing of the 1965 output surge, which pushed the unemployment rate to 4%, is consistent with a lagged response to the tax cut. The economy's perfor-mance in 1965 can lead one to believe that the tax cut did exactly what its Keynesian designers predicted.

There is room for doubt, however. Monetarists have contended all along that the expansion of the early to middle 1960s was fueled by the rapid growth rate of the money supply from 1961 through 1965. While the unemployment rate was slow to show the progress owing to brisk growth in the labor force, output had begun a healthy expansion in 1961 that carried it above the economy's long-term trend well before taxes were cut. Output, which had climbed at a 5.5% annual rate in the two years before the tax cut, continued on this strong growth path until 1966. The expansion was three years old when taxes were cut, and it continued until 1966, when monetary policy took a sharp contractionary turn.

Another significant measure weakens the case for the tax cut's impact. Pure fiscal policy affects aggregate demand through the velocity of money. The tax cut, if it truly did lead to a surge in aggregate demand that can be separated from the demand growth already in progress for three years, should have set off a rise in velocity. It appears it did not. We saw earlier that velocity was on a downward course in the early 1960s. Velocity was constant or dropping from the time of the tax cut until the last quarter of 1965, when it started to rise. Though aggregate demand and output were booming upward in 1965, velocity was not. By the process of elimination, one can conclude that aggregate demand was being driven upward by the money supply before and after the tax cut. That conclusion strongly suggests that while the tax cut had great significance from the standpoint of the history and development of fiscal policy, it may have done very little to change the level of aggregate demand and the economy's course.

The actual influence the tax cut had on aggregate demand may never be determined. Nevertheless, the tax cut was certainly perceived as enormously successful. Keynesian fiscal policy reached an all-time high in terms of its level of acceptance in the mid-1960s. The economy's strength, rightly or wrongly, was associated with the tax cut. Confidence in fiscal policy was so great that policymakers' biggest concern was when the next tax cut would be needed to avoid future fiscal drag, since the economy continued to expand and generate more tax revenues. As it turned out, the Vietnam War and its effect on expenditures eliminated worries about too much taxes.

☐ **Fiscal Failures** The coalition of support that, as a result of the tax cut, formed around the New Economics of the Kennedy-Johnson economists showed some cracks with the fiscal effects of the war, and those cracks widened with the failures of the 1968 surtax. By the end of the decade, the control of the budget was increasingly out of the hands of economic advisers, and international and domestic political forces were becoming more important than theoretical or practical economic considerations. As policymakers had to deal more and more with the problems of inflation, their faith in fiscal policy waned and they turned to other tools, including wage and price controls.

No sooner had fiscal policy achieved the triumph of the tax cut than policymakers began to tarnish its image. The Johnson administration increased America's commitment in Vietnam and declared war on poverty at home. That meant large increases in government expenditures. After holding steady in 1965, those expenditures leapt upward by more than 13% in 1966, 17% in 1967, and 13% in 1968. Spurred by the rapid growth in income, tax revenues climbed rapidly as well, but not rapidly enough to keep up with spending. Fiscal policy was highly expansionary, all the while unemployment was below 4%.

Everybody knew this policy was inflationary. Assuming no reduction in expenditures, the only solution was a tax increase. But the president hesitated to support a "war tax" in 1966, and then Congress refused in 1967. One reason expenditures were allowed to outrace taxes was that Secretary of Defense Robert McNamara persistently underestimated (or underrevealed) military expenditures on the war. Nevertheless, a deficit of any size under these circumstances was contrary to Keynesian doctrine. Arthur Okun, the new head of the Council of Economic Advisors, knew this as well as anyone, but he was powerless. Fine-tuning had taken a backseat to war and politics. Besides, in 1967 the economy was experiencing a slowdown associated with the credit crunch. Some in Congress did not see the wisdom in raising taxes to battle excess aggregate demand when demand appeared to be so slack. Meanwhile, the deficit bulged to nearly $25 billion in 1968 (over $90 billion in 1991 dollars).

It was not until June 1968 that Congress finally got around to raising taxes. The Revenue and Expenditure Control Act of 1968 levied a 10% surtax on personal income back-dated to April and corporate income back-dated to January. The surtax was a simple way of temporarily raising taxes without changing the underlying tax rates. After calculating their taxes for 1968, taxpayers tacked on an extra 10% of that amount to their tax bill. Designed to generate nearly $10 billion in new revenues, the surtax was not enough to eliminate the entire deficit. But at least it was the right kind of fiscal policy in an inflation-threatened economy operating beyond full employment.

When Nixon entered office in 1969, he set out to further narrow the deficit gap by holding down on the spending side. Spending was cut from Johnson's 1969 budget, and expenditures grew by less than 3% (a reduction in real terms). Tax revenues caught up to expenditures, and a budget surplus was created.

The surplus of 1969 was a fiscal policy landmark. After all, the annual budget had been in the red since 1960, and it has been ever since. But the tax increase came a good two years too late. Fiscal policy's stature had to endure a major blow with this episode. Not only did the policy suffer from the delay, but the surtax apparently had little effect on aggregate demand. The law may have said the surtax was "effective" as of early 1968, but aggregate demand did not begin to slow until late in 1969, after the Fed had significantly reduced money supply growth. One reason may have been that the full-employment budget still showed a deficit until 1969. That suggests the tax increase may have been too small.

In the aftermath, many theorists argued that a temporary tax increase does not cause consumers to adjust their spending in any significant manner, since households make decisions based on long-term income projections. The surtax, two years late, may have been doomed as a policy tool regardless of the timing because consumers essentially ignored it. The surtax was too little, too late, and too temporary. A look at what velocity did in 1968, 1969, and 1970 confirms the surtax did not slow spending: velocity climbed steadily during the two-and-a-half-year period the surtax existed. Aggregate demand theory predicts a decline in velocity with a tax increase. Once again, fiscal policy in practice did not live up to its Keynesian theoretical standards.

The Nixon administration placed economics as a high priority because Nixon had promised to harness inflation, but fiscal policy was destined to take a backseat. Nixon's advisers leaned to the conservative side. Paul McCracken and Herbert Stein believed the way to fight inflation was with "gradualism," a slow reduction in the growth rate of aggregate demand. They looked to the Fed to institute such a policy, with an emphasis on slower money supply growth rates. As we saw earlier, however, Martin, at the Fed, threw a monkey wrench into that plan with a tightening of the money supply in 1969 that was anything but gradual. The resulting recession in 1970 put political pressure on Nixon, and he passed that pressure on to both fiscal and monetary policymakers. They were called upon to return policy to an expansionary stance, and that meant the end to gradualism before it was ever really applied. With both policies switched to expansionary, the administration eventually turned elsewhere to fight inflation—that is, to wage and price controls.

Fiscal policy was not completely abandoned by the Nixon administration. In fact, when the recovery from the 1970 recession appeared stalled in 1971, the Council of Economic Advisors employed the now-familiar full-employment budget to press for a more expansionary spending program that concentrated more on purchases and less on transfers. A small tax cut, passed at the end of 1971, reinforced this stance. During the election year of 1972, expenditures rose rapidly, supplementing the monetary boost to aggregate demand already being provided by Burns at the Fed. Burns was not the only one to draw criticism for shaping policy around election-year politics; the administration was also suspected of advancing an unnecessarily expansionary policy for political gain. A look at the full-employment budget figure confirms that fiscal policy in 1972 was in its most expansionary stance since 1968, another election year. Presidents of both parties used what freedom they had with expenditures to boost the economy and make political hay. Fiscal and monetary policies both developed a cyclical pattern that had a four-year period suspiciously paralleling election dates.

With the election in hand, the policy pendulum swung from fighting unemployment to fighting inflation. Fiscal policy became mildly contractionary as Nixon armed himself with the veto stamp and brought the growth rate of expenditures below that of tax revenues, which were being propelled upward by an economy fast approaching full employment. The budget deficit narrowed in 1973 and 1974, and the full-employment budget was actually balanced by the third quarter of 1974.

☐ **More Fiscal Politics**   The recession of 1974 and the ascension of Gerald Ford to the presidency brought on an interesting display of the influence of politics on fiscal policy. In the fall of 1974 Ford, along with an overwhelming majority of Americans, judged inflation to be the country's biggest problem and proposed a list of demand and supply policies designed to fight it. At the top of the list was a tax increase, a temporary surtax of all things. Even though the economy was well into a serious recession and the 1968 surtax was so ineffective, Ford prescribed a dose of what came to be called, somewhat derisively, "old-time religion." His goal was to "Whip Inflation Now" with an old-fashioned austerity plan of reduced aggregate demand. Sure, that would deepen the recession, but Ford could afford the political costs, since the country was so sympathetic to him in the immediate post-Watergate atmosphere and since future ambitions were limited. Besides, here was an opportunity to truly stop inflation if policymakers were determined.

The tax hike plan in the middle of a recession was decidedly against the Keynesian grain and was not well received. It did not matter, because Ford experienced the aforementioned political conversion and decided to run for president in 1976. That decision was politically inconsistent with raising taxes and worsening the recession. The goal of stopping inflation was discarded in favor of stimulating a recovery. In January 1975 Ford called for a tax cut. The demands of an approaching election once again prompted policymakers to abandon efforts to slow inflation and to design self-serving expansionary programs. By March, Congress happily cooperated and passed the Tax Reduction Act of 1975, calling for a 10% rebate on

1974 income taxes up to $200 per household, a bonus payment of up to $50 for social security recipients, and a reduction in 1975 taxes, with most of these checks going out in the summer of 1975.

Keynes would have given Ford and Congress a fairly high grade for their fiscal recovery package in 1975 and 1976. The actual and full-employment budgets were both pushed well into the deficit zone. In fact, Ford himself presented this picture in an explanation for the record-breaking deficit that developed. He pointed out that while it was true that the deficit was $75 billion, a major portion of it could be blamed on the recession's automatic impact on the budget. The rest of the deficit was attributable to the tax cut, which reduced revenues by almost $22 billion. Embarrassed though he was to be running such a large deficit—Ford, after all, was a conservative Republican—the president was admitting to a discretionary boost in that deficit that made him a closet Keynesian when it came to fighting a recession. Of course, this meant there was no chance of any real progress on the inflation front. Once again, policymakers showed the inflationary bias with which Keynesian policy was applied. The price the economy paid for Ford taking a more aggressive Keynesian approach than Eisenhower had 20 years earlier was a loss of control over the inflation rate. One-sided Keynesian policy was definitely proving to be inflationary.

Policymakers were faced with a conundrum: every time contractionary policy was applied in an effort to battle inflation, the drop in aggregate demand set off a recession. As we already have established, the inflation rate does not respond quickly to a drop in aggregate demand, because inflationary expectations continue to propel prices upward. Progress on the inflation front does not show up for as long as three years after the application of restrictive demand policy. During that time, unemployment climbs, and political pressures mount on the incumbent president. The pressures were too much for Nixon in 1971 and for Ford in 1975. They could not wait for the inflation rate to come down, and they used their powers to change fiscal policy to expansionary and to persuade Arthur Burns to do the same with monetary policy. If policymakers are going to apply old-time religion to fight inflation, they must be ready to stick with it for more than a year and a half. Approaching elections drowned out patience in 1971 and 1975. Politics ruled over sound economics and would continue to do so for the rest of the decade.

Carter used the high unemployment and inflation rates in 1976 to his political advantage. A midyear slowdown in the recovery (which had started in the spring of 1975) in the election year placed the emphasis on stimulating aggregate demand, and Carter proposed an expansionary fiscal package that included tax cuts. No sooner had Carter taken a seat in the Oval Office, however, than the expansion revived and the need to boost aggregate demand passed. As the economy climbed back toward full employment in 1977 and 1978, fiscal policy remained neutral, and the actual and full-employment budgets deficits were allowed to gradually shrink.

The rapid growth in money income, attributable to both output and prices rising, pushed tax revenues up at a brisk pace. Taxpayers were faced with *tax bracket creep*—as prices drove up money incomes, taxpayers were pushed into progressively higher tax brackets. Inflation was creating a backdoor tax increase, and Americans were beginning to notice and complain. Congress tried to soften that blow with a tax cut in late 1978. Nevertheless, the budget deficit (actual and full-employment) continued to shrink until a balanced budget was within sight in 1979.

By 1979, inflation was worsening but Carter was within reach of two goals, a balanced budget and full employment. The actual deficit was the smallest since 1970, dropping below $20 billion, and unemployment was down to 5.7%, not far from a stated goal of 5%. Actually, Carter's original goal for unemployment had been the old 4% target set in the early 1960s, but his advisers reviewed labor market conditions and concluded that 5% was more realistic, given the increases in teenage and female unemployment. Interestingly, Congress was still calling for unemployment rates as low as 3% in the Humphrey-Hawkins Bill. As its turned out, even Carter's 5% goal was probably too ambitious. Most economists now agree that the natural rate of unemployment in 1979 was probably closer to 6% than to 5%. Policymakers may not have recognized it in 1979, but the economy was already at full employment.

In 1979 most everyone in Washington was operating under the assumption that a recession was imminent. The combination of monetary restraint and inflationary expectations sent interest rates into the double digits. Coincidentally, the crisis in Iran was driving oil prices toward $30 a barrel, thereby reducing aggregate supply and worsening both the inflation and the unemployment pictures. Somehow, output managed to creep slightly upward, but the economy was mired in stagflation quicksand. Very little faith was left in fiscal or monetary policy to control inflation. The White House had turned to voluntary wage and price constraints with much fanfare but to no avail, and fears of compulsory wage and price controls abounded. Carter had to do something to calm the fears and expectations. As we saw earlier, he asked Americans for restraint and made inflation fighting primarily the responsibility of the Federal Reserve and Paul Volcker.

By this time, stabilization policy was out of the hands of fiscal policymakers. The monetarist counterrevolution was taking hold, and the great Keynesian experiment in fiscal stabilization was coming to an end. It had been ruined by the inherent weaknesses in the tools and biases of the policymakers. During the 1960s and 1970s, fiscal policy had proved to pack far less impact than its designers and supporters had believed. Even the exulted 1964 tax cut owed much of its apparent clout to expansionary monetary policy. Had fiscal policy been conducted correctly along Keynesian guidelines without lags, it probably still would have been found less effective than Kennedy's advisers kept predicting. Unfortunately, we will never know, because fiscal policy after 1964 was so politicized that it became a greater source of instability than stability. Policy changes were made often, and they were in the wrong direction as often as in the right. Political impatience and unemployment paranoia left fiscal policy with a definite inflationary bias. Keynes had said deficits were needed sometimes. By the 1970s, policymakers made deficits a permanent fixture, even in times of full employment. The revolution in economic theory and policymaking had soured not only because of shortcomings in the theory and tools but also because of the failure of policymakers to implement the policies their designers had prescribed.

9

Disinflation and Deficits: 1980–1990

DURING THE PRESIDENTIAL DEBATE IN October 1980, Ronald Reagan asked the American people if they felt they were better off than they had been four years earlier. Faced with all those sorry economic data we listed at the beginning of chapter 8—such as interest rates in the teens, a misery-index reading above 20, and falling real earnings—the answer was a resounding no. The people were ready for a change. Where Jimmy Carter had been telling them inflation was the result of their living too well, Reagan contended the problem was that the government itself was living too well. Reagan argued that the economy and the country needed a dramatic change from the liberal policies of more government. He offered a plan whose foundation was less government intervention, indeed less government period.

The Reagan plan became known, at times somewhat derisively, as Reaganomics, and it aimed to reverse the growth in government and release the economy from the constraints conservatives felt had developed as the government became larger and more involved in the marketplace. Although voters may have been ready for a change, it turned out that Congress was not so adaptable. Congress was cooperative about lowering tax rates, but the people on Capitol Hill could find little about the government that they were willing to eliminate or even scale back. As a result, the federal budget deficits bloomed early in the decade and refused to shrink right on into the 1990s. The size of the federal deficit and its many perceived effects on the economy became the most important and controversial economic issue of the era. The perennial deficits were blamed for, among other things, high interest rates, movements in the value of the dollar, growth of equally enormous deficits in the balance of trade, explosive growth of the federal debt, apparent conversion of the United States from a net creditor to a debtor nation, and both the cause and the cure of the 1981–82 recession (so much for consistency). By the end of the decade, economic reports were dominated by struggles to reduce the dual deficits on the budget and the balance of trade. Reaganomics became equated with deficits more than anything else.

What is striking about the economy's performance during the 1980s is that it defied prediction. Doom-and-gloomers continuously predicted that Reaganomics and what it had wrought would send the economy into some sort of crisis. Yet, as Table 9 shows, the economy, after recovering from the recession early in the decade, embarked on an expansion of near record length. Output climbed essentially without interruption from the very beginning of 1983 right into 1990. Moreover, the inflation rate was dramatically reduced by 1982 to less than 4%, where it stayed until creeping up to 4.5% in 1989. While inflation was not conquered, it was contained to a far more acceptable level. Policymakers accomplished disinflation far more successfully than many at the beginning of the decade believed possible. While the process required a recession, that contraction was actually less severe and protracted than many had predicted, and the expansion was far more robust and prolonged than anyone could have imagined. The economy achieved a degree of stability by the end of the 1980s that would have been the envy of policymakers in the early 1960s. The irony is that this stability was achieved in an era of reduced government intervention—that is, with a virtual abandonment of fiscal policy and restrained use of monetary policy.

We begin this chapter with an examination of Reaganomics, its roots, its themes, and its harsh realities. We then turn to the Federal Reserve to see how it managed to pull off the disinflation after the highly inauspicious way it had started the decade. By the middle of the decade, Volcker was lauded for at least caging the inflation dragon—a stark contrast to the cries for his impeachment in 1981. His successor, Alan Greenspan, carried on the fight in hope of actually slaying the monster and returning the inflation rate to 1950s levels. From a discussion of the Fed, we return to the topic of the budget deficits, expanding on their invincibility throughout the decade and trying to sort out the

Table 9. Economic Indicators, 1980–1990

	Q	M1	M2	P	CPI	GE	GR	Surplus Deficit	UN	Prime Rate
1980	−0.2	6.8	8.9	9	12.5	591	517	−74	7.1	15.3
1981	1.9	6.5	9.9	9.7	8.9	678	599	−79	7.6	18.9
1982	−2.5	8.5	8.8	6.4	3.8	746	618	−128	9.7	14.9
1983	3.6	9.6	11.8	3.9	3.8	808	601	−207	9.6	10.8
1984	6.8	5.7	8.2	3.7	3.9	852	666	−186	7.5	12.4
1985	3.4	12.4	8.4	3	3.8	946	734	−212	7.2	9.9
1986	2.7	17	9.6	2.6	1.1	990	769	−221	7	8.3
1987	3.7	3.5	3.3	3.2	4.4	1,004	854	−150	6.2	8.2
1988	4.4	5.1	5.5	3.3	4.1	1,064	909	−155	5.5	9.3
1989	2.6	0.6	4.5	4.1	4.8	1,143	991	−153	5.3	10.8
1990	0.5	4.0	3.2	4.0	5.3	1,252	1,031	−221	5.6	10.0

Q = Percent change in real GNP (output)
M1 = Percent change in M1 (currency plus checking account deposits)
M2 = Percent change in M2 (currency plus checking and savings accounts)
P = Percent change in GNP Implicit Price Deflator
CPI = Percent change in Consumer Price Index
GE = Federal government expenditures (billions of dollars)
GR = Federal government revenues (billions of dollars)
Surplus/Deficit = GR minus GE
UN = Average unemployment rate (percent)
Prime Rate = Average prime rate of interest (percent)

Sources: See Bibliographic Essay.

many linkages to other economic conditions. Finally, we look at the long expansion and the monetary policy that aided it.

☐ Reaganomics

As the economy said good-bye to the second worst decade of the century, the many faults that had developed during that period led economists and policymakers to rethink what was wrong with the economy and what direction policy should take to rescue it from the malaise of the late 1970s. Although many stubborn Keynesians were trying to stave off the conceptual attacks of their conservative colleagues, the tide was turning in favor of the idea that government policies had been the problem not the solution to the economic woes of the previous decade.

☐ **The Plan**   Reaganomics came from many sources, including Reagan himself. What had become apparent was that the Keynesian prescriptions, all of them involving manipulations of aggregate demand, had become increasingly ineffective in battling stagflation. Efforts to slow inflation with reductions in aggregate demand worsened unemployment, and boosts to aggregate demand designed to lower the unemployment rate led to surges in inflation. Demand-side policy was always half-right and half-wrong. It was natural for people to eventually look to the supply-side. An increase in the level of aggregate supply, which always causes output to rise and prices to fall, simultaneously fights both inflation and unemployment. A policy that brings forth such a change would be perfect for fighting stagflation. Hence, it was natural for supply-side economics to rise out of the ashes of Keynesian demand-side policy.

Increased emphasis on aggregate supply arose in unison with increased awareness of variables that affect aggregate supply. As noted earlier, improvements in labor productivity slowed from an annual rate of 2% in the 1950s and 1960s to zero from 1975 into the early 1980s, and this development attracted much attention among both economists and politicians. If labor productivity stalls, so does economic growth, which means that living standards stagnate. One cannot expect to do battle with inflation and be successful in such an economic environment.

Noting stagnant labor productivity is one thing; determining its cause is another. Conservative supply-siders were unanimous in placing the blame on the government. At the top of the list were tax rates. During the inflation years, American's money incomes rose almost as fast as prices, because every time prices rise in our economy somebody's money income also rises. That left Americans' real pretax income almost as high but shifted every taxpayer into progressively higher tax brackets—tax bracket creep. A graduated tax system like ours is always susceptible to bracket creep during periods of inflation, but it took on painful proportions in the 1970s, when prices and money incomes were climbing at such alarmingly fast rates. The median marginal tax rate—that is, the rate paid by the average taxpayer on the last or next dollar earned—climbed steadily during the 1970s, from 27% in 1970 to 36% in 1980. Families with modest incomes found themselves moving up into tax brackets previously associated with far wealthier people. Even a young economics professor of moderate means whom I happen to know encountered a 43% tax rate on any additional income he could muster.

Many economists argued that these high rates discouraged effort on the part of labor and reduced the level of capital investment by businesses. Investment was also harmed by the damper these high income tax rates put on savings. Supply-siders insisted that lower tax rates would increase the supply of savings in the loanable funds markets; more savings would in turn push real interest rates down and investment up. The tax system had become a major disincentive and a handicap to economic growth. The consensus was that tax rates should be lowered and the whole revenue system overhauled.

Tax reductions were a time-honored tradition among conservative Republicans. You may remember chapter 3's discussion of the postwar tax cuts of the 1920s. It was believed then, as in 1980, that lower tax rates, particularly in the upper brackets, would stimulate investment and economic growth, which would benefit all income brackets. This concept has often been called the "trickle-down" effect by critics, because the benefits are most directly visible to the rich, with parallel long-term benefits trickling down to lower income brackets. Supply-siders are firm believers in the idea that economic growth benefits all, and any policy that stimulates growth leaves everyone with a higher standard of living. A corollary phrase commonly used was "A rising tide lifts all boats."

When looking for a demonstration of their ideas, supply-siders pointed to the 1964 tax cut as an example of how lower tax rates benefited all. They did not interpret the effects of the tax cut in the same manner as its demand-sider architects, who focused on increases in aggregate demand. Supply-siders saw an increase in aggregate supply as well. How else, they argued, could one explain the shrinking of the deficit and the relatively slow inflation in 1964 and 1965? Like a weatherman and a rain dancer enjoying a drought-breaking rain, the rivals would never agree on exactly what happened after the tax cut even though both sides liked the results.

A traditional roadblock to any tax cut has been the existence of a continuing budget deficit. Andrew Mellon had no such problem in the 1920s, but the Kennedy-Johnson team did in 1964, and so did many tax cutters in 1980. The shrinking of the deficit in 1965 after the tax cut was one weapon in the supply-siders' arsenal. Another came from Arthur Laffer, a conservative economist from California who considered the effects of different marginal tax rates on total tax revenues coming into the Treasury. He noted that tax revenues rise as the tax rate rises from zero. But logic insists that tax revenues must be zero when the marginal tax rate reaches 100%: there would be no incentive to earn an income at a 100% rate; therefore, no income would be produced, and no tax revenues would be generated. This means that while tax revenues rise with tax rates at lower tax rates, there must be some point beyond which revenues begin to fall as rates continue to rise. Legend has it that Laffer casually drew this relationship between tax rates and tax revenues on a napkin, and the infamous Laffer curve, a mound-shaped curve resembling a large anthill, was born. Whatever the truth about its origins, the Laffer curve had a vast impact on policy in the 1980s.

The existence of a Laffer-like relationship is indisputable; tax rates of nearly 100% will undoubtedly inhibit growth. Where the battle lines are drawn is over the shape of the curve and on which side of the peak the United States rested in the late 1970s. Supply-siders argued in 1980 that tax rates were so high that the nation was on the downslope. It followed that lower tax rates would be likely to produce more tax revenues, not less. Others argued that the nation was on the upslope, where higher tax rates brought in more revenues, albeit at a progressively slower pace. The supply-siders began calling for tax cuts during the Carter administration. The Kemp-Roth tax bill—named after its authors, Rep. Jack Kemp and Sen. William Roth—was the first shot in the supply-side offensive, but it failed to pass in 1978. Its sequel was more successful in 1981.

Urged on by Kemp and others, candidate Reagan adopted a tax cut as one of the four major planks of his economic platform. The second plank dealt with the absolute amount of government spending and the composition of that spending. Extrapolations of Carter's budgets showed a continued rise in the ratios of both taxes to GNP and government expenditures to GNP. Reagan was determined to stop and reverse the growth of the federal government. He called for significant reductions in the absolute level of spending in an effort to bring down the ratio of government spending to GNP. Despite the federal government's bigger bite out of the nation's total income, the percentage of national income going to defense spending had been on a secular decline in the 1970s. Carter sought to redress this situation himself in his final two budgets. But Reagan proposed a far more aggressive increase in arms spending. "Peace through strength" was one of his mottoes. Thus, the second plank of Reaganomics called for a substantial increase in defense spending coupled with a reduction in total spending. Obviously, some nondefense programs would have to be cut back drastically.

The reduction in the size of the government effected by the first two planks was expected to stimulate private economic activity by freeing resources and funds. To give aggregate supply an even bigger boost, the third plank of Reaganomics called for less government regulation. Each year, up to $100 billion of costs were and still are being incurred by businesses simply trying to comply with government regulations and red tape. The process of deregulation had got off to a strong start during Carter's term as policy was enacted to free oil and natural gas, airlines, and financial services industries. Reagan planned to carry that ball much farther, or at least so he said.

The fourth plank concentrated on the inflation rate. Reagan's policy advisers, who included supply-siders and monetarists, believed the success of the whole package depended on the Federal Reserve's ability to slow the inflation rate. The Reagan people were unable to tell Volcker and his people what to do; nevertheless, both Reagan and his advisers called for a monetarist program of slow and steady growth of the money supply. They could not implement such a policy, but they could certainly let the Fed and the public know they were backing the Fed's efforts at disinflation all the way. This was a new and vital approach from a president and his advisers, and it proved beneficial to the Fed's efforts and credibility.

This aspect of Reaganomics was influenced by another relatively new philosophy, rational expectations, a theory held by a small but rapidly growing group of conservative economists. This theory holds that participants in the marketplace develop expectations about the course of economic variables based on knowledge of past patterns. Included in those patterns are the effects of government policy programs. Rational expectationists argue that as people become progressively more knowledgeable about policy and its effects, they respond to policy changes by taking actions for their own benefit based on their expectations of the effects of the policies. The best example concerns the money supply and interest rates. If moneylenders continue to observe, as they did during the inflation years, that increases in the money supply lead to inflation, they will rationally respond to an increase in the money supply by expecting inflation. To hedge against the expected inflation, they will raise market interest rates immediately on learning of the policy action. As a result, the money supply increase fails to lower real rates and leads to higher market rates. The theory of rational expectations was often used to argue that Keynesian monetary policy moves would be ineffectual, because interest rates would not move in opposition to the money supply.

More important to Reaganomics, the implications of rational expectationists' conclusions helped provide a disinflation strategy. Reagan's advisers convinced him that if the Fed announced that monetary policy henceforth would lock on a slow and steady money supply growth path without variation and if Reagan reinforced that policy with his approval and commitment, the markets could immediately begin expecting a deceleration of inflation in the near future—assuming, of course, the markets believed the Fed and the president. Not only would market interest rates fall, but so would labor demands for wage increases. In general, inflationary expectations could be dampened rapidly. By radically shortening the lag between the money supply slowdown and its effect on the inflation rate, the job of slowing inflation would become significantly easier. That in turn would make the economic contraction necessary to break inflationary expectations much less severe and prolonged, perhaps even unnecessary. In other words, a painful recession or a lengthy depression could be avoided, while the disinflation medicine was applied by the Fed.

This last point became a keystone of the Reagan plan. The optimistic predictions Reagan's advisers made about the economy under their plan foresaw disinflation without a recession. In fact, they surprisingly predicted—many said, incredibly—robust years with moderate to low interest rates during the early 1980s. Of course, much of that scenario was based on the premise that the stimulative effect on the level of aggregate supply of the first three planks of the plan would be so strong as to outweigh any negative demand-side effects of the monetary slowdown.

If inflationary expectations could be eliminated overnight by presidential proclamation, it would be theoretically possible to accomplish a monetary slowdown and disinflation without setting off a recession. This was the weak link in the Reagan plan. No rational person in America could have lived through the previous two decades capped off by the debacle of 1980 and believe the Fed was finally going to get its act together and do exactly what the monetarists wanted. The Fed governors encountered those doubts when they asked bankers, in early 1981, what they expected the inflation rate to be at the end of the year: the unanimous response was in the double digits.

Many critics of Reaganomics complained about its inconsistencies, but such critics were often interpreting the plan from a Keynesian, demand-side point of view. A tax cut combined with a monetary slowdown sounds contradictory if we view the tax cut as a boost to aggregate demand and the money slowdown as a reduction in demand. That leaves demand unchanged and the economy unaffected. But if the tax cut is seen as an aggregate supply stimulant, the policy combination creates a simultaneous increase in supply and decrease in demand. That would cause no net change in output but a drop in the price level. That means a reduction in inflation without a recession, which is perfectly consistent—at least, theoretically. The real world may not have responded as Reagan's advisers predicted and the plan may have been overly optimistic and based on unrealistic assumptions, but its parts were reasonably consistent.

The optimistic picture the Reagan people painted came to be known as the "rosy scenario." It certainly would have been a pleasure to have lived out that scenario. The predictions made by Reagan's advisers in 1980 for Reagan's first term were as follows:

> Output—up every year; +1.4% in 1981, +5.2% in 1982, +4.9% in 1983, and +4.2% in 1984
>
> Money GNP—an average increase of more than 11% per year
>
> CPI inflation rate—10.5% in 1981, 7.2% in 1982, 6.0% in 1983, and 5.1% in 1984
>
> Unemployment—up to 7.8% in 1981, but down each subsequent year to 6.4% in 1984
>
> Interest rates—down every year to 7% in 1984
>
> Budget deficit—down every year and eliminated by 1984 or 1985

The central goal was to achieve a reduction of inflation without a drop in output and with only a minor uptick in unemployment. Reagan was proposing, as one critic put it, a "costless disinflation," and there was ample reason to doubt the likelihood of that scenario.

Where Reagan's plans were most vulnerable to complaints of inconsistencies, or at least escapes from reality, was in the area of the budget. It would take more than a supply-side perspective and a rosy scenario to conclude that Reagan could accomplish his tax cut and defense buildup while still managing to balance the budget by 1984. Here political realities became as important as economic ones.

☐ **Economic and Political Realities**   During the 1980 Republican presidential primary debates, fellow candidate George Bush called Reagan's economic plan "voodoo economics." He was mainly referring to Reagan's promise to balance the budget despite tax cuts and increases in defense spending. At that stage, Reagan spoke of reducing government spending by eliminating wasteful programs and cutting the waste in those which remained. Yet he gave no specifics about where the budget ax would fall. After the election, much of the carving fell into the hands of David Stockman, the brash young U.S. representative appointed to head the Office of Management and Budget (OMB). His Herculean task was to make the voodoo into reality. He quickly discovered that the rosy scenario was based on assumptions that were going to be impossible to fulfill in actuality. The economy was not going to perform as miraculously well as the scenario outlined; nor was Congress going to accept the budget cuts necessary to avoid grand deficits. Faith in the Reagan plan was fated for a head-on collision with reality.

Stockman discovered it was tough to cut the budget given the parameters set by Reagan. The defense department was essentially immune to cuts, since Reagan intended to expand spending in that area. Caspar ("Cap the Knife") Weinberger, the new defense secretary, had forged a reputation as a budget cutter in a previous stint at the OMB. Nevertheless, absolute savings were ruled out with the defense buildup, and besides, Weinberger fell prey to the urge many defense secretaries have to be empire builders and weapons buyers. With defense spending ruled out, 25% of the budget was untouchable.

In addition, Reagan insisted throughout the campaign that he would not cut down the "safety net," the income transfer payments to the poor and/or elderly included in social security, Medicare, Medicaid, and so on. That put as much as another 40–50% of the budget off-limits to Stockman's search for areas to cut. Back when Eisenhower was struggling rather unsuccessfully to trim the budget, he faced a reverse image of Stockman's foe. At that time, the safety net made up less than 25% of the budget while defense had a share of more than 50%, and defense spending was Eisenhower's primary target for cuts. Reagan's campaign promises had protected 75% of the budget. Another 10% of the budget went to interest payments on the national debt. All Stockman could hope for was the predicted decline in interest rates that would whittle down that untouchable portion of the budget.

That left as little as 15% of the budget available for carving, and the spending reductions would have to be severe in order to meet the overall budget goals. Spending in these programs would have to fall by at least one-third. Stockman targeted billions of dollars in many of the programs when he made his budget projections; however, he soon found out that targeting was much easier than actually cutting. He also discovered something his service in Congress should have taught him: just how faithful the members of Congress from both parties were to these programs. Promises to eliminate entire cabinet departments like energy or cut back programs like agricultural supports drew harsh opposition. Although some significant cuts were made, many were simply temporary accounting charades, and they all fell well short of what was necessary to accomplish Reagan's budgetary goals. Stockman's struggles and ultimate failures to reduce government spending, summed up in the title of his memoir, *The Triumph of Politics*, showed that Reagan would not only be unsuccessful at balancing the budget but also at curbing, let alone reducing, the growth of government. The government-spending-to-GNP ratio was destined to rise instead of fall for political reasons far more than economic ones. By 1985, real spending was 15% higher than Reagan's projections, an excess that explains entirely the real growth in the structural deficit during Reagan's first term.

Stockman's budget-balancing projections did not pan out for other reasons. In 1980 most everyone predicted a balanced budget by 1984 because of how rapidly inflation was driving up tax revenues through tax bracket creep. Stockman's budget projections were based on assumptions of much higher inflation rates than actually occurred. As the inflation rate began to tumble in the latter part of 1981, the gap between taxes and expenditures began to widen. Tax revenues were on a much slower growth path than expected. To make matters worse, interest rates were significantly higher than predicted. That enlarged the interest payments on the debt and sent government expenditures up enough to cancel out the spending cuts Congress did manage to swallow.

The tax cut, or more officially the Economic Recovery and Tax Act (ERTA) of 1981—a revival of the Kemp-Roth tax bill—led to lower taxes than expected. Reagan asked for a three-year program with tax rates cut by 30%, but Congress, concerned about the current deficit, trimmed the cut to 25% over two and half years. But this does not mean the tax cut was smaller than requested. In actuality, by the time Congress got done with changes in the proposal designed to make the tax bill more equitable, tax revenues were reduced by more than Reagan requested. When this program took effect, it widened the deficit gap even more. The tax rate reductions actually did nothing more than counteract impending tax bracket creep. Nonetheless, there was no scenario or voodoo spell under which tax revenues would catch up to government expenditures in the foreseeable future.

Then the unspeakable began—the recession. No matter how hard the Reagan faithful wanted to believe a contraction was avoidable, it was inevitable. Monetary policy and the inflation rate were simply on a collision course that was bound to produce a recession of some sort unless inflationary expectations disappeared overnight. Here is where one can find a glaring contradiction in the rosy scenario. Referring to the projection figures presented earlier, we can see that a money GNP growth rate of more than 11% was projected through 1985. That would require a similar M2 growth rate, since M2 and money GNP have the same average growth rates. In keeping with the goal of disinflation, however, the Fed was setting money supply targets well below this level. The M2 target range was between 6% and 9%. As long as the inflation rate was as high or higher than the M2 growth rate, there was no room for output expansion. As we have seen and will see further in the next section, the Fed did little to dampen inflationary expectations with the wild gyrations through which it put the money supply. That guaranteed the persistence of expectations and the onslaught of a recession.

The recession was one more dose of reality for the budget. It had the usual effect of pushing up expenditures and driving down tax revenues. As early signs of the recession began to brew in the summer of 1981, it became apparent to Reagan's advisers that the imminent recession was going to bloat the deficit even as Congress was deciding whether or not to cut taxes. Inside the White House, the rosy scenario was history, discarded in favor of more realistic and pessimistic numbers. But that pessimism was not allowed to show through to the public, particularly Congress. To do so would possibly derail the tax cut, since many supporters would back off in the face of the true deficit projections. The administration continued to predict output expansion until the tax cut was passed. Warnings to members of Congress from other sources, including people at the Fed, that the cut would drive interest rates upward and possibly increase the likelihood of a recession did not deter Congress from passing the tax reduction bill.

The deficit more than doubled, to almost $100 billion, by fiscal year 1982. In relative terms—such as in 1991 dollars or as a percentage of GNP—the deficit was not unusually high in 1982. Indeed, it was a bit smaller in relative terms than the peak deficit during the 1974–75 recession. Nevertheless, the growth of the deficit underscored the difference between the rosy scenario and reality. Output was falling, not rising, and interest rates were rising, not falling. By 1982, people began blaming the deficit for causing the high interest rates and prolonging the recession. This view did not make any Keynesian sense, but Reaganomics had a way of confusing even Keynesian economists. What was more striking than the rise in the deficit owing to the recession was the rise in the full-employment (or structural) deficit, the part not attributable to the recession. The recession's additions to the deficit were temporary phenomena; the underlying budget was getting deeper in the red in a far more permanent fashion. The deficits were only going to get worse and become the issue of the decade, and we will return to them shortly.

☐ The Fed Battles Inflation

When we last saw the Fed in the previous chapter, it had just completed a totally abysmal year of attempting monetary targeting. The result was wide variations in the growth rate of M1, interest rates, and output. The economy had been put through a whiplash ride in 1980, and the Fed was starting over again with its monetarist experiment. The goal was still to bring down the inflation rate, and the hope was to accomplish that in a far steadier fashion. Many believed in the fall of 1980 that the previous 12 months had been wasted. The Fed had a chance to slow both demand and inflation and to begin the disinflation process. But as a result of clamping down too hard on the money supply for the first six months and overdoing the easing in the last six, all the Fed had done was to give the country a short recession and to magnify inflationary expectations. The inflation rate was just as high as it had been in 1979.

In reality, though, the Fed was getting closer to the fruits of its anti-inflationary efforts. The effects of the deceleration of the money supply—which started in late 1977—on the inflation rate had been delayed by the usual lag factors, as well as additional ones connected to foreign trade. The inflation rate was due to come down in 1981 and stay down for many years. By bringing the average rate of growth of the money supply down from the double-digit range, the Fed was successful in reducing inflation. But the Fed's erratic month-to-month performance greatly contributed to extraordinarily high interest rates, which drove the economy into a recession by the end of 1981.

☐ **Disinflation**   The disinflation breakthrough finally came in 1981. The CPI had risen throughout 1979 and 1980 at double-digit annual rates almost without interruption. In March 1981 the increase was at a rate of only 7.5%, and the average increase for the next three months was the same. Another double-digit spurt followed during the third quarter, but that was the inflation monster's last roar. By 1982, the now-tamer inflation rate settled into a holding pattern of below 4%, where it stayed until the latter part of 1988, when it quickened a bit. From the beginning of 1981 to the end of that year, the inflation rate as measured by the CPI came down 8%, and the rate as measured by the GNP deflator tumbled by 6.5% (see Figure 4). The Federal Reserve's efforts to slow the money supply growth rate had borne fruit in 1981, and the Fed—especially Paul Volcker—got most of the credit for the accomplishment, even if a recession came with the package.

As was established in the previous chapter, the disinflation work actually started in late 1977 when the Fed, during Burns's last months, decelerated M2 growth below 10% after almost three years of money expansion in excess of 12%. Then under Miller, the Fed managed to hold the M2 growth rate to an annual rate near 8%. Before the slow-down, the money supply growth rate of 1975–78 was consistent with an inflation rate of 8–9%, which is exactly the rate observed in 1978 through 1980 on the GNP deflator. A distinct three-year lag is apparent in both the inflation surge in 1978 and the eventual decline in 1981. The slower post-1977 M2 growth rate was consistent with an inflation rate of near 5%. Given the three-year lag, the disinflation would have been right on schedule had it started as 1980 gave way to 1981. As it was, the breakthrough was a few months late, but it was a totally consistent manifestation of monetary policy from late 1977 onward. The disinflation seeds were planted for two full years before Volcker took the Fed's helm. This was apparent to very few at the time, and still escapes most accounts, which give the Volcker regime virtually all the credit.

Actually, Volcker's and his colleagues' actions during their first months of supposed money targeting simultaneously both confirmed the disinflation and delayed it. On one hand, despite the monthly variations M2 grew by 8.6% during the first 16 months—from October 1979 to January 1981. That extended the streak of slower money growth beyond three full years and further cemented the eventual stabilization of the inflation rate in the 5% range. Had Volcker accomplished this average rate with a far steadier hand, it is more likely that the disinflation would have begun on schedule. Instead, the money supply, as we know, grew very slowly during the first six months of targeting and extremely rapidly during the next six. The latter surge fueled a renewed burst of inflationary expectations, which had dropped off drastically during the spring 1980 recession. The expected inflation rate jumped back over 10%, and that in turn propelled the inflation rate upward for another several months, thereby delaying the disinflation break until later in 1981. The dent the 1980 recession put into inflationary expectations was wasted by that money surge.

The movements of the inflation rate during this time can be tricky to interpret. First, one has to be aware of the three-year lag that we have emphasized but was lost on most observers. The 1981 disinflation was the inevitable result of the monetary policy change more than three years earlier. Second, it is necessary to take into account the effect of foreign influences on American prices. The CPI inflation rate of 12% per year in 1979 and 1980 was 3–4% higher than the lagged money supply growth rate would have predicted. One problem was that the CPI in those years tended to exaggerate the inflation rate because of technical reasons. Contributing coincidentally to a more rapid consumer inflation rate were the effects of rising energy prices caused by OPEC supply restrictions and rising import prices caused by the declining exchange value of the dollar. Energy prices jumped 37% in 1979, 20% in 1980, and 12% in 1981. Foreign variables not only magnified the inflation rate in those three years but also contributed to the tardiness of the disinflation.

These same foreign variables, moving in the opposite direction, worked to exaggerate the degree of the disinflation after 1981 by helping to reduce the inflation rate below the 5% rate the money supply growth rate would have predicted. The value of the dollar bottomed out in the middle of 1980 and began a climb that took it to record levels by the end of 1984. As the value of the dollar rose, import prices fell and domestic producers were forced to become more price competitive. The result was a further dampening of the measured inflation rate during this four-and-a-half-year period of dollar escalation. Superimposed over the deflationary effects of dollar appreciation was the big decline in oil prices that started gradually in 1983 and 1984 but turned into a collapse by the end of 1985. The price of a barrel of crude fell from the $35 level to near $10. The oil price bust temporarily drove the inflation rate to zero in 1986. Together, these two forces held the inflation rate artificially lower through 1986.

In short, the domestic "core" inflation rate was fundamentally not as high as it appeared just before disinflation began; nor was it as low as it looked for several years after 1981. Nevertheless, the fundamental cause of the change in the underlying domestic inflation rate was the change in monetary policy dating back to late 1977, when the M2 growth rate was reduced to a less inflationary pace—a pace similar to that of the early 1960s and consistent with an inflation rate of 5%. That the inflation rate dipped below this level was the happy coincidence of the foreign variables and declining velocity.

□ **The Tardy Recession**   After studying so many recessions, we have surely established by now what consistently causes them in this country. In virtually every case, the drop in output has been preceded by a significant decline in the growth rate of the money supply. And we have seen that time after time, the contraction has started within a year after monetary tightening. The deflationary effects of the tightening have then consistently followed, but after approximately two more years have elapsed. It will come as no surprise, therefore, to discover that this recession too was caused by a monetary slowdown. Nonetheless, the 1981–82 recession is probably the most difficult recession of all to explain. Because the monetary slowdown began in 1977, it is perplexing that this recession occurred four years later, after the disinflation had already begun.

If we look back to late 1977, it is possible both to see that the roots of the 1981–82 recession stretch back that far and to explain why the recession was so slow in arriving. Given the economy's track record, it would have been reasonable to predict a recession for 1978 or 1979. And many people did. Instead, output rose by a robust 6.2% in 1978, faster than the previous year. What kept the economy from sliding into a recession was an incredible surge in the velocity of money. Driven upward by inflationary expectations and rising interest rates, velocity began rising in late 1977 and jumped up by more than 6% in 1978 (see Figure 5). Thus, even though the 1978 M2 growth rate was down by about 4% from a year earlier, the aggregate demand growth rate, riding the boost from velocity, was actually 2% swifter in 1978. No wonder the economy performed better in 1978 than 1977; demand was rising faster in 1978 despite the money slowdown.

The velocity surge continued at a slower pace throughout 1979. As a result, aggregate demand growth was off somewhat that year, and the economy responded appropriately with a stagnant year of less than 1% expansion. In all, the two-and-a-half-year elevation of velocity raised the rate of money turnover by more than 9%. That almost entirely offset the contractionary effects of the money slowdown and delayed the serious impact of the Fed's new policy by as much as two years—much as the decline in velocity in the early 1960s had delayed the impact of the money growth acceleration.

This brings us to Volcker's first year, which we discussed in chapter 8. The money supply growth rate was turned down another notch during the first six months of money targeting, starting in October 1979, as M2 grew at a 5.4% rate. With velocity snapping back downward as well, aggregate demand growth came to a halt by the second quarter of 1980. A nasty drop in output occurred during that quarter. The recession that had been put off for two years appeared to begin with a vengeance. But the Fed panicked and flooded the economy with money from May through August. At the same time, velocity, spurred by inflationary expectations, shot back upward. Aggregate demand surged ahead and pulled the economy out of the brief recession. The net result over this one-year period was a rate of increase in aggregate demand of nearly 10%, which was faster than in the previous two years. The money targeting strategy was designed to help the Fed slow aggregate demand, and for the first six months it did. But by the end of the first year, the money supply surge outweighed the earlier tightening and left aggregate demand growing distinctly faster than before. The 1980 roller coaster gave us a preview of the "tardy" recession, but in the end that recession was delayed another year.

After three years of slower money supply growth, the economy had avoided the kind of recession that had previously occurred shortly after such slowdowns. During that time, money growth had been reduced by a total of 12% relative to the growth path projected had money growth stayed on the 1975–77 course. Such a money supply deceleration usually drags down aggregate demand and sets off a recession. A combination of factors, dominated by velocity, held the recession at bay. During the same three-year period, velocity rose by more than 12%, completely canceling in the end the overall effect of the monetary slowdown. The economy had dodged the recession bullet for three years because of a totally unpredictable swing in velocity. That was the good news. The bad news was that, given that M2 velocity has a zero trend over the long run, such an extraordinary upward swing in velocity was sure to be followed by a downward swing that was at least as extraordinary. When that reversal occurred, a major drop in aggregate demand finally sent the economy into the long-dreaded recession. The reversal came in 1981. As a result, the recession came about nine months after the much-delayed fall in aggregate demand finally began. The recession was actually right on schedule; it was the drop in aggregate demand that was three years late.

The Fed tried once again in 1981 to hold the money supply within its target ranges. Unfortunately, the governors soon discovered that hitting M1 targets, a task difficult enough in the previous year, had become doubly difficult because of bank deregulation legislation that took effect in 1981. The Monetary Control Act of 1980, among other things, formalized the creation of interest-bearing checking accounts (NOW accounts). These accounts were included with other checking accounts in both M1 and M2, while savings accounts and certificates of deposit continued to be counted only the more encompassing M2. Anytime market interest rates on the NOW accounts climbed, many people shifted funds from savings to checking accounts. The result left no change in M2, or the amount of money available in the economy, but it created a bulge in M1. A drop in interest rates produced the opposite flow. M1 figures became increasingly buffeted by the shifts in funds, making the interpretation of M1 data very difficult and potentially misleading. One solution was to target M2 instead, as some monetarists had called for all along. But the Fed had promised to target M1 and had made such an issue about it that Volcker was determined to stick with the plan. Doing so would not be easy.

Shocked by a March/April 1981 surge in the money supply numbers that sent M1 up at an annual rate in excess of 20% (and M2 up at a 17% rate), the Fed was uncertain how to respond. Was this a short-term aberration that should be ignored or at least discounted, or should the Fed relive 1980 and counteract this surge with a major correction? The debate among the governors and between the Fed and the White House was animated. The governors decided to take a middle course but to lean in the contractionary direction. After the overreaction of the preceding summer, which Volcker was still trying to live down, he hoped any errors in 1981 would be in the direction of slower money growth. The White House concurred. M1 growth was halted for six months, while M2 growth was slowed to a moderate 7.8%.

By October 1981, the second year of the Fed's avowed money targeting showed a 9% M2 growth rate and a 5% M1 rate. Neither figure was particularly striking in either direction. For all its fanfare, the two years of money targeting had produced no significant change in the money supply growth rate from the rate achieved during the preceding two pre-Volcker years. Many accounts of this period emphasize that the monetary tightening that occurred during Volcker's first two years precipitated the 1981 recession. Those assessments are based strictly on interpretations of interest rate movements; money supply figures simply do not bear out the view. Despite the wide month-to-month variations in the money supply growth rates, the annual M2 rates were quite steady, around the 9% level. The Fed could have been charged with drunken driving for swerving its car out of both sides of its lane, but in its own defense it could point out that it did average down the center of the lane.

What finally set off the recession was the plunge in velocity, which began in 1981, and the effect it had on interest rates. By 1981, the contractionary effects of almost four years of decelerated money supply growth had been stored up and temporarily neutralized by the climb in velocity. In the middle of that year velocity started to plunge, falling 6% by the end of the year. That was enough to counteract most of the growth in M2, and it dropped the growth of aggregate demand from the 10% and faster rates prevailing over the previous three to six years down to 3%. Aggregate demand stalled, and the Fed was determined not to rush in and try to rescue the economy from a recession this time. From 1981 to early 1983, velocity fell as far as it had risen during the preceding three and a half years. In doing so, it finally brought to bear the effects of the monetary slowdown, and it concentrated those effects in 1981 and 1982. The economy would now have to get used to the slower growth in aggregate demand, and it would have to do that all at once.

The velocity nosedive had a substantial impact on interest rates. When velocity falls, that means people are holding on to more money and holding it for longer periods. This means an increase in the demand for money, and it makes money more scarce. This surge in money demand in the spring of 1981 came just as the Fed was counteracting the March/April money bulge. Thus, at the same time the Fed was squeezing the money supply, money demand was rising. The mechanics of supply and demand produced a jump in interest rates as the prime rate soared above 20%. Though interest rates had shot up this way in 1980 and set off a recession, this episode would be worse. The 1981 interest rate escalation came at a time when the inflation rate had begun to subside. With market rates shooting up and the inflation rate sliding down, real interest rates jumped to more than 10% for the first time since the Great Depression. Over the past 150 years of American economic history, the five previous episodes of real interest rates in excess of 10% have been associated with serious economic contractions—as in 1839, 1920, and 1930. The 1981–82 recession would be no exception.

Real interest rates remained above the 10% level for five quarters. The inflation rate had subsided to near 5% by early 1982, but market interest rates remained in the upper teens. The real cost of borrowing money, especially in the short term, was suffocatingly exorbitant. The sectors of the economy that were struck hardest by the recession were those most sensitive to interest rates. Capital investment and exports took the brunt of the contraction, while consumption and government spending did not fall. Every time the real interest rate moved up, capital spending dropped dramatically in the face of such high borrowing costs. During the fourth quarter of 1981 and all of 1982, domestic investment plummeted 26%. That same five-quarter period saw exports drop by more than 15%.

The loss of exports resulted from a chain reaction that started with the high real interest rates. Foreign financial investors were attracted to the high real rates of return on American securities. Many foreigners brought their savings to the United States to invest in its financial markets. To make these purchases, the foreigners had first to acquire dollars, an aspect that drove up the demand for the dollar. As a result, the value of the dollar soared. Although we have already noted that this movement helped bring down the inflation rate, it also depressed U.S. exports by making them so much more expensive to potential foreign buyers.

The recession was concentrated in the industrial and agricultural sectors, which relied on capital investment and exports, respectively. The service sector went virtually untouched. The national unemployment rate reached almost 11% by the end of 1982, with most of the lost jobs located in the Northeast and the upper Midwest. Many southern and western states escaped the recession entirely. The price of slowing money growth and the inflation rate was borne disproportionately by only part of the population. Such persons were punished for the Fed's ill-advised policy of excessively rapid money growth in the 1970s, its inability to bring the growth rate down in an orderly fashion, and the inflationary expectations fostered by both these failings.

As the recession worsened throughout 1982, the Fed became the target of progressively more heat from the White House and Congress. When an upward surge in M1 occurred at the beginning of the year, the Fed was forced into another targeting corner, and Volcker began to squirm under the pressure. His avowed targeting was itself the target for most complaints. The surge pushed interest rates down and renewed hopes for an early recovery. But it also prompted the Fed to tighten the screws, and that sent interest rates shooting back up again. The level of interest rates and the intensity of complaints were positively related. Even though money growth was still on the same general path as it had been, falling velocity continued to exert its upward pressure on interest rates. And the large federal deficit did not help, since it increased the demand for loanable funds. To bring rates down would require the Fed to abandon its anti-inflation course. Given that the slogan coming from the White House was "stay the course," Volcker decided to stick to his plan at least a little longer.

By July 1982, the summer heat was magnified by the criticism the Fed was getting from all directions. The financial markets were in disarray because of the mounting foreign debt crisis. American banks had lent Third World nations tens of billions of dollars in the late 1970s, and the interest rates on these loans had shot up with other American rates. Mexico and other countries found themselves unable to keep up with their payments, and this situation put many American banks' survival in peril. Weary of the recession and the targeting debate, the Fed quietly moved in July to bring interest rates down. M1 growth was accelerated dramatically, and the discount rate was forcefully pushed down step by step. In other words, the Fed formally abandoned money targeting and returned to interest rate targeting. There was no great fanfare, as there had been three years earlier when the new system was adopted. In fact, the official pronouncement did not come until October, and the press was informed secondhanded. But the change was already obvious to almost everyone. By the end of the year, short-term rates fell by 6% and long-term rates dropped by 4%.

It is not that the Fed increased the money supply so much that rates fell. M2 growth increased only slightly. By taking the interest rate–oriented action, however, the Fed dramatically changed market expectations. Why that happened is hard to say. But it is clear that with very little effort the Fed was able to convince the markets that interest rates were coming down. When enough people believe interest rates are going to fall, their reactions will cause those rates to fall. Once convinced, the market did most of the work, for the demand for securities rose, rapidly driving their prices up and sending interest rates down. Furthermore, inflationary expectations finally came down in line with the current inflation rate. That too put downward pressure on rates and helped bring real interest rates down from 11% to 6% in just a few months. With real interest rates at 6%, investment was sure to rebound, and the economic turnaround was only a few months away. In fact, industrial production headed back up starting in December 1982, and the economy set off on a robust recovery and a lengthy expansion.

☐ One Deficit Leads to Another

Both the Fed and the White House basked in the glow. They took full credit for bringing down the inflation rate and setting off a strong and prolonged expansion that was not accompanied by the standard reacceleration of inflation. In fact, both did deserve some praise. Although the Fed gets low grades for its month-to-month recklessness, its chief accomplishment was that it did "stay the course" and keep the money supply growth rate from returning to the double-digit level of the 1970s. And Reagan helped the anti-inflation battle by consistently favoring slow money growth and generally supporting the Fed's goals, if not its exact operations. The Reagan-era deficits may have made Volcker's job tougher, but that was outweighed by Reagan's commitment to adhere to his original policy of disinflation and minimal government intervention. Reagan was the first president since Eisenhower to ignore the urge to use expansionary policy for short-term political gains. He did not call for easier monetary policy, and he actually agreed to a tax increase, as we will see, in 1982. By 1983 and 1984, the combined picture of monetary and fiscal policies had been quite successful at putting the economy on a low-inflation growth path. The big drawback was the ever-expanding budget deficit. Nobody liked it, but nobody was able to stop its growth, and many worried it endangered the newly established prosperity.

☐ **Budget out of Control**   What caused the budget deficit to grow so much? That is a good question, one that draws a variety of responses, even from the people who made the policy in the Reagan administration. Three main sources can be identified:

1. The Economic Recovery Tax Act (ERTA), which (a) cut marginal tax rates in 1981, 1982, and 1983 and (b) established tax bracket indexing to begin in 1985
2. Increases in government spending or failures to reduce spending
3. The recession

ERTA was really designed simply to end tax bracket creep by counteracting the increases in tax rates and revenues that were expected to occur until 1985, when tax rates were scheduled to be indexed. Thus, the bill's designers sought only to halt the rise in the tax-to-GNP ratio. As discussed earlier, the tax cut had more bite than originally planned. Congress broadened the tax cuts and increased their revenue reduction impact by 25%. Worried as early as 1982 about the ballooning deficit, Congress passed the Tax Equity and Fiscal Responsibility Act (TEFRA), which left income tax rates alone but raised enough revenues from other sources to counter the extra tax cut added into the ERTA.

Of more lasting influence on tax revenues after 1981 was the rate of inflation, which fell faster than White House advisers or anybody else expected. Disinflation slowed tax bracket creep well below projections and turned the ERTA into a cut in real taxes rather than merely a prevention of inflation-induced real increases. Consequently, the ERTA slowed the growth of tax revenues faster than expected. Some blame the tax cuts—which by 1988 had probably reduced tax revenues by $500–700 billion—for the growth of the deficits; they have a valid point, since taxes were cut more than anyone planned.

Others blame the growth in federal spending, which persisted unabated during the Reagan years. One truly must wonder how rapidly government spending would have grown under a president who was not an avowed fiscal conservative and budget cutter. By the end of 1984, government spending in real terms was 15% higher than Reagan's advisers had predicted four years earlier. That amounts to close to $130 billion of extra spending annually after adjusting for inflation. Subtract those excess expenditures from actual outlays, and all growth in the real deficit is more than eliminated. Of course, to note that expenditures ran above the Reagan projections is somewhat meaningless when we consider that the Reagan projections of spending cuts were so unspecified and in many cases totally unrealistic. Nevertheless, it can still be argued that the growth of the deficit and the failure to balance the budget as projected can be blamed primarily on the failure to meet the original aggregate spending goals. Whose fault is that? With close to 85% of the budget declared off-limits by Reagan, and the rest viewed as equally untouchable by Congress, the White House and Congress must clearly share the blame for the growth in spending.

Regardless of which causal factor—spending or taxes—deserves more blame for increasing the structural deficits, there is no debate over the impact of the recession on the actual deficits. As we know, the Reagan projections for GNP in the rosy scenario were not consistent with the disinflation policy being conducted by the Fed. Had the administration made more realistic assumptions, those allowing for a major slowdown or contraction in the economy, it might have been more apparent that bigger deficits were guaranteed to arise. Serious adjustments to the tax cut or spending plans might have been made. As it was, the recession, by driving tax revenues down and pushing transfer expenditures up, greatly magnified the deficit. In fact, the recession doubled the deficit in 1982 and increased deficit paranoia enough to prompt the midrecession tax hike (TEFRA). But by 1985, the effects of the recession on the budget had passed. By then, the gap between the actual and the structural deficit had almost disappeared. The remaining deficit, which had risen from 2% of GNP in 1981 to more than 4%, was by that time solely attributable to some combination of the tax cut and spending increases.

While there can be no denying that the deficits would have been substantially smaller had Congress not passed the tax cuts, spending increases obviously contributed a great deal to the expanding deficits. After the recovery began in 1983 and the final phase of the ERTA took effect later that year, the temporary decline in tax revenues came to an end. In fact, tax revenues leapt up by 22% in 1984 and 1985. Nonetheless, the deficit increased. Even when tax revenues were rising at their fastest rate, they could not keep up with the increases in government spending. All in all, by 1990 the economy had experienced eight straight years of expansion, during which time tax revenues flowing into the Treasury were annually bolstered by increased economic activity. From 1983 to 1990, tax revenues rose by 76%, faster than money GNP. In the past, economic expansions of virtually any length had led to a shrinking of the deficit as tax revenues rose and transfer payments fell. But that was not the case in the 1980s. Clearly the inability to control the growth of government spending allowed the deficit to (a) expand in the immediate postrecession years and (b) persist unchecked for the rest of the decade.

What is not so clear is whether higher tax rates and greater tax revenues would have helped prevent or narrow the deficit. Spending might simply have increased more rapidly without the deficit as a constraining factor. As George Bush insisted in 1988, it was not for a lack of tax revenues that the budget ran a deficit. He too had a good point. There had been a minority opinion within the camp of the tax cut supporters that the only way to bring spending down was to take away Congress's allowance, first by cutting taxes. If a deficit arose, all the better in contributing to a crisis atmosphere that might force Congress to cut spending. Those who had hoped the tax cut would force Congress to trim spending were certainly guilty of wishful thinking. The economy survived quite well despite the deficits. No crisis occurred. Congress soon realized that large deficits and a ballooning national debt were not such an issue, and that realization took away a major incentive to shrink the deficit. Meanwhile, the fact that the economy continued to hum along added no urgency to deficit reduction plans.

At this point, the Gramm-Rudman (eventually titled Gram-Rudman-Hollings Act) amendment came into the picture. Whereas the existence of the deficits did not create a crisis atmosphere to motivate Congress, the Gramm-Rudman bill was designed to create an artificial crisis. This 1985 bill set descending deficit targets for future years. If Congress failed to meet these targets, automatic across-the-board spending cuts would be mandated. Of course, most of the safety net was made immune to the cuts. But all those dollars spent on defense and other discretionary programs would come under the indiscriminate budget knife. The bill's clout was greatly reduced when a constitutionality question forced a reworking of the rules. Ultimately, both Congress and the president figured out a variety of "creative accounting" methods to meet the bill's requirements without really cutting the deficit. Some of the early tricks included postponing spending plans to later budget years and selling off federal property—Band-Aid solutions. Later, during Bush's presidency, surpluses in the social security trust fund were borrowed to cancel out enough of the deficit to meet the targets.

By 1990, the budget deficit without the social security transfer was nearly $300 billion, and the government was no closer to solving the deficit problem than it had been in 1985. After eight years of prosperity, the government had no excuse for not balancing the budget—except the inability of government to control its spending. And the voting public was no help, since Americans consistently refused to accept either the tax hikes or the spending cuts necessary to eliminate the deficit. The budget was out of control.

☐ **Deficit Consequences**   The budget deficits of the 1980s and their effect on the rapidly growing federal debt became a cause of increasing but changing concern throughout the decade. Early on, the anxiety concentrated on how the deficits might derail the expansion.

Later, after the expansion proved immune to the deficits' effects, appre-
hension mounted over the long-run effects of growing internal and external debts on economic growth, the living standards of future generations,
and the independence of the American economy. The ramifications of the
deficits and debt were much more far-reaching and complicated than
simple Keynesian concerns about aggregate demand management or politicians' warnings about leaving the nation's grandchildren so many debts
to pay. In fact, through all the interdependencies of the economy, the
state of the macroeconomy was linked to the deficits, and one cannot
understand the economy of the 1980s—or the future, for that matter—
without a clear picture of how it all works together. Fortunately, even
though most people did not have this picture, to tune it in is quite simple.

   We have looked at part of the picture earlier in the chapter, but let
us go over all the interconnections between budget deficits and the rest
of the economy.

1. Large government deficits greatly increase the demand for
   loanable funds.
2. Increased loan demand drives up interest rates.
      At this point policymakers reach a fork in the road and
      must choose between two paths.

   Path A:

3. The Fed increases the money supply to hold down interest
   rates. Large deficits lead to large increases in the money supply and to a probable acceleration of inflation after two or
   three years. Economists call this monetizing the deficit.
4. Inflation acts as a tax on the private sector, reducing households' and businesses' share of the national income so that the
   government can hold on to its increased share. Inflation also
   increases the demand for imports, while making exports too
   expensive for foreigners. The net outflow of dollars from the
   country drives down the value of the dollar in the world currency market.

   Or Path B:

3. The Fed does not increase the growth rate of the money supply
   but does allow interest rates to increase. No inflation results,
   but interest rates do go up.
4. High interest rates discourage capital investment, which economists call the crowding-out effect. The excess of government
   spending over taxes, or government dissavings, soaks up a major portion of savings-fed loanable funds and leaves less for

capital investment. Investment falls in proportion to the size of the deficit. Excess government spending crowds out private spending.

5. High interest rates also draw foreigners with savings to invest their savings in American financial markets. The inflow of funds helps alleviate the relative scarcity caused by government borrowing and allows interest rates to subside enough to encourage capital investment. Investment is no longer crowded out by government borrowing and high interest rates. Government borrowing is essentially financed directly and indirectly by the inflow of foreign funds.

6. Foreign investments in American financial markets (foreigners buying corporate and government interest-earning securities) drive up the demand for the dollar. The value of the dollar in world currency markets rises.

7. The rise in the value of the dollar makes imports cheaper and exports more expensive and leads to a major widening of the balance of trade deficit. Because the flow of currencies into and out of the country is naturally balanced every year by movements in the value of the dollar, every dollar flowing into the financial markets must generate a dollar flowing out in the goods market. The crowding-out effect hits American producers of exports and producers of goods competing with imports.

Path A (3 and 4) accurately describes the economy during the 1960s and the 1970s. In an effort to hold down interest rates in the face of large government deficits, the Fed moved to progressively higher plateaus of money growth. Inflation and eventual stagnation were the results. In the 1980s Path B (3–7) was followed, as the Fed held down the money supply growth rate in the face of growing federal budget deficits. From 1983 on, investment avoided most of the crowding-out effect because the massive inflow of foreign savings into the American financial markets kept U.S. interest rates down. The value of the dollar soared until 1985, and the balance of trade deficit ballooned, placing the burden of the deficit spending on the trade sector.

The period 1981 to 1985 was a difficult one for the country's industrial sector. The recession, as noted, struck hardest there because of the unusually high real interest rates. Another factor was the impact of the rising value of the dollar. Whenever the dollar rose in currency markets, the price of American goods to foreigners went up as well. Between 1980 and 1985, the trade-weighted value of the dollar soared 82% and the price of American exports climbed proportionately. Much was made about the lack of American competitiveness, how American products were not as good as foreign products, how these products were more expensive, and how American workers were not as productive as their foreign counterparts.

Most of that talk was off the mark. How could American products compete with an 82% surcharge tacked onto their price? This was not the producers' or workers' fault. Nor was it the fault of any new unfair foreign trade practices supposedly adopted in the 1980s by America's trading partners. Many members of Congress thought the solution to the trade deficit problem lay in restrictions on imports, and Reagan was forced to fight trade restriction bills to the point of using his veto. The blame should have been directed at the rising dollar and the forces driving it up—federal budget deficits and the consequent high interest rates. There was nothing wrong with American workers that a balanced budget could not have solved.

Regardless of the blame, many jobs were lost in the industrial-manufacturing sector. Much was made of the stagnation of the Rust Belt, the geographic area from Pennsylvania westward to Illinois, where many factories, including steel mills, auto plants, and tire works, were closed permanently. This market was taken over by import substitutes, seemingly all from Japan. On the other hand, American producers were forced into programs to improve efficiency, cut costs in light of the impacts of the rising dollar, and specialize in products wherein cost advantages still existed or could be created. By the latter part of the decade, when the dollar returned to its 1980 level, the economy was a significantly leaner and more competitive production machine. Interestingly, a leading sector, and at times *the* leading sector, in propelling the continued expansion became exports.

Slowly but surely, exports began catching up to imports and the trade deficit progressively narrowed. But by 1990, that gap still remained at more than $100 billion a year. By that time, the balance of payments (trade, services, and capital flows) had established a fairly stable equilibrium, and the value of the dollar had settled down from its ascent and descent in the 1980s. The inflow of currency into the American financial markets was being balanced by the trade balance deficit. The surge in foreign buying of American financial assets was creating some interesting developments.

In 1985 the United States, according to government measurements, became a net debtor nation for the first time since 1914 (see chapter 2). This means that the sum of American assets (both public and private) owned by foreigners was now more than the sum of foreign assets owned by Americans. From 1980 to 1985, the federal government had added more than $880 billion to the federal debt. A large majority of that excess government spending was financed by the savings of foreigners, because American households and corporations were barely saving enough to keep up with domestic capital investment. In other words, the federal budget deficits were primarily being financed by foreign funds. That does not mean most of the government securities being issued by the Treasury were being bought by foreigners; rather, it means the amount of American securities in general annually being bought by foreigners was almost equal to the amount of newly issued Treasury debt. Foreign funds annually were making up the difference between the total supply of savings by American consumers and corporations (about $650 billion in 1985) and the total demand for those savings by consumers, corporations, and the borrowing federal government (about $760 billion in 1985). Take away the federal deficits, and the demand would not have exceeded the supply, interest rates would not have been so high, foreign funds would not have been needed, and the United States would not have become a net debtor nation. The dollar amount of the swing in America's financial position vis-à-vis the rest of the world in the 1980s from net creditor to net debtor was very similar to the amount by which the federal debt grew during that time.

Matters seemed only to get worse toward the latter part of the 1980s. The consumer savings rate continued on the downward course it had been on since the early seventies, and corporate savings dipped as well. By 1987, the American private sector's savings rate was down from more than 20% to 15% and the gap between the demand for loanable funds and the domestic supply was widening. Foreign funds automatically flowed in to fill that gap. By 1990, consumers were saving somewhat more, but the net indebtedness of the United States to the rest of the world was measured to be well past $600 billion and climbing. Many economists and lawmakers began sounding alarms.

In actuality, this ballooning indebtedness was more apparent than real. Under closer scrutiny, it was discovered that the government calculations of indebtedness were biased. The government assessed the value of an asset at its original purchase price, rather than its current market value. This meant that most American-owned foreign assets were drastically undervalued in the calculations, because they had been acquired many years earlier, whereas most foreign-owned American assets were recent purchases. Net annual income payments on all these assets were still flowing into the United States at the end of the 1980s, thereby indicating that the country had not really become a net debtor—yet. Nevertheless, federal budget deficits had much to do with the swing in the country's position during the decade. If the inflow continued in the financial markets, the debt situation would only deteriorate further, and it would continue as long as federal budget deficits pushed the demand for loanable funds beyond the supply.

The bright side of the story was that the funds that had flowed into the country had helped fuel a substantial amount of economic growth. From that increased capacity, the future bills would have to be paid. The United States had followed the route of many entrepreneurs by borrowing heavily to increase the nation's capital stock. Americans' wealth and income was much higher as a result, but so were their debts.

☐ Keeping the Expansion on Course

In spite of one doomsday prediction after another, the worst stock market crash since 1929, the uncontrollable budget deficit, the savings and loan crisis, and numerous other threatening forces, the expansion that started in 1983 continued unabated right on into 1990. Economic history suggested that a recession was inevitable, since every expansion had ended sooner or later with a recession. No peacetime expansion had stayed afloat so long or so stubbornly in the face of so many seemingly lethal torpedoes. Economists made it a habit to predict "no recession this year but maybe next year." As a result, they were half-right every year. Like the little train that thought it could, the economy chugged right along.

The durability of the expansion said much about the status of stabilization policy before the 1980s relative to the course established by policymakers near the end of the decade. A review of all the recessions we have studied throughout this book shows that almost every one was touched off by a change in government policy that pushed down aggregate demand. Most of those contractionary policy moves were engineered to battle inflation or to head off anticipated inflation surges, and most of those policy moves came from the Federal Reserve. The Fed has had a nasty habit of turning the money faucet on too fast and then turning it down hard as a reaction, as if the faucet handle had been sticking because of rust. One can make a strong argument for the case that, particularly since 1960, had the Fed avoided the upward surges in the money supply, it could have avoided the downward corrections. In so doing, the Fed would have avoided many of the problems encountered from 1960 to 1990.

During the last half of Volcker's eight-year term, which ended in 1987, and during Alan Greenspan's first two years at the Fed's helm, the Fed managed to avoid the extended upward surges in money supply that had previously prompted the negative corrections. After giving the economy a two-quarter surge in the money supply right at the beginning of 1983, the Fed settled into a dependable pattern of moderate money growth. As Table 9 and Figure 3 clearly demonstrate, the money supply growth rate was on a downward trend from 1983 to 1989. In fact, the average annual M2 growth rate of less than 5% from the beginning of 1987 to the middle of 1989 was the best display of noninflationary policy since the 1950s. Even though the Fed was no longer paying lip service to official monetary targeting, its policy had come closer to monetarist standards of slower and steadier money growth. None of those annual rates of money growth was high enough to push the core inflation rate out of the 3–5% zone in which it had stayed for a surprising eight years. Since there was no extended surge of inflation, there was never a need for a significant contractionary slowing of the money supply. The money supply and aggregate demand stayed on a fairly smooth growth path, and so did output and prices.

In addition to a minor dip in 1986, the economy had to weather the great stock market crash in 1987. The economy ignored that crash for two reasons. First, the Fed acted promptly and added liquidity to the financial markets in the face of the stock sell-off. Second and more important, this crash, like the one in 1929, had a modest effect on aggregate demand. Even a crash of that magnitude is likely to lower aggregate demand by less than 2% at maximum. So long as the money supply and velocity do not take a nosedive, a stock market crash will not cause a recession. In 1987 the Fed made sure such a recession did not happen. The 1987 experience proved that the 1929 crash did not cause or even greatly contribute to the Great Depression. It was a symptom, not a cause.

After 1987, the next threat to the expansion came in 1989. By the middle of 1988, unemployment had fallen below 5.5%. This was a striking accomplishment, considering how many economists had unwisely stated that the economy had reached full employment in 1985 and 1986, when the unemployment rate stalled at just over 7%. These assessments came despite the fact that capacity utilization was well below standards associated with full employment. As the unemployment rate approached 5%, everybody agreed that unemployment was at or near its natural rate, since capacity utilization was finally approaching full-employment levels. Not wanting to allow the economy to catch a new batch of demand-pull inflation after avoiding it for so many years, the Fed was determined to slow aggregate demand but to do so in such a way as to not set off a recession. This would be delicate work given the sometimes uncontrollable or unpredictable nature of the money supply and velocity. Greenspan hoped to slow the growth of the money supply just enough to engineer what became widely known as a "soft landing," wherein output rises a bit slower than is preferred but the inflation rate stays the same. In other words, the Fed was trying to keep the economy in equilibrium near full employment—without going past that goal and causing inflation or falling short of it and setting off a recession.

Much to the surprise of many, Greenspan was temporarily success-ful at accomplishing the soft landing, although output expansion had slowed to a crawl. Not that Greenspan had no problems. He undoubt-edly slowed the M2 growth rate too much—2.6% from mid 1988 to mid 1989. With M2 rising so slowly, Greenspan was steering the econ-omy periously close to a recession. He tightened M2 so much because he made the common error of forgetting about the three-year lag and thinking the current year's inflation rate is the product of the current year's monetary policy. In 1989 he was battling an inflation surge whose roots reached back to a money surge in 1986 (see Figures 3 and 4). Matters were made worse by inflationary supply-side shocks from a bad harvest caused by a persistent drought. A 3% rise in short-term interest rates clued the Fed into the fact that money was too tight and a recession was near. The governors responded with a year of over 6% M2 growth from mid 1989 to mid 1990, and the economy eked out small output increases into the summer of 1990.

Although interest rates continued to attract most of the Fed's atten-tion during the Greenspan years, a new gauge of the relative inflation-ary impact of monetary policy was also being applied. The measure, called P*, was based on the quantity of money equation we have used so often:

$$P^* = \frac{M2 \times \text{average M2 velocity}}{\text{full-employment real GNP}}$$

P* rises at the rate by which M2 growth exceeds the rate of increase in full-employment output (about 3% annually). Because M2 velocity varies around an unchanged average (the Fed used 1.59), actual prices (P) do not rise at the same rate as P* each year. But because M2 velocity regularly returns to its average, the rates of increase in P and P* ap-proach each other. When P* has been rising faster than actual prices, an acceleration of inflation has followed; when P* has lagged behind P, a deceleration of inflation has followed. A look back at the relative move-ments of P* and P shows that P* can be an accurate predictor of accelera-tions and decelerations of inflation.

P* fell below P in 1978 and stayed there until 1985. The P* guide would have stubbornly predicted that a deceleration of inflation was coming starting in 1978, and it would have continued to do so until 1985. This corresponds precisely to our discussion of the monetary slowdown that started in late 1978 and the deceleration of inflation that finally started in 1981 and continued until 1986. P* exceeded P from 1985 to 1989, and the inflation rate accelerated from 1986 through 1989. By 1989 P* was back below P as a result of Greenspan's slow money growth, and the possibilities of a deceleration of inflation in 1990 looked promising once the supply-side impact of the record winter cold wave worked its way through the economy early in the year.

That the Fed was using a gauge based on the quantity of money equation at the end of the decade is significant. Monetarism, after becoming the "in" economic philosophy at the beginning of the decade, went through a period of serious public doubt during the mid 1980s. The performance of the Fed during the three-year period of avowed money targeting had done monetarism almost irreparable damage. The Fed took interest rates and the economy on such a wild ride, capped off by the recession in 1981 and 1982, that anything associated with monetarism was earmarked for public disdain. Even though true monetarists disavowed themselves of what the Fed was doing—it never came close to hitting its month-to-month targets and never really abandoned interest-rate manipulations—they still suffered from guilt by association. Then some monetarists earned the public disapproval by making several highly inaccurate predictions. By 1985 nobody was listening to monetarists anymore. Their stay on the top of the mountain had lasted only five years.

The monetarist problems revolved around the unreliability of the M1 measure of the money supply compared with that of M2. M1 became a misleading datum with the advent of interest-bearing checking accounts; it was going through wide variations that simply were not true reflections of monetary conditions. In addition, M1 velocity radically changed its secular pattern. Throughout the previous three decades, M1 velocity had risen at a fairly steady pace of 3% a year, and money GNP had risen at an average annual rate equal to the rate of M1 growth plus this 3%. Beginning in 1981, M1 velocity began to fall, and it kept on falling. The quantity equation stopped working. The big topic of discussion and research became the "velocity puzzle." Much effort was expended to determine that M1 velocity had for 30 years risen with interest rates and in the 1980s was falling with interest rates.

To make monetarists look even worse, some of them insisted on predicting a serious inflation acceleration back into double digits through-

out the early 1980s based on those hefty M1 growth figures. Why they
chose to concentrate on M1 figures is a bigger mystery than what velocity
did. Milton Friedman had championed the use of M2 in his book *Monetary History*. Had everyone used M2 figures as a guide, all would have
seen that the money supply was growing in the 9% range, which was
consistent with an inflation rate near 5%. These inaccurate predictions
made all monetarists look bad.

Furthermore, had everyone paid more attention to M2, no one
would have been so puzzled by the movements of velocity. While M1
velocity was breaking a 30-year mold, M2 was performing as usual. It
was still varying, albeit quite widely during the early 1980s, around its
secular average near 1.6. After M2 velocity reached its 30-year peak at
1.8 in 1980, everyone should have anticipated that it was due for a steep
decline. As we noted earlier, every zig in M2 velocity is likely to be
followed by a zag of similar proportion. By 1986 velocity had sunk to
1.55, its lowest level in 30 years. The exorcising of inflation and inflationary expectations produced a major seismic event on the M2 velocity
chart, but by 1989 M2 velocity had returned to its long-run average.
From 1980 to 1990 M2 growth (114%) almost equaled money GNP
growth (103%). Given that output rose by 30% during the decade, 57%
inflation made up the difference:

	Money Supply (M2)	×	Velocity	=	GNP	=	Output	×	Prices
1980	100	×	1.00	=	100	=	100	×	1.00
1990	214	×	0.95	=	203	=	130	×	1.57

Once again, the figures for an entire decade show that the inflation rate
is directly related to the excess of money growth above the increase in
output. In the 1990s the excess was radically lower than in the 1980s,
and the annual inflation rate averaged near 5%.

No wonder the Fed was finding the P* formula such a productive
tool. The quantity of money equation had not lost any of its ability to
predict long-run inflation trends. Had all monetarists remained true to
the equation, monetarism would not have lost so much respect in the
1980s. The monetarist goals once again looked appropriate for putting the
economy on a stable course. In fact, Greenspan set a goal for the economy
of a zero inflation rate. He threw his support behind a proposed congressional bill that would make that goal a policy priority. To meet that goal,
Greenspan needed to squeeze the M2 growth rate down to 3% or lower.
Some strongly doubted whether the economy was able to achieve zero
inflation and maintain full employment. Indeed, in 1989 and 1990 labor
costs were rising at a pace of nearly 5%. As long as wages were rising so

fast, prices would retain upward momentum, and the goals of zero inflation and continued expansion would be incompatible.

The economy's anemic performance in 1989 and early 1990 should have persuaded Greenspan that his plan to reach zero inflation was at that time not in the economy's best interest. Instead, he pressed on in the spring of 1990 and lowered the M2 growth rate to near 2%. For the last eight months of the year M2 grew at a 2.3% annual rate—even slower than during the 1988–89 period and over 4% slower than in the preceding 12 months. History tells us that a money-growth deceleration of 4% is almost certain to cause a recession. With prices rising faster than the money supply, real aggregate demand was falling. Output would surely follow before the end of the year, and the long expansion would finally end.

Whether monetary policy alone would have knocked out the expansion in 1990 we will never know, because the economy received another one-two punch in August 1990. The beginning of the Persian Gulf crisis had oil prices soaring and consumer confidence plummeting. As oil prices doubled to $40 a barrel in a matter of weeks, aggregate supply shrank; and as consumers became more cautious with their spending, aggregate demand was dampened beyond what the tight monetary policy was already doing. The same combination—tight money and expensive oil—that seemingly had caused the two previous recessions made most people predict a recession. The end of the 1980s expansion finally came in the fall months as industrial production and retail sales dropped rapidly. GNP figures for the fourth quarter confirmed that a recession had begun, as output fell at a 1.6% annual rate.

In spite of the fact that the presence of a recession was apparent to all, the Fed pursued its tight money policy right through the end of the year and on into the next. The M2 growth rate slowed to a mere 1.1% during the final quarter of the year, and the January figure was an even 1%. As output sank, the Fed was further slowing money growth as if the board members of the 1920s were back. Why would the Fed pursue such a contractionary policy in the face of a recession? It did so for two reasons: (a) it was more concerned about the inflationary effects of the oil price increases than the negative impact on output, and (b) it was once again using interest rates rather than the money supply as the indicator of relative money ease or constraint. The first reason was consistent with Greenspan's compulsion to fight inflation; the second is another manifestation of reading the wrong signal.

Interest rates were falling during the second half of 1990, particularly during the last quarter. A drop in interest rates is typical during a recession. Many, including the people at the Fed, mistakenly interpreted the falling rates to mean monetary policy was easing. Because M2 growth was slowing, the opposite was true. Greenspan could not understand why there was so much talk in banking circles throughout the year about a credit crunch while interest rates, including the Fed's discount rate, were falling. Besides, the monetary base was rising rather briskly. The answer was right there in the money supply data. Greenspan obviously was not looking in that direction. The Fed seemed to look at everything but M2.

After the Persian Gulf War was swiftly completed in early 1991, the only thing the economy needed to return to its natural expansion path was a money-supply growth rate consistent with expansion. In other words, ending the recession and resuming the expansion was up to the Fed. Economic stability revolved around the Fed's skills. With fiscal policy no longer an operational tool because the budget remained out of control, monetary policy had become the government's sole avenue to a stabilization policy. After the hard-learned lessons of the previous decades, the hope in 1991 was that the Fed would be the source of stability that its actions in the latter half of the 1980s had suggested it was becoming. But the policies of 1989–90 and the weaknesses they revealed also suggested that the search for economic stability was far from completed.

10

Learning from History

THE SEARCH FOR ECONOMIC STABILITY in the United States has entered its ninth decade. The journey, which began with the creation of the Federal Reserve, led the economy through several contractions of varying severity, as well as one serious and lingering bout of inflation, and it carried policymaking through theoretical and practical revolutions and counterrevolutions. In retracing that journey over the preceding nine chapters, we have discovered that economists and policymakers have learned many lessons. Modern stabilization policy has benefited from this learning experience. The continued search for a stable path is much more likely to be successful in future decades because of these experiences. But we have also found that other lessons—made apparent to us by the perspective of retracing the entire journey—await complete acceptance in both academic and government circles. Let us review the journey and some of the more important lessons.

☐ Steps toward Stability

The panic and suspension of payment in 1907, as well as the economic contraction that followed, convinced Congress that the financial system should no longer be permitted to act as a source of economic instability. Political leaders finally decided that a centralized source of liquidity was needed to support the banking system in times of deposit withdrawals and money supply shrinkage. The Fed was born, but it was thrown into the policy arena without the proper tools to control the money supply. Moreover, its directors lacked knowledge about the impact of money supply variations on the economy. The Fed was powerless to battle pre–World War I inflation, and the domination of the Treasury and the White House over the Fed during and after the war reduced monetary policy to a mere vehicle for financing wartime deficit spending.

In an effort to bring postwar inflation under control, the Fed overreacted and drastically reduced the money supply in 1920 and 1921. This overdose of anti-inflation policy precipitated a serious contraction and deflation. Instead of serving as a guarantor against a monetary contraction and economic decline, the Fed's first independent policy move of significance caused both. During the period 1922 to 1929, the Fed seemed to be maturing and developing into a source of economic stability—ironically, far beyond the parameters envisioned by its designers. The development of open market operations provided the Fed with a tool that held out the promise of countercyclical capabilities. The Fed's use of this tool before and during the minirecessions of 1924 and 1927 suggested that the Fed might be able to manipulate aggregate demand. From a more cynical point of view, such use also revealed that the Fed might be capable of setting off recessions as well. Nevertheless, the experiences of the 1920s led the public to believe that the Fed had the power and the skills to promote stability. That was a colossal misjudgment.

Misled by the conviction that the rise in stock prices would necessarily come to a dramatic end and that the ensuing stock market retreat would drag the economy down with it, the Fed turned all its inexperience toward slowing the 1920s bull market. Unable to slow loans for stock purchases, the Fed succeeded only in halting the growth of the money supply and aggregate demand, and thereby triggered the economic contraction that began in 1929. Eventually, those results slaughtered the bull market as well as the illusion of stability. The Fed's reaction to the bank panics that began in 1930 showed it was not even ready to do what it had been assigned to do—that is, provide emergency liquidity to a panic-plagued banking system—let alone act as the economy's gyroscope. The tools were there, but the understanding was not. Misguided by misinterpretations of the level of excess reserves and interest rates (market versus real), the Fed allowed the money supply to shrink by one-third, and it let real interest rates soar into the teens. Money was very scarce and very expensive; aggregate demand plummeted. The Fed's ill-fated excursion beyond its purview into the affairs of the stock market precipitated the economic downturn, and the Fed's irresponsible failure to perform its most fundamental duty turned the downturn into the economy's worst depression.

The inability of Federal Reserve Board members to ward off the depression was interpreted by almost everyone as irrefutable evidence that the Fed itself was incapable of providing economic stability. Those searching for better results headed off in two directions. The New Deal supporters acted on their belief that the economy was inherently so unstable that government needed to build a scaffolding of programs to provide stability. Their efforts succeeded only in weighing down the economy. Simultaneously, the Keynesian revolution was hatched, wherein compensatory fiscal policy was offered as an alternative to monetary policy. The continued mistakes at the Fed (the reserve requirement increases in 1937) and the White House (the bankrupt reflation plans and the continued efforts to balance the budget) lent support to the need for bold new fiscal policy.

The prosperity of World War II offered tangible support for the Keynesian approach. All theoretical policy discussions in the 1940s and 1950s revolved around how best to implement Keynes's prescription for fiscal policy. With the Fed playing a supporting role for the Treasury's wartime deficit financing, fiscal policy was the preferred stabilization tool among the academics. The actual implementation of the fiscal game plan, however, did not come until the Kennedy and Johnson administrations in the 1960s. In the meantime, the Fed's governors spent the 1950s revitalizing monetary policy and reestablishing its potency. As if replaying the 1920s scenario, the Fed confirmed that swings in the money supply growth rate could both start and reverse a recession—that monetary policy had the potential for being a source of either instability or stability, depending on how it was applied.

While the New Frontier economists battled with Congress to activate their fiscal plan, the Fed inconspicuously set off on its own new policy program. The money supply growth rate accelerated dramatically in 1960, and for the next four years the money supply grew significantly faster than output for the first time in peacetime since before World War I. The Fed fueled rapid growth in aggregate demand that propelled the economy to full employment by 1965 and provoked an acceleration of inflation that began as early as 1964.

At this time, the 1964 tax cut ushered in what was supposed to be the beginning of fiscal fine-tuning and the end of the business cycle. Taking full credit for boosting the economy to full employment, even though the tax cut had joined the trip to full employment at the next-to-last stop, fiscal policymakers looked forward to future applications of

Keynesian economics. Many believed the search for stability was over, the solution found.

That optimism was quickly dispelled, and the reliability of fiscal policy came into doubt. The inability of the Johnson administration and Congress to raise taxes to finance increased spending from 1966 to 1968 gave the first hint that fiscal policy was a tool far too politically hot to handle on a regular basis. Visions of frequent adjustments of government spending and taxes to stabilize aggregate demand were dashed by the realization that the political system would not allow such timely and sensitive policymaking. A stabilization tool is of little use if it cannot be used often or requires a long waiting period. To make matters more discouraging, the 1968 tax increase had little or no apparent effect on slowing aggregate demand. That raised the possibility that fiscal policy was not only less reliable but also less potent than previously thought.

Although fiscal policy was not abandoned, policymakers began to turn increasingly to monetary policy as potentially the more effective stabilization tool. The experiences of the late 1960s and early 1970s appeared to confirm that changes in monetary policy had a significant effect on aggregate demand and output. The monetary slowdown in 1969 and 1970 did what the 1968 surtax failed to do—slow aggregate demand—and set off a recession. The acceleration in money growth that followed, from late 1970 through 1972, pulled the economy out of the recession and pushed it to full employment. Then the monetary slowdown in 1973 and 1974 touched off another recession, and the subsequent resumption of rapid money growth produced another recovery. Monetary policy was proving to be a potent tool, but so far its application was producing more, rather than less, instability.

Monetarists argued that monetary policy was in fact potent and could be a source of stability if applied correctly—something that had not occurred in recent years. They contended that a more steady hand on the money supply would automatically bring forth more stability in the growth of aggregate demand and output. Moreover, monetarists claimed that inflation could be greatly reduced, possibly even eliminated, if the growth rate of the money supply was slowed to match the average growth rate of output. Slow and steady money growth was the preferred route to noninflationary stability.

The monetarist prescription slowly gained support throughout the 1970s. That was partly due to the persuasiveness of the argument and the supporting evidence. It can also be attributed to the decline in confidence in fiscal policy as a viable tool for stabilization. The politicization of the budget in the late 1960s and early 1970s greatly handicapped fiscal policymakers. The state of the budget was being determined not by macroeconomic policy considerations but by the whims of special interests. Furthermore, the 1975 tax cut's failure to have a measurable impact on aggregate demand added further doubt about the efficacy of fiscal policy in nondepression situations. By the end of the 1970s—with the budget showing deficits every year regardless of the state of the economy—it became apparent that the search for economic stability was turning increasingly away from fiscal policy. Managing the budget proved to be both politically impractical and economically ineffective.

While the consensus was convinced that swings in monetary policy could touch off movements in output in the same direction with a high degree of reliability, monetarists had a difficult time convincing other economists and policymakers that monetary policy should be based on steady money supply targets. Many doubters feared such a strategy would handcuff policymakers and prevent them from using the money supply as a stabilizing force to counteract other variables that buffet aggregate demand. There was also considerable doubt that the cure for inflation was simply slower money growth. A "slow and steady" approach, many argued, was just too naive. Nevertheless, by the end of the 1970s the policy cupboard was bare except for monetary policy. The monetarist approach looked like the only alternative left. The Fed grudgingly, and only halfheartedly, adopted the monetarist technique in late 1979.

With nonbelievers at the Fed trying to use money supply targeting to exorcise inflation from the economy, the early results were total disarray in 1980 and a recession in 1981 and 1982. Money supply growth rates were anything but steady. The Fed fueled rather than dampened inflationary expectations and greatly increased instability in all markets. Fortunately, even though money supply growth rates were far from steady, starting in late 1977 they were markedly slower on average. With the predictably delayed reaction, the inflation rate began to fall in 1981, and it stayed down for the rest of the decade. The "slow" half of the monetarist prescription proved correct. With money supply growth rates resembling those of the early 1960s, the inflation rate subsided to 1960s' levels. Furthermore, as the Fed became more adept at hitting the lower target ranges—particularly for M2—the economy achieved a stability it had not seen since the early 1960s. It had become apparent to all that the best way to avoid a recession was first to avoid an inflationary surge that would force the Fed to cut down on money supply growth. And the best way to avoid the inflationary surge was to not allow the money supply to grow too fast. Therefore, whether it should be called monetarism or not, slow and more steady became the prescription at the Fed in the mid 1980s.

By 1990 the search for economic stability, which had started with the Fed in 1913, had led back to the Fed. Whether the Fed had the capability to be the ultimate source of stability in the economy remained unclear—particularly after the 1990 recession—but the signs were encouraging. Nonmonetarists insisted that if the Fed was to remain the provider of stability, it had to be able to adapt its policies to changing economic conditions. In other words, the Fed still had to be able to reverse direction whenever necessary and lean into the wind regardless of direction. That required monetary flexibility. While nonmonetarists pictured a small boat on a stormy sea and a very busy captain, monetarists (who had great faith in the inherent stability of the economy) envisioned a large boat on automatic pilot on a mildly choppy sea. Monetarists contended that most of the economy's instability in the stagflation era—indeed, most of the instability throughout the twentieth century—had been primarily caused by the Fed. They maintained that the Fed's inability to determine the wind's force and direction led it to spend more time leaning *with* the wind and magnifying instability. Monetarists contended that the slow and steady approach would act on the economy like ballast on a boat, preventing the boat from swaying too far from side to side. Which view is ultimately right may be determined in the 1990s, or the debate may continue into the next century. Regardless of the preferred policy approach, by process of elimination Americans had settled on the Federal Reserve as their best hope for government-enhanced economic stability.

□ Important Lessons

It is possible to look back at the last 80-odd years and pick out a few lessons that should have been learned by 1990. Some of these lessons have already been incorporated into marked improvements in policymaking. Other lessons, which become apparent on reviewing the journey the economy has taken in the search for economic stability, await acceptance by analysts and/or policymakers before their benefits can be enjoyed. As long as policy is guided by ideas that do not square with these lessons, efforts to achieve stability will be handicapped.

Two lessons involve identifying what was responsible for the acceleration of inflation in the 1960s and the deceleration in the 1980s. It is high time we stopped associating the acceleration of inflation with the Vietnam War and its effects on government spending. First, we saw in chapter 8 that the inflation acceleration predated the expenditures boosts by about two years. Second, given the lagged behavior of movements of the inflation rate, the cause of the acceleration must be traced back to the early 1960s. The money supply grew much faster than in the 1950s and much faster than output. The lag and declines in velocity may have obscured the reasons for the inflation acceleration, but the cause is obvious today. The inflation came from the Fed, and there was no excuse, since budgets were balanced when the Fed hit the money accelerator in 1960.

The credit for slowing the inflation in the early 1980s is usually given to the Fed, and it deserves credit. But the Volcker Fed does not deserve as much of the credit as it is often given; nor does the 1981–82 recession deserve much of the blame. The policy that brought the inflation rate down starting in 1981 was initiated in late 1977 during Arthur Burns's last months in office and continued through the 20 months of William Miller's tenure. The annual M2 growth rate was lowered by 4–5% to around 8%, and the average inflation rate dropped by the same amount. The Reagan administration deserves some credit for being consistently supportive of the disinflation policy throughout the 1981–82 recession, when it would have been easy to opt for expansionary policy. The inflation rate stayed down for the rest of the 1980s because money growth was held to a moderate pace.

Even though most economists and policymakers have been won over to the idea that the key determinant of the economy's inflation rate is the rate of growth of the money supply, many have still missed a pair of important lessons identified in this book. It is apparent that even people within the Fed either do not know or fail to remember that the inflation rate in year X is determined by the rate of growth of the money supply two or three years prior to that year. The decades of the 1960s, 1970s, and 1980s are a testimony to the lag between changes in monetary policy and changes in the inflation rate. Despite this fact, it is common to hear even the Fed's chair discussing this year's inflation rate and this year's money growth rate as if they were closely related. Alan Greenspan tried to fight an inflation surge in 1989—caused by a money surge in 1986—with tight money in 1989, even though history teaches us over and over that the policy would probably affect the inflation rate in 1992. Until the lag mechanics are incorporated into policy decisions, monetary policy will be less stabilizing than we would like.

That same argument goes for recognizing the difference between real and market interest rates and making policy decisions based on real rates rather than the misleading signals sent out by market rates. One cannot explain either the Great Depression or the 1981–82 recession without making the distinction between real and market rate. The inability of some economists to recognize the significance of the double-digit real rates during the monetary contraction of 1929 to 1933 prevents them from properly assessing the impact of the money supply collapse, just as it handicapped the judgement of board members at the Fed. The incredibly low real interest rates in the 1970s clearly show that money was overly abundant and inflationary regardless of the high level of market interest rates. And the return of double-digit real rates in 1981 and 1982 precipitated the contraction in those years.

The search for economic stability has included the birth, development, and retirement of fiscal policy as a stabilization tool. I recently read an article concerning the budget deficit reduction plans that referred to "time-tested fiscal principles." It is easy to guess what those principle are—they are in Keynesian economics sections of every textbook—but, given the track record fiscal policy has established since the 1950s, it is very difficult to believe that fiscal policy has passed the tests of time. After closely studying the tax cuts of 1964 and 1975 and the tax hike of 1968, as well as observing the effects of many budget deficits, it is hard to find solid evidence of fiscal policy having a substantial independent effect on aggregate demand. The impact of World War II spending on the depression remains the only good example of "time-tested fiscal principles." As long as lawmakers can cite these alleged fiscal principles as an excuse for not cutting the budget deficit because "we do not want to cause a recession," the budget may never be balanced. One lesson that arises from our historical survey is that it is time to quit using Keynesian economics as an excuse rather than a guide.

When viewing the entire time period covered in this book, I cannot help but notice that the overwhelming majority of the recessions suffered since 1914 have been primarily caused by bad government policy—and more specifically, bad monetary policy. The recessions that began in 1920, 1929, 1937, 1948, 1960, 1970, 1973, 1980, and 1981 was unambiguously preceded by a major dose of contractionary monetary policy, and the lag between the policy change and the beginning of the output contraction was usually a matter of months. The other recessions, which began in 1953 and 1957, were preceded by milder tightenings of monetary policy. Fiscal policy also contributed somewhat to recessions in 1937, 1953, and 1970. The most important point here is that little evidence supports the notion that the economy tumbles into recessions of any consequence all by itself. The economy has consistently been pushed off the cliff by government policy; it rarely, if ever, jumped.

Economic historians, when discussing the causes of the Great Depression, continue to present the underconsumption theory as a possibility, when it was not a significant factor. Major out-of-the-blue drops in consumption simply do not occur, and such a plunge in consumption did not set off the Great Depression. Private sector spenders, consumers, and business capital investors are simple animals who spend when money is cheap and cut back their spending when money becomes scarce and expensive. Consumption and capital investment fell dramatically from 1929 to 1933 because the money supply fell by one-third and real interest rates rose into the teens. Thinking otherwise defies the over-whelming weight of the evidence. A shadow of a doubt may remain in some people's minds because they have failed to properly consider real interest rates, just as the Fed did in the 1930s. That should not prevent us, however, from placing the preponderance of blame for the severity of the great contraction on the Fed and its failure to do its job. We should close the case on the cause of the Great Depression and declare the Fed—which certainly was aided and abetted by fiscal policy and tariffs—guilty.

The sooner we straighten out our perception of the past, the sooner we will be able to understand the present and anticipate the future. As we saw in the previous chapter, pundits consistently and incorrectly predicted a recession throughout the late 1980s. Their predictions were based on the idea that recessions have periodically occurred in the econ-omy, and the economy was overdue for another. Of course, history does lead one to believe that a recession will inevitably end any expansion, because it has always happened that way. But we have seen that history also tells us that recessions are neither necessary nor predetermined. They are consistently handmade by policymakers in Washington, D.C. As long as the Fed does not allow the money supply to grow too rapidly and touch off inflation or inflationary fears, there is no need for it to decelerate money growth by enough to cause a recession. Moderate M2 growth will ensure that a reasonable amount of money will continue to be available at a reasonable real price and that private-sector spending will continue to grow. Only a major supply-side shock could derail such an expansion. But when the Fed makes a mistake and fuels an inflation-ary boom, a recession can be expected eventually to follow whenever the Fed applies the brakes. But until that mistake occurs, expansion is more an inevitability than is a contraction—that is, unless the Fed makes a similar mistake, as it did in 1990, and tries to eliminate 4% inflation in one year. As long as money decelerations of 3% or more are avoided, the chances of recessions are greatly reduced.

☐ Future Prospects

Even though the search for economic stability has come full circle back to the Federal Reserve, we cannot conclude that the search has been entirely successful, not yet. While there is no doubt the Fed today is much more reliable than the Fed of the 1930s, we must be careful not to be taken in too much by the existence of relative stability. To place the sole responsibility for economic stability on an institution with such a spotty track record is quite risky. But the potential for far greater stability than previously achieved is certainly present because of the lessons we have learned. If the Fed extends the trend of slowing the average money growth rate, which is so evident in Figure 3, continued low inflation rates in the 1990s are a strong possibility. Yet much could still go wrong and make this most recent episode of stability as much of an illusion as was the tranquillity of the 1920s.

The biggest danger facing the Fed in the 1990s will probably come from the many pressures to increase the money supply that built up throughout the 1980s. As long as the annual federal budget deficit continues to exceed $100 billion, the resulting upward pressure on real interest rates will cause many to call for more rapid money growth. The enormous projected costs of the bailouts of savings and loans and insured pension programs are likely to add to that pressure. Major defaults on Third World debts to American banks could still lead to financial crises that the Fed would have to meet with increases in the money supply. And with America on the verge of truly becoming a net debtor, the temptation will be there to debase the value of the dollar and thereby the debts with increases of the money supply. Moreover, there is always the possibility that serious supply-side shocks, such as an energy crisis, could force the Fed to battle aggregate supply reductions with money supply injections. Any one of those motivations could precipitate a monetary expansion that would reignite dormant inflation and set off a series of events all too common in the 1970s. That would bring an end to the latest period of relative economic stability. In the face of those pressures to make monetary policy more expansionary, the Fed chair must proceed virtually alone in the search for the ultimate in economic stability, a full-employment economy with a low inflation rate.

CHRONOLOGY

1913	Creation of the Federal Reserve.
1914–1917	Gold-fueled monetary inflation.
1917–1919	Fed monetizes wartime and postwar deficits; officials at Treasury and Fed disavow blame for inflation.
1920	Major discount rate increase and money supply reduction set off recession of 1920–21.
1923	Fed establishes Open Market Investment Committee after discovering influence of open market operations on money supply.
1924 and 1927	Expansionary monetary policy, designed to aid British efforts to reestablish gold standard, helps boost economy out of mild recessions.
1928–1929	Fed efforts to slow stock market speculation halt money supply growth.
1929	Economic contraction begins in summer; stock market crashes in October.
1930–1933	Series of bank panics drive down money supply.
1931	Fed increases interest rates to prevent gold outflow.
1932	Congress passes major tax increase designed to eliminate budget deficit; Fed tries and abandons expansionary open market operations.
1933	President Roosevelt declares bank holiday; eventually, only 75% of the remaining banks reopen. Roosevelt takes United States off the gold standard and devalues the dollar.

1934–1935	Major banking reform legislation enacted, including creation of the FDIC and the empowerment of the Fed to change reserve requirements. National Industrial Recovery Act drives up wages and prices.
1936–1937	Fed doubles the reserve requirement; money supply falls. Roosevelt abandons pump priming and sets balanced budget as an attainable goal.
1937–38	With economy far from completing its recovery, it suffers a relapse recession. Fiscal policy is contractionary, as government expenditures fall and tax revenues rise both years despite the recession.
1941–1942	Surge in military spending and expanding money supply propel economy to full employment.
1942–1946	Money supply doubles.
1943–1945	Budget deficits exceed $50 billion (50% of 1929 GNP) annually; federal debt exceeds GNP.
1946	With the Employment Act of 1946, federal government takes responsibility for maintaining economic stability. Bretton Woods trade agreement establishes fixed exchange rate system, with dollar as international currency.
1947–1948	Budget deficit replaced by surplus.
1948	Fed raises reserve requirement, and money supply falls for a year. Recession begins at midyear. Congress passes tax cut.
1951	Treasury and Fed reach an "accord" whereby Fed is no longer compelled to hold down interest rates as an aid to Treasury deficit financing. William McChesney Martin begins two-decade tenure as chair of the Board of Governors.
1952	Congress and President Truman use a tax hike and spending cuts to ward off inflation.
1953	Tight policy by Fed early in year contributes to a mild financial panic, which the Fed greets with reductions in reserve requirements.
1953–1954	Post–Korean War "rolling adjustment" recession. President Eisenhower reluctantly accepts a budget deficit, and Fed uses all three monetary policy tools to speed money growth.

1957	Fed stops money supply growth.
1957–1958	A brief recession elicits a switch to a very expansionary monetary policy; Eisenhower tolerates his second recession deficit.
1959–1960	From mid-1959 to mid-1960, Fed pushes the money supply down.
1960	The Eisenhower administration suffers third recession and its accompanying budget deficit.
1960–1965	Fed adopts inflationary policy stance, with 8% annual M2 growth rates.
1964	Inflation acceleration begins. Congress passes major tax cut.
1966–1967	Vietnam War and Great Society spending pushes budget from a surplus to a deficit, with economy already at full employment. Anti-inflationary monetary policy drives interest rates up and sets off a "credit crunch"; the Fed responds by switching policy back to rapid money growth until end of 1968.
1968	Congress passes surtax, an anti-inflationary tax increase.
1969	The Fed greets Nixon's election with a dramatic braking of money supply growth. A combination of contractionary fiscal policy—a federal budget surplus—and tight monetary policy sets off a recession by the end of the year.
1970	Arthur Burns replaces Martin at Fed, and money growth soon rockets to double-digit rates to ward off financial uneasiness caused by Penn Central Railroad bankruptcy. M2 growth averages near 12% for next 30 months. Recession deepens while inflation persists.
1971	President Nixon implements wage and price controls and sets the dollar free from the Bretton Woods system. The value of the dollar begins to sink to true market level.
1973–1974	Fed cuts the money growth rate in half. OPEC oil embargo leads to a quadrupling of oil prices.
1974–1975	Tight monetary policy and surge in oil prices drive output down.

1974   President Ford calls for tax increase and continued restrictive monetary policy to "Whip Inflation Now."

1975   In January, Ford proposes tax cut to battle recession; Congress passes tax rebate later in year. Burns pushes money supply growth rate to 13% level, where it stays until mid-1977.

1977–1979 During Burns's last months and short tenure of G. William Miller, money growth is slowed from 13% to under 9%.

1979   Paul Volcker takes over at the Fed and soon implements stated goal of money supply targeting. In actuality, Fed sets off on year of unequaled monetary instability.

1980   A halting of money growth early in year and a drop in consumer borrowing triggered by announcement of credit controls set off a sharp drop in GNP. The Fed responds with an enormous surge in money growth, and the economy begins to expand again.

1981   Disinflation policy finally shows results, as inflation rate drops from double digits to near 6%. High real interest rates drive investment and exports down as long-awaited recession begins. Congress passes three-year, three-stage tax rate reduction designed by supply-siders to spur economic growth.

1982   Impact of tax cut and recession sends federal budget into deep deficit. As the unemployment rate tops 10%, Fed moves away from money targeting in an effort to bring interest rates down. Congress enacts tax hike in middle of recession to narrow the budget deficit.

1983   Surge in money supply and drop in interest rates touch off a robust recovery.

1985   Value of dollar ends four-year, record climb, during which high U.S. interest rates drive up demand for the dollar and high-valued dollars create record trade deficits. The dollar begins three-year decline. Gramm-Rudman deficit reduction plan enacted.

1987–1989   Alan Greenspan replaces Paul Volcker as Fed chair in 1987 and pursues further reduction in infation rate. M2 growth slows to near 4.5%.

1988–1989   With economy at full employment, Greenspan tries for a "soft landing"—that is, to avoid an inflation acceleration without causing a recession—with mildly restrictive policy. The expansion slows to a crawl.

1989–1990   Fed boosts M2 growth to over 6% for 12 months ending in May 1990 then slows M2 growth to just over 2% for rest of year. Persian Gulf crisis doubles oil prices to $40 a barrel and sinks consumer confidence. Drop in output in fourth quarter brings end to long expansion.

BIBLIOGRAPHIC ESSAY

☐ Chapter 1

The sources for the data in the tables are as follows:

Output—1914–1939, *Historical Statistics of the United States: Colonial Times to 1970*, Series F 31.
1940–1990, *Economic Report of the President*, Table C-2.
M1 and M2—1914–1959, calculated from Friedman and Schwartz, *A Monetary History of the United States*, Table A-1.
1960–1990, *Economic Report of the President*, Table C-67.
P—1914–1939, calculated from *Historical Statistics*, Series F 5.
1940–1990, *Economic Report of the President*, Table C-3.
CPI—*Economic Report of the President*, Table C-58.
GE—1914–1939, *Historical Statistics*, Series Y 466.
1940–1990, *Economic Report of the President*, Table B-76.
GR—1914–1940, *Historical Statistics*, Series Y 352.
1940–1990, *Economic Report of the President*, Table B-76.
UN—1914–1959, *Historical Statistics of the United States*, Series D 86.
1960–1990, *Economic Report of the President*, Table B-110.
PR—Tables 2–6, *Historical Statistics of the United States*, Series X 445
Tables 7–9, *Economic Report of the President*, Table B-71.

When it comes to the big picture of the entire period covered by this volume (or at least most of the period), a few books are excellent sources. On the side of monetary policy, two unbeatable books are *A Monetary History of the United States, 1867–1960* (1963), by Milton Friedman and Anna J. Schwartz, and *The American Monetary System* (1987), by Robert A. Degen. Nothing can compare to the Friedman and Schwartz book as an encyclopedic source for data and interpretation. The material in this book was the foundation of the rebirth of monetarism. Unfortunately, its coverage ends in 1960. Degen's book provides a much more concise summary of monetary institutional and policy changes from the turn of the century to the present. *Secrets of the Temple* (1987), by Wiliam Greider, concentrates on the 1970s and 1980s, but its flashbacks also provide good accounts of earlier periods, such as those during the creation of the Fed and during the depression.

A survey of all forms of economic policies from 1917 to recent years can be found in Anthony Campagna's *U.S. National Economic Policy, 1917–1985* (1987). Although his analysis seems at times to favor outdated sources and Keynesian interpretations, his coverage of fiscal policy is comprehensive. Another source for White House policy from Hoover to Reagan that understandably focuses on fiscal policy is Herbert Stein's *Presidential Economics* (1988), which provides an insider's view that only a former member of the Council of Economic Advisors could give. Finally, current economic history textbooks, like Jonathan Hughes's *American Economic History* (1990), Robert Puth's *American Economic History* (1988), and Gary Walton and Hugh Rockoff's *History of the American Economy* (1990), offer multichapter summaries that are quite informative.

☐ Chapter 2

The best sources for background material on the economy in the days just before the Federal Reserve was created, plus accounts of the Fed's early years, are Friedman and Schwartz's *Monetary History* (chapters 4–5) and Degen's *American Monetary System* (chapters 1–2), as well as James Livingston's *Origins of the Federal Reserve System* (1986) and Robert West's *Banking Reform and the Federal Reserve, 1863–1923* (1977). This last book is probably also the best source for the actual political process that brought about the Federal Reserve Act, but all three are valuable for their insights into the forces behind the creation of the Fed and its first years of operation. For details from insiders' contemporaneous points of view, one can turn to Paul Warburg's *The Federal Reserve System, Its Origins and Growth* (1930), Henry Parker Willis's *The Federal Reserve System* (1923), or W. P. G. Harding's *The Formative Period of the Federal Reserve System* (1923). These three authors are men who were deeply involved in the Fed's early years. One more insider book is *Interpretations of Federal Reserve Policy in the Speeches and Writings of Benjamin Strong* (1979), edited by W. Randolph Burgess, which probes the ideas of one of the most influential men at the Fed in the 1910s and 1920s. On Federal Reserve policy during and after the war, Elmus Wicker's *Federal Reserve Monetary Policy, 1917–1933* (1966) is invaluable for its in-depth investigation of the men and motivations behind monetary policies. A useful source of raw information and interpretation about wartime financing is *Financial History of the United States* (1952), by Paul Studensky and Herman Krooss.

☐ Chapter 3

For the same reasons they were cited in the previous chapter, the most reliable sources for monetary policy in the 1920s remain Friedman and Schwartz's *Monetary History* (chapter 6), Degen's *American Monetary System* (chapter 3), and Wicker's *Monetary Policy*. Harold Reed also packs plenty of information into *Federal Reserve Policy, 1921–1930* (1930). Since this was the decade when Benjamin Strong was so influential at the Fed, Lester Chandler's definitive biography, *Benjamin Strong, Central Banker* (1958), is an important source, as is Benjamin Anderson's less complimentary picture of Strong in *Economics and the Public Welfare* (1979). Chandler provides another excellent view of monetary policy leading up to the depression in *American Monetary Policy, 1928–1941* (1971). Campagna's *National Economic Policy* contributes a good summary of the fiscal policies of the Republican administrations of the 1920s, particularly the tax rate reductions.

For the stock market crash, most people read John Kenneth Galbraith's *The Great Crash, 1929* (1954), but its views are not standing up well to the tests of time, particularly since the 1987 crash. More recently developed ideas can be found in Robert Sobel's *The Great Bull Market* (1968), G. J. Santoni's "The Great Bull Markets 1924–29 and 1982–87: Speculative Bubbles or Economic Fundamentals" (St. Louis Federal Reserve Bank *Review*, 1987), Gerry Gunderson's *A New Economic History of America* (1976, chapter 16), and my own "Macroeconomic Causes and Consequences of Major Stock Market Reversals" (in *Essays in Economic and Business History*, 1989).

☐ Chapters 4 and 5

To avoid repetition, the suggested readings for the two chapters on the Great Depression are combined. Monetary policy during the depression receives thorough coverage from four sources that were useful in the preceding chapter, including Friedman and Schwartz's *Monetary History* (chapters 7–9), Degen's *American Monetary System* (chapter 4), Chandler's *American Monetary Policy*, and Wicker's *Monetary Policy* (up to 1933). Debates over the causes of the depression can be found in Peter Temin's *Did Monetary Forces Cause the Great Depression?* (1976); in *The Great Depression Revisited* (1981), edited by Karl Brunner; and in Thomas Mayer's "Money and the Great Depression: A Critique of Professor Temin's Thesis" (in *Explorations in Economic History*, 1978). See also my own "Depression or Deflation . . ." (in *Essays in Economic and Business History*, 1981) and "Real Interest Rates and Economic Contraction . . ." (*EEBH*, 1986). Entirely different points of view can be found in Murray Rothbard's *America's Great Depression* (1975) and Charles Kindleberger's *The World in Depression, 1929–1939* (1973).

Perhaps the best and most readable single book on the economics of the depression is Lester Chandler's *America's Greatest Depression* (1970), but Michael Bernstein's *The Great Depression* (1988), which takes a more technical and in-depth look at the economy's performance, is also very informative.

When it comes to New Deal policies, in addition to the sources already listed two must-reads are Michael Weinstein's "Some Macroeconomic Aspects of the NIRA" in Brunner's *The Great Depression Revisited* and Cary Brown's revealing "Fiscal Policy in the Thirties: A Reappraisal" (*American Economic Review*, 1956). Of course, John Maynard Keynes's *The General Theory*, "The Means to Prosperity," and his famous *New York Times* open letter of 31 December 1933 (probably the best critique ever of the New Deal's reflation strategy) offer insights into the great theoretical debate over pump priming, as do a series of journal articles in the *History of Political Economy* in 1978 and 1980 by Byrd Jones and Lauchlin Currie. Two books that do a fine job of retracing the steps of the Keynesian revolution are Robert Lekachman's *The Age of Keynes* (1966) and Herbert Stein's *Fiscal Revolution in America* (1969). Once again, Campagna's *U.S. National Economic Policy* is particularly helpful in the area of fiscal policy.

☐ Chapter 6

While monetary policy takes a backseat to fiscal policy in this chapter, the two were inextricably intertwined because of the extraordinary demands of financing the war. Two sources for monetary policy familiar from previous chapters—Friedman and Schwartz's *Monetary History* (chapter 10), and Degen's *American Monetary System* (chapters 5–6)—continue to be useful and necessarily overflow somewhat into fiscal policy in the area of war financing. Campagna's *U.S. National Policy* covers both fiscal and monetary policies.

The best two sources on the evolution of fiscal policy out of Keynesian theories are Stein's *Fiscal Revolution* and Lekachman's *Age of Keynes*. To get a flavor of the development of fiscal policy theories and practices in the 1930s and 1940s, one can scan the articles in the American Economics Association's *Readings in Fiscal Policy*. Wilfred Lewis's *Federal Fiscal Policy in the Postwar Recession* (1962) is also helpful with respect to the 1948 recession. Two excellent interpretive sources on the Bretton Woods agreement are Richard Gardner's *Sterling-Dollar Diplomacy* (1956) and Henry Hazlitt's *From Bretton Woods to World Inflation* (1984).

☐ Chapter 7

Apparently the 1950s were too dull for most economists, for there is a limited supply of sources on this decade alone. Three worth investigating are Harold Vatter's *The U.S. Economy in the 1950s* (1963), Bert Hickman's *Growth and Stability in the Postwar Economy* (1960), and Daniel Ahearn's *Federal Fiscal Policy Reappraised, 1951–1959* (1963). Better sources are those which include the events of the 1950s as part of the bigger postwar picture extending into the 1960s. Well worth reading are Stein's *The Fiscal Revolution in America* and Wilfred Lewis's *Federal Fiscal Policy in the Postwar Recessions* for fiscal policy. Robert Gordon's article "Postwar Macroeconomics: The Evolution of Events and Ideas" (in Martin Feldstein's *The American Economy in Transition*, 1980) and G. L. Bach's *Making Monetary and Fiscal Policy* (1971) provide excellent coverage of both fiscal and monetary policies. Friedman and Schwartz's *Monetary History* (chapter 11) and Degen's *The American Monetary System* are solid on monetary policy. And Campagna has a good chapter on the Eisenhower years in *U.S. National Economic Policy.*

☐ Chapter 8

There are many books about the Kennedy-Johnson years, but few were truly useful to this study of stabilization policy. To understand the fiscal policy of the Kennedy team, Walter Heller's *New Dimensions in Political Economy* is required reading. (In fact, it *was* required in my introductory political science class in 1968 at the College of William and Mary.) An excellent sampler of theories and thinking behind the Keynesian politics of the 1960s can be found in Smith and Teigen's edition of *Readings in Money, National Income, and Stabilization Policy* (1970), which was required reading for economics graduate students at Indiana University in the early 1970s, and also in the Hall and Doyle edition of *Inflation* (1969). The Kennedy years are the ultimate goal of Stein's *The Fiscal Revolution in America*, which was so helpful in the preceding two chapters. Other good sources for the 1960s include Bach's *Making Monetary and Fiscal Policy*, Arthur Okun's *The Political Economy of Prosperity* (1970), and Seymour Harris's *Economics of the Kennedy Years* (1964).

Some of the very best analysis of both fiscal and monetary policy during the 1960s and early 1970s can be found in *The American Economy in Transition* (edited by Feldstein), especially Gordon's article, "Postwar Macroeconomics." Hugh Norton provides a fly-on-the-wall view of the inner workings of the Council of Economic Advisors that is particularly interesting during these two decades in his *The Quest for Economic Stability: Roosevelt to Reagan* (1985). Once again, Degen's *The American Monetary System* comes through for monetary policy, and Campagna's Keynesian biases in *U.S. National Economic Policy* are well suited to these years. Friedman and Schwartz's *Monetary History* ends in 1960, but its sequel, *Monetary Trends in the United States and the United Kingdom* (1982), extends their empirical coverage to 1975. *The Secrets of the Tem-*

ple, by Greider, is unequaled in its account of the Carter years. Maxwell Newton and John Wooley both do investigative reports on Fed policy during the 1970s and the early Volcker years in *The Fed* (1983) and *Monetary Politics* (1984), respectively. Two worthwhile books on the 1970s by well-known economists are *Our Stagflation Malaise* (1981), by Sidney Weintraub, and *The Great Recession* (1978), by Otto Eckstein. Finally, browsing through the annual editions of the *Economic Report of the President*, particularly for the 1960s and 1970s, can give enlightening insights into policy strategies.

☐ Chapter 9

Several books deal with Reaganomics, but the ones I found the most useful come from two insiders: Michael Boskin's *Reagan and the Economy* (1987) and William Niskanen's *Reaganomics* (1988). Both men were economic advisers to the Reagan-Bush team. They may be a little biased, but since they sometimes disagree in their interpretations a comparison of the two provides an excellent perspective. Both authors take hard, informative looks at the deficits and their probable short- and long-run effects. An interesting and sometimes eye-opening analysis of the deficit and debt can be found in Robert Eisner's *How Real Is the Federal Deficit?* (1986). Other books on Reaganomics that are worth investigating for their economic content are Bruce Bartlett's *Reaganomics* (1981); Paul Craig Roberts's *The Supply-Side Revolution* (1984); *Economic Policy in the Reagan Years*, edited by Charles Stone and Isabel Sawhill (1984); *The Reagan Record*, edited by John Palmer and Isabel Sawhill (1984); *The Legacy of Reaganomics*, Edited by Charles Hulten and Sawhill (1984). Of course, for the ultimate inside view of the budgetary process and the political theater associated with it during the Reagan years, there is David Stockman's *The Triumph of Politics* (1986); should be titled "The Triumph of Politics over Economics." Good sources for background material on the Reagan program and supply-side economics include Jack Kemp's *An American Renaissance* (1979) and George Gilder's *Wealth and Poverty* (1981).

There is no better source for the monetary policy story of the Volcker years than William Greider's *Secrets of the Temple*, which was also listed for the previous chapter. In fact, this massive (700-page) study, which reads like a novel but educates like a textbook, provides countless insights into the entire history of the Federal Reserve and monetary policy. A quicker read than *Temple* but with interesting coverage on the Volcker years can be found in Newton's *The Fed*. Beyond that, there were numerous articles during the 1980s in the Federal Reserve Bank reviews, particularly the St. Louis Fed *Review*, that are easy to read and address such issues as the plight of monetarism, the best choice for policy targets, the M1 versus M2 debate, the velocity puzzle, and the recent use of P*. I strongly recommend browsing through the 1980s volumes.

SELECTED
BIBLIOGRAPHY

Ahearn, Daniel S. *Federal Reserve Policy Reappraised, 1951–1959*. New York: Columbia University Press, 1963.

Anderson, Benjamin M. *Economics and the Public Welfare*. Indianapolis: Liberty Press, 1979.

Bach, G. L. *Making Monetary and Fiscal Policy*. Washington, D.C.: Brookings Institute, 1971.

Barro, Robert J. ed. *Modern Business Cycle Theory*. Cambridge, Mass.: Harvard University Press, 1989.

———. "Output Effects of Government Purchases," *Journal of Political Economy* 87 (October 1979).

Bartlett, Bruce R. *Reaganomics*. Westport, Conn.: Arlington House, 1981.

Berman, Peter. *Inflation and the Money Supply, 1956–1977*. Lexington, Mass.: D. C. Heath, 1978.

Bernanke, B. S. "Non-Monetary Effects of the Financial Collapse in the Propagation of the Great Depression. *American Economic Review* 73 (June 1983).

Bernstein, Michael. *The Great Depression: Delayed Recovery and Economic Change in America*. New York: Cambridge University Press, 1988.

Blinder, Alan S. *Economic Policy and the Great Stagflation*. New York: Academic Press, 1979.

Boskin, Michael. *Reagan and the Economy*. San Francisco, Calif.: ICS Press, 1987.

Brown, E. Cary. "Fiscal Policy in the 'Thirties: A Reappraisal," *American Economic Review* 46 (December 1956).

Brunner, Karl, ed. *The Great Depression Revisited*. Boston: Klawer Nijhoff, 1981.

Burgess, W. Randolph, ed. *Interpretations of Federal Reserve Policy in the Speeches and Writings of Benjamin Strong*. New York: Harper and Row, 1930.

228

Burns, Arthur. *Reflections of an Economic Policymaker.* Washington, D.C.: American Enterprise Institute, 1978.

Cagan, Phillip. *Persistent Inflation.* New York: Columbia University Press, 1979.

Campagna, Anthony S. *U.S. National Economic Policy, 1917–1985.* New York: Praeger, 1987.

Chandler, Lester V. *American Monetary Policy, 1929–1941.* New York: Harper and Row, 1971.

———. *America's Greatest Depression, 1929–1941.* New York: Harper and Row, 1970.

———. *Benjamin Strong, Central Banker.* Washington, D.C.: Brookings Institute, 1958.

Council of Economic Advisors. *Economic Report of the President.* Washington, D.C.: U.S. Government Printing Office.

Currie, Lauchlin, "Causes of the Recession (1938)." *History of Political Economy* 12 (Fall 1980).

Degen, Robert A. *The American Monetary System.* Lexington, Mass.: D. C. Heath, 1987.

Eckstein, Otto. *The Great Recession.* New York: North and Holland, 1978.

Eisner, Robert. *How Real Is the Federal Deficit?* New York: Free Press, 1986.

Feldstein, Martin, ed. *The American Economy in Transition.* Chicago: University of Chicago Press, 1980.

Friedman, Milton. "The Role of Monetary Policy," *American Economic Review,* 58 (March 1968).

Friedman, Milton, and Anna J. Schwartz. *A Monetary History of the United States, 1867–1960.* Princeton, N.J.: Princeton University Press, 1963.

———. *Monetary Trends in the United States and the United Kingdom.* Chicago: University of Chicago Press, 1982.

Galbraith, John Kenneth. *The Great Crash.* Boston: Houghton Mifflin, 1954.

Gardner, Richard. *Sterling-Dollar Diplomacy.* New York: Oxford University Press, 1956.

Gilbert, Charles. *American Financing of World War I.* Westport, Conn.: Greenwood Press, 1970.

Gilder, George. *Wealth and Poverty.* New York: Basic Books, 1981.

Goldenweiser, E. A. *Federal Reserve System in Operation.* New York: McGraw-Hill, 1925.

Gordon, Robert J. *Macroeconomics.* Glenview, Ill.: Scott, Foresman, 1990.

———. "Postwar Macroeconomics: The Evolution of Events and Ideas." In *The American Economy in Transition,* edited by Martin Feldstein. Chicago: University of Chicago Press, 1980.

————. "Understanding Inflation in the 1980s." *Brookings Papers on Economic Activity* 16, no. 1 (1985).

Greider, William. *Secrets of the Temple.* New York: Simon and Schuster, 1987.

Gunderson, Gerald. *A New Economic History of America.* New York: McGraw-Hill, 1976.

Hall, R. J., and Peter Doyle, eds. *Inflation.* Baltimore, Md.: Penguin, 1969.

Hamilton, James D. "Monetary Factors in the Great Depression," *Journal of Monetary Economics* 19 (1987).

————. Oil and the Macroeconomy Since World War II," *Journal of Political Economy* 91 (April 1983).

Harding, William P. G. *The Formative Period of the Federal Reserve System.* New York: AMS Press, 1923.

Harris, Seymour. *Economics of the Kennedy Years.* New York: Harper and Row, 1964.

Hazlitt, Henry. *From Bretton Woods to World Inflation: A Study of Causes and Consequences.* Chicago: Regnery Gateway, 1984.

Heller, Walter. *New Dimensions of Political Economy.* New York: W. W. Norton, 1967.

Hickman, Bert. *Growth and Stability in the Postwar Economy.* Washington, D.C.: Brookings Institute, 1960.

Historical Statistics of the United States: Colonial Times to 1970. Washington, D.C.: U.S. Department of Commerce, 1975.

Holmans, A. E. *United States Fiscal Policy.* New York: Oxford University Press, 1961.

Hughes, Jonathan. *American Economic History.* Glenview, Ill.: Scott, Foresman, 1990.

Hulten, Charles R., and Isabel V. Sawhill, eds. *The Legacy of Reaganomics.* Washington, D.C.: Urban Institute Press, 1984.

Jones, Byrd L. "Lauchlin Currie and the Causes of the 1937 Recession." *History of Political Economy* 12 (Fall 1980).

————. "Lauchlin Currie, Pump Priming, and New Deal Fiscal Policy, 1934–1936." *History of Political Economy* 10 (Winter 1978).

Kemp, Jack. *An American Renaissance.* New York: Harper and Row, 1979.

Keynes, John Maynard. *The General Theory of Employment, Interest, and Money.* London: Macmillan, 1949 (reprint).

————. "The Means to Prosperity." In *The Collected Works of John Maynard Keynes,* vol. 9. London: St. Martin's Press, 1972.

————. "An Open Letter." (Reprinted from *New York Times,* 31 December 1933). In *Readings in Fiscal Policy,* edited by the American Economic Association. Homewood, Ill.: Irwin, 1955.

————. *A Tract on Monetary Reform.* London: Macmillan, 1924.

————. *A Treatise on Money.* London: Macmillan, 1930.

Kimmel, Lewis H. *Federal Budget and Fiscal Policy, 1789–1958.* Washington D.C.: Brookings Institute, 1959.

Kindleberger, Charles P. *The World in Depression, 1929–1939.* Berkeley: University of California Press, 1973.

Lekachman, Robert. *The Age of Keynes.* New York: McGraw-Hill, 1966.

Lewis, Wilfred. *Federal Fiscal Policy in the Postwar Recessions.* Washington, D.C.: Brookings Institute, 1962.

Livingston, James. *Origins of the Federal Reserve System.* Ithaca, N.Y.: Cornell University Press, 1986.

Macesich, George. *The Politics of Monetarism.* Totawa, N.J.: Rowman and Allanheld, 1984.

Mayer, Thomas. "Money and the Great Depression: A Critique of Professor Temin's Thesis," *Explorations in Economic History* 15 (April 1978).

———. *The Structure of Monetarism.* New York: W. W. Norton, 1978.

McCullum, Ben T. "The Current State of the Policy Ineffectiveness Debate," *American Economic Review* 69 proceedings (May 1979).

Meyer, Laurence. *The Economic Consequences of Government Deficits.* Boston: Kluwer Nijhoff, 1983.

Mills, Gregory B., and John L. Palmer. *Federal Budget Policy in the 1980s.* Washington, D.C.: Urban Institute Press, 1984.

Mitchell, Broadus. *Depression Decade.* New York: Rinehart, 1947.

Newton, Maxwell. *The Fed.* New York: Times Books, 1983.

Niskanen, William A. *Reaganomics.* New York: Oxford University Press, 1988.

Norton, Hugh S. *The Quest for Economic Stability.* Columbia: University of South Carolina Press, 1985.

Okun, Arthur M. *The Political Economy of Prosperity.* New York: W. W. Norton, 1970.

Palmer, John L., and Isabel V. Sawhill. *The Reagan Record.* Cambridge, Mass.: Ballinger, 1984.

Pisciotta, John, and Mark Vaughn, eds. *Macroeconomics.* Guilford, Conn.: Duskin, 1987.

Puth, Robert C. *American Economic History.* New York: Dryden Press, 1988.

Reed, Harold. *Federal Reserve Policy, 1921–1930.* New York: McGraw-Hill, 1930.

Roberts, Paul Craig. *The Supply Side Revolution.* Cambridge, Mass.: Harvard University Press, 1984.

Rothbard, Murray. *America's Greatest Depression.* New York: Richardson & Snyder, 1983.

Santoni, G. J. "The Great Bull Markets 1924–29 and 1982–97: Speculative

Bubbles or Economic Fundamentals?" [St. Louis Federal Reserve Bank] *Review* 69 (November 1987).

Savage, James D. *Balanced Budgets and American Politics.* Ithaca, N.Y.: Cornell University Press, 1988.

Silk, Leonard. *Nixonomics.* New York: Praeger, 1972.

Smith, Warren L., and Ronald L. Teigen, eds. *Readings in Money, National Income, and Stabilization Policy.* Homewood, Ill.: Irwin, 1970.

Sobel, Robert. *The Great Bull Market.* New York: W. W. Norton, 1968.

Soule, George. *Prosperity Decade.* New York: Harper and Row, 1947.

Stein, Herbert. *The Fiscal Revolution in America.* Chicago: University of Chicago Press, 1969.

———. *Presidential Economics.* Washington, D.C.: American Enterprise Institute, 1988.

Stockman, David. *The Triumph of Politics.* New York: Harper and Row, 1986.

Stone, Charles F., and Isabel V. Sawhill. *Economic Policy in the Reagan Years.* Washington, D.C.: Urban Institute Press, 1984.

Studenski, Paul, and Herman Krooss. *Financial History of the United States.* New York: McGraw-Hill, 1952.

Temin, Peter. *Did Monetary Forces Cause the Great Depression?* New York: W. W. Norton, 1976.

Vatter, Harold. *The U.S. Economy in the 1950.* New York: W. W. Norton, 1963.

Walton, Gary M., and Hugh Rockoff. *History of the American Economy.* New York: Harcourt Brace Jovanovich, 1990.

Warburg, Paul M. *The Federal Reserve System, Its Origins and Growth,* vol. 1. New York: Macmillan, 1930.

Weiher, Kenneth. "Depression or Deflation: A Comparison of the 1930s and 1840s." *Essays in Economic and Business History* 2 (1981).

———. "Macroeconomic Causes and Consequences of Major Stock Market Reversals: An Historical Study." *Essays in Economic and Business History* 7 (1989).

———. *Macroeconomics, Aggregate Theory, and Policy.* St. Paul, Minn.: West, 1986.

———. "Real Interest Rates and Economic Contractions: A Comparison of the 1982 Recession with Other Great Contractions." *Essays in Economic and Business History* 4 (1986).

Weinstein, Michael M. "Some Macroeconomic Impacts of the National Industrial Recovery Act, 1933–35." In *The Great Depression Revisited.* Boston: Kluwer Nijhoff, 1981.

Weintraub, Sidney. *Our Stagflation Malaise.* Westport, Conn.: Quorum Books, 1981.

West, Robert Craig. *Banking Reform and the Federal Reserve, 1863–1923.* Ithaca, N.Y.: Cornell University Press, 1977.

Wicker, Elmus R. *Federal Reserve Monetary Policy, 1917–1933.* New York: Random House, 1966.

———. "A Reconsideration of the Causes of the Banking Panic of 1930." *Journal of Economic History* 40 (1982).

Willis, Henry Parker. *The Federal Reserve System.* New York: Ronald Press, 1923.

Wooley, John T. *Monetary Politics.* New York: Cambridge University Press, 1984.

INDEX

THE AUTHOR

Kenneth Weiher is an associate professor of economics at the University of Texas at San Antonio (UTSA). After receiving his B.A. in economics from the College of William and Mary and his Ph.D. in economics from Indiana University, he began teaching at UTSA in 1975. He has received multiple awards for outstanding teaching and has written numerous articles in urban economic and macroeconomic history. He is the author of *Macroeconomics*, an intermediate textbook, and an active member of the Economic and Business Historical Society. His more recent publications—on economic instability and government stabilization policies—in the society's journal, *Essays in Economic and Business History*, set the stage for the writing of this book.